Wayne Rainey

Wayne Rainey

HIS OWN STORY

Second edition

Michael Scott

Haynes Publishing

First published in hardback in August 1997
Reprinted in 1997 (twice) and 1998
This paperback edition, with additional material, published in June 2010

A catalogue record for this book is available from the British Library

ISBN 978 1 84425 862 8

Library of Congress catalog card no 2010921626

Published by Haynes Publishing,
Sparkford, Yeovil, Somerset BA22 7JJ, UK
Tel: 01963 442030 Fax: 01963 440001
Int.tel: +44 1963 442030 Int.fax: +44 1963 440001
E-mail: sales@haynes.co.uk
Website: www.haynes.co.uk

Haynes North America Inc.,
861 Lawrence Drive, Newbury Park, California 91320, USA

Designed and typeset Dominic Stickland
Printed and bound in the USA

Cover illustrations
Front: Historic champion. *(Getty)*
Back: Rainey leads Kevin Schwantz and Eddie Lawson – rivals of a golden age *(Gold & Goose)*

CONTENTS

WAYNE RAINEY'S DEDICATION
To my son Rex who I love very much

ACKNOWLEDGEMENTS

The author would like to thank the following
for their time and memories:
Chris 'Itchy' Armstrong, Paul Butler, Paul Carruthers, Dave Dewey,
Don Grigsby, Mike Lane, Eddie Lawson, Gary Mathers,
Rob Muzzy, Kevin Magee, Dean Miller, Mike Minnig, Sandy, Ila,
Rodney and Renee Rainey, Shae Rainey, John Reed, Peter Richards
FRCS, Kenny Roberts, Rob 'Burnout' Salerno, Kevin Schwantz,
Bubba Shobert, Mike Sinclair, Shell Thuet, Robert G Watkins MD,
and many others.

AUTHOR'S DEDICATION
To Jennifer, Ripton, and Rebecca

FOREWORD

by Kenny Roberts, three times 500cc World Champion, winning team
owner, and new racing motorcycle manufacturer

All my life, it seems, I've had to spend a lot of time persuading people outside motorcycle racing that it is a worthwhile sport. I want them to know what I know – that racing means something. It has a nobility like any other sport, and a value all of its own.

I've made a lot of progress too. Wayne Rainey was a powerful part of that persuasion. As a rider and as a character he had it all: courage, determination, intelligence, decency, honesty . . . and of course skill.

I just loved the way he'd work at it, always going for more, right until the end. And I loved watching the way he'd spring off into the lead on cold tyres, spinning and sliding as if he was in turn one of the Ascot oval. I especially loved how when things were against him, he'd just work harder. He'd never give up trying to avoid getting beat.

I felt shattered when he got hurt in 1993. Everybody did.

Looking at Wayne now, I see we needn't have worried. As Dr Costa said to me on the day he crashed: 'Wayne has a new life now – and he's going to be good at it'.

Wayne's spirit and honesty are a shining light in his new life. In this book he is also fearlessly honest about his life, his career and his rivals.

I have also been involved, in a way, with author Michael Scott, who has always been fair and in search of the truth. He has interviewed me and many others involved with Wayne, to get fresh insights into the truth behind the legend.

I'm proud of my association with Wayne. I'm proud of what he achieved in my team. I'm proud to face him now as a rival team manager – he's someone worth trying to beat. And I'm proud to be his friend.

March 1997

PROLOGUE

It was over. A shining light had been extinguished. As the news spread like a shock wave, others came to the same realisation. For us, racing would never be the same again. Michael Scott, Misano, 1993

When Wayne Rainey crashed and snapped his spine at Misano on 5 September 1993, the damage was instant, and permanent. The cord was severed. There was never any question that he would walk again.

It happened at 1.29pm, lunchtime on a sunny Italian Sunday. In the harrowing minutes, hours and days that followed, the world of racing reeled. Accidents happen, and sometimes they are worse. But not to the likes of Wayne Rainey. He was one of the greats, and his god-like status as ruler of the elite 500cc class was far too elevated for devotees to accept how suddenly and how radically it had changed.

I was at Misano, as I had been at almost every one of Wayne Rainey's grand prix races, and by fate became aware of the gravity of his injuries even before he'd left the track. It was over. A shining light had been extinguished. As the news spread like a shock wave, others came to the same realisation. For us, racing would never be the same again.

The circumstances of this awful event had assembled with inexorable precision over the preceding 32 years and longer, driven by a perfectionist determination that ran in the family. Psycho-analysing the drive that took Wayne – takes any top athlete – to the obsessive levels of the World Championship would be a book in itself. It is something to wonder at, something to envy and admire. And, often as not, even to pity.

It starts with an inner drive, the same one that drove his father Sandy headlong into a racing life, as a rider, a builder and tuner. It wasn't just winning that mattered. *It was doing it differently, then winning.*

The same drive, or an even stronger version, was a good friend to the little blond-haired Wayne, helping him to show precocious talent as a schoolboy racer. It spurred him on round and round the endless ovals of the US dirt-tracks. It provided the determination that took him all the way to the Grand Prix series, the pinnacle of motorcycle racing. And when he got there, the drive turned into disappointment, and a rage that almost destroyed him.

This crash was the culmination of three years of increasing torment. Wayne's success as a racer had been illuminated because it came during an era rich in exceptional talent. The latest in a line of American multiple champions, he had achieved dominance in a company that included Eddie Lawson, four times World Champion; Wayne Gardner, the Australian bulldog; Michael Doohan, who would take over his own mantle; and Texan Kevin Schwantz. Especially Kevin Schwantz. Schwantz was a rider with a genius level of natural talent, who had been the other half of Wayne's racing equation for almost ten years.

Wayne beat these gifted rivals by working harder, thinking harder, by being more dedicated – by being more complete. It made him rich, popular and widely admired. Here was a good-looking, well-mannered hero who had done it all. Strangely, though, that brought him no fulfilment. When he won the World Championship in 1990 he felt joy for a moment, then it was gone. The 1991 and 1992 titles were no better. This dissatisfaction puzzled him deeply. His response was typical. He tried to achieve more. When he crashed at Misano, he was reaching out for a historic fourth successive championship.

Back home in California, the sun had not risen yet. While stunned television viewers in Europe watched the broken hero flapping his arms ineffectually in the scattered gravel trap (oh, the symbolism in that pitiful image) Wayne's family in America were stirring uneasily.

In Los Angeles, in the old family home in Norwalk, his mother Ila waited in turmoil. The night before, Wayne had called, as he always did after practice. He was going to break the track record, he told her. Well, don't do anything that doesn't feel right, she said. Then it was night. In the early morning she woke suddenly, after a horrible nightmare about Wayne falling, of sand scattering, a disjointed dreadful dream.

In Hickman, outside Modesto, his father Sandy had got back after 1am from Lodi dirt track where he'd been working with Kenny Roberts's young step-son Tyson, a learner-racer. Sandy was sleeping in a trailer-home at Kenny's ranch when he was woken by a savage cramp, a charley-horse, in his leg. He had to leap up, and stagger lop-sided round the trailer to walk it off. He'd just got back to bed when the bang came on the door. *Sandy. It's the phone. You'd better come quick.* In the predawn chill, Sandy threw on some clothes and hurried to the main house to call Italy and hear the worst about his first-born child. He called Ila directly. 'I said, Hon . . . And she knew. She just said, oh no. And hung up.'

In Monterey, at Wayne's fine hilltop house, his infant son Rex slept, but his wife Shae was wide awake. Usually they'd have been at the track. This was the first race she'd missed for months, coming home early to prepare for the US GP the next weekend, just down the hill at Laguna Seca.

SHAE'S JOURNAL: *It was a strange morning. I woke at 4.30am. I knew Wayne was still racing. I didn't have a good feeling. I just lay there. Ten minutes later the phone rang. It was Scott. I knew something terrible had happened. He said: Wayne crashed, but he's OK. I think that is the stock line to tell somebody's wife. Then he said: They are going to take him to hospital by helicopter to have him checked out. I said: If he is going by helicopter, he is not all right. Looking back now, Wayne must have crashed about the time I woke up.*

Waiting for that early morning Grand Prix call was routine. A routine ordeal. In the past ten years it had come 95 times, from racetracks around the world. Twenty four times it was exultant: 'I won the race.' Only three times – once in 1989 and twice in 1992 – had the message been the one they dreaded: 'I crashed.' Until now it had always been followed with: 'But I'm OK.' The dread had deepened over the years.

At Misano, amid all the confusion, the facts were soon known. Wayne was alive, but critically hurt. In the medical centre, the diagnosis was instant. A text book case. The on-track neurosurgeon Dr Peter Richards had read how when the spinal cord snapped in this way, the victim would sweat profusely above the injury, but not at all below it. It was rarely seen, however. For one thing, injuries like Wayne's are usually fatal. The aorta, the main artery, is attached to the spine at that point, and this amount of displacement generally tears it, causing a massive internal haemorrhage and rapid death.

Kenny Roberts, himself a triple World Champion, and now owner of Wayne's Marlboro-sponsored factory Yamaha team, heard of the crash while he watched from the pits. But he hadn't rushed to the medical centre. They'd told him: looks like he got his collarbone. He's breathing, and he's conscious. 'I wasn't unduly concerned.'

Kenny had been an integral part of Wayne's GP career from the very start. He'd paved the way for the new generation of Americans, storming into the GPs to win three years straight from 1978 to 1980. Before that, he'd been US champion twice – a series based around oval dirt-tracks – and he was the first to bring the wheelspinning, tail-sliding style to the World Championships. After retirement, he'd run a rather half-baked 250 effort in 1984 with Wayne as one of two riders. When the two joined up again in 1988 he was the owner of a full-on big-budget factory 500 team, running Yamahas in Lucky Strike colours. In the meantime the two men had gone from mentor and apprentice to the closest of friends – more like brothers, says Kenny, or father and son. And together they'd achieved domination.

That day Kenny watched his other rider, Luca Cadalora, for a couple of laps – he was leading now, and would go on to take the hollowest of home wins. Then he and team physiotherapist Dean Miller went over. They were soon aware of the full gravity of the injury. Kenny couldn't hide this knowledge. It was his face more than anything that made Wayne realise just how badly he was hurt. Until then, he'd hoped perhaps his body was in shock, that the feeling would come back. Now he knew otherwise. Although for the present, sucking on the oxygen with damaged lungs, he was rather more preoccupied with simply staying alive.

SHAE'S JOURNAL: *I received another call from Kenny about 10 minutes later. He said: Wayne can't feel his legs. I didn't know what to think. I guess I wasn't thinking. He was going to call me from the hospital. I was sitting in the family room. I waited for about an hour,* *then I went back to bed. Then Kenny called again. Somehow I knew in his voice. He said: It's not good. I said nothing. He said: He'll probably never walk again. I said: I know Wayne. He'll walk. Then I think I broke down. It's kind of foggy. I hung up, walked in a stupor to my mom, woke her up. Mom. Wayne will never walk again. Just as calm as anything. I must have been in shock. I kept saying: Don't worry. Wayne's OK. I'm OK.*

Kevin Schwantz knew his arch rival had fallen, and that this was his chance to regain the championship lead he'd lost one race before. He didn't want to think beyond that, forcing himself not to notice the frantic activity around the prone rider by the trackside. 'I knew it was at a really dangerous spot.' When the helicopter rushing him to Cesena Hospital, outside Bologna to the north, took off just after the race was over, Schwantz told himself: maybe it's not a medical helicopter. Just a TV thing or something.

It was some time after the ceremonies and press conferences when an Italian TV reporter banged on the motorhome door and said: Hey, Kevin. How does it feel to be World Champion? 'I said: I'm only five points in front, with two races left. What are you talking about? And they said: Wayne's not going to race again. I said it then and I'll say it again: I'd much rather have gotten beat and still be racing him than to win it like this.' Schwantz had never had to think before about how much racing against Wayne had inspired his own brilliant career. It took a year more before the truth sank in. Without Wayne to race against, there wasn't really much point racing.

For Wayne, the equation balanced differently. Advised by the similarly though more seriously injured Formula 1 team owner Frank Williams, he threw himself straight back into the sport. Less than seven months after the accident, pale and wasted, still coming to grips with his wheelchair and all the implications of that, he returned to the first round of the 1994 World Championship in Australia, where it was announced he was to take over Kenny Roberts's 250 team, which would henceforth be known as Team Marlboro Rainey.

Looking back, this was all rather premature. He wasn't ready yet, and anyway, he wanted his own team, not one that in truth still belonged to Kenny. But nobody knew of the hardship he was suffering. He kept it to himself – the times of despair.

As if the family had not suffered enough, Shae's mother finally lost her battle against cancer while Wayne was in Australia. It had been a long and painful ordeal, stretched out over two years that had taken a heavy toll on those close to her. Her death was a grievous blow to his Shae, so brave and strong. It was when Wayne saw her falling into a deferred depression 18 months later that he realised it was up to him to pull the whole thing round. Start living again so she didn't have his misery to carry along too.

With redoubled determination, at least as much as he had expended as a rider, he built up a racing team of his own through 1995 and 1996 and, though thwarted by circumstances from achieving the World Championship success he craved, in 1997 he was back again, with Yamaha's official works squad under his total control, and the avowed and serious intention of winning the 500cc title.

SHAE'S JOURNAL: *I flew to San Francisco, met Sandy, Ila and Gary (Howard, Wayne's business manager) in the lounge. I start to cry again. Ila doesn't want me to tell her anything. She doesn't want to know what's wrong with Wayne. Delta (Airlines) were very kind to us. They must have known we were on a medical emergency trip. The flight was very long, naturally. I sat with Gary. This was the first time in my life I couldn't eat anything. I kept thinking I was going to wake up. We landed in Frankfurt, switched planes. Paola (Martignoni) from Cagiva was waiting for us, to take us to the hospital in their helicopter. That was very nice of them. We all fell asleep on the way to Forli airport. Then Chuckie (Aksland) and Scott (Copeland, her nephew) took us to the hospital. I could see Maekawa, Sakurada and Nakajima (Yamaha factory staff) up there. Then immediately I was taken to see Wayne. On the way to the Intensive Care Unit, I started to cry again.*

The news at the Cesena hospital near Bologna was predictably bleak. X-rays confirmed that the sixth thoracic vertebra – T6 – had snapped clean in half. Other injuries included bruised and bleeding lungs. Nothing could be done about the paralysing back injury.

The immediate concern was to keep the patient alive. 'I came close to dying in the helicopter, because I couldn't get the next breath. I needed that oxygen. That's what kept me alive. Man, I didn't want to die. I didn't care how bad I was, or how I'd end up, I just wanted to live. I remember when we got to the hospital it seemed like there were 200 fans there, clapping and stuff. I needed something for the pain, but they couldn't give me nothing until they knew what was wrong. I remember these doctors sticking a tube in me to drain my lungs. They put a centrepunch under my armpits each side and just hit it through my skin and flesh and into the lung. I remember going: Ooohhff!'

In the next bed lay another motorcycle accident victim, a young Italian who had crashed on his way to watch the grand prix. He never arrived, and never knew that the person next to him, trying to talk him back into the world – 'Hey, Paolo, can you hear me: this is Wayne, this is Wayne Rainey' – was the rider he'd gone to see.

In one sense, they were just two routine trauma cases, as you might find in any intensive care unit in the developed world. One would live, one would die. On that first night, thirsty and wanting ice cubes to suck, unable to yell, Wayne tried to get the attention of the nurses, but they had the radio cranked up loud and were dancing. Or was this a halucination? Yet, as Wayne would observe a few days later, when he was more in a position to notice such things, even the case-hardened doctors were upset to see what this great champion had been reduced to. He lay there for five days. He remembers on the last night the floor-doctor coming in, crying. 'He was devastated that Wayne Rainey was paralysed.'

SHAE'S JOURNAL: *I went up to the ICU. You had to put on gowns, hats, shoes. Then I saw Kenny for the first time. He seemed to be doing OK. I think he was better when he saw Wayne. So I went in. Wayne was very happy to see me.*

One among many ironies was the fact that Wayne had crashed at his favourite circuit. He'd loved Misano from the first time he raced there – on a 250 in 1984, during a first isolated GP season that many have forgotten. The crash was not particularly unusual, except in the way both he and the bike were sent somersaulting together through the gravel trap. A basic rule for minimising injury when you crash is: Slide, Don't Roll. In this case, both went flipping end over end. The spine injury was a direct consequence.

There was a reason. In a new but growing track fashion the gravel was raked into a series of wide ripples. This had proved effective in quickly taming wayward racing cars; but when Wayne inadvertently ran across similarly raked gravel during testing at another Italian track earlier that year, he'd discovered that it was rather different on a bike. It turned into a bucking bronco. Even worse, as we now saw, when the bike wasn't on its wheels. 'I didn't say anything about it then. It was only after my accident that they started raking the gravel-traps smooth for the bikes.'

SHAE'S JOURNAL: *He had a black eye. The whites of his eyes were completely red. He had bruises on his face. I felt so much better now that I was with him. He was so upbeat. He gave me his spiel that 'I have no regrets. I'm happy that I did it racing and I was on top.' I was so happy that he was so positive. He just made me feel so good. He gave everyone the same spiel though. Soon I was beginning to wonder how long he could keep saying this before he got mad about it. His mom came in and Wayne took a picture of us. He was still smiling.*

Shae had never known Wayne as anything but a racer. She was just 12 when she met him, play-riding a minibike of her own. He, then 14, was quite simply 'the cutest boy I ever did see.' From teenage crush to dating to love and marriage occupied the next decade or so: in retrospect it seems pre-ordained, as good marriages often do. Shae had always managed to remain detached about watching the man she loved risking his life: as if when he put his helmet on he became a different person. In this way, when he was going through his growing torment, she was unaware of the depth of his pain. If he was short, if he kicked his leathers up and down the motorhome, well, he was having a frustrating year. She knew he wasn't enjoying it, and that things couldn't go on this way. But he kept the worst of it to himself. 'I didn't realise how obsessed he was, until it was too late.'

How she wished, how she still wishes, she'd been with him at

Misano. Because what she had been able to do during the last difficult year was say: Hey. Remember to go and have fun. Enjoy the racing. If she'd been able to say that at Misano, perhaps he'd not have tried too hard. Perhaps none of this would have happened.

SHAE'S JOURNAL: *I spent a couple of hours with Wayne the first night, then I went to my hotel. It was night time. We had dinner. There was an Italian man helping – a friend of the hotel owner. They made a fabulous dinner for all of us. Ila didn't last through the meal. She started crying, and left. I could see that Kenny was upset. I went to my room, and the phone rang. It was Dean. He said to come up to his room, that Kenny was very upset. I went there: Kenny was crying hysterically. I tried to comfort him, but he blamed himself for Wayne's accident. He said it was all his fault.*

Wayne never blamed anybody but himself. He took comfort from the fact that it had happened when he was leading the race and the World Championship, and had the throttle open. The only regret was that he'd tried too hard.

This had never been a weakness before. He could always see the big picture, appraise each race as part of the championship rather than an isolated event to be won at any cost. The difference this year was that his works Yamaha had taken a wrong turning in chassis development. The bike had hindered his style and, as Schwantz moved steadily ahead on points, Rainey was obliged to over-ride his motorcycle just to try and stay in touch. Always able to go right to the limit, he was now forcing himself to ride beyond that. It wasn't the kind of racing he liked, or was used to. It was risky and mentally exhausting. Yet it led to his proudest victory and, at a time when he'd ceased to enjoy being a racer, to his most enjoyable race. Not to mention a strange, out-of-body experience.

This happened at the Japanese GP at Suzuka, third race of the season. Wayne's pride was that he had already been beaten when, some way into the race, his tyres 'went off' (lost grip as they heated up). This freed him from the bad handling problems of his Yamaha, since now he could slide the bike in a way that the opposition could not, intimidating them by his demonstration of sheer control.

During this ride, coming through from 12th place to win by less than a tenth of a second, his conscious mind actually seemed to leave his body. 'It was while I was catching up. I still had no idea I might win. But I was enjoying myself so much sliding the bike. It happened as I came up to outbrake Beattie into the hairpin for third.

Suddenly for about two tenths of a second I was looking down on myself, watching my bike slip past his. And I was conscious of laughing out loud, because I was having so much fun.'

SHAE'S JOURNAL: *(On the first night), I had my sister fax me some Scripture to read. I desperately needed some guidance from the Lord. It did help me and I slept fairly well. Wayne's night did not go so well. The ICU room is not what you think it should be. There were four beds in one room, divided by curtains. Most of the people in there were brain dead, except Wayne.*

Two years after the crash Wayne looked at his racing leathers for the first time. We were working together on this book at his home in Monterey; his cousin Mike Lane and nephew Ryan were visiting, and he sent the three of us up the steep steps to the attic over his garage, where several years worth of riding gear were carefully stored.

The detailed inspection of the scuffed racing suit was a time of few words and strong emotions. Until then, Wayne believed he'd snapped his spine in his final twisting jacknife into the gravel. He'd landed upside down and backwards, his head folded forward by the impact, his knees coming up towards his shoulders, his back bowed outwards. Almost a birthing position. Now he noticed a slight green mark and impact bruising on the leather right at the point of the injury. Was it the bike, the front forks, that dealt the crucial blow? 'Yet if I'd broken it earlier in the fall, I wouldn't have landed straight out.' Perhaps it was a combination of the two, the full damage caused by two impacts. Either way, it was not pleasant to think about.

Wayne's next actions alarmed the rest of us. Yamaha, his employers (so to speak) then and now, and loyal all the way, had given him two prototypes of a vehicle they had tested but never produced. The Yamaha 'Magic Carpet' is a wheeled platform powered by a motorcycle engine and steered by handlebars, onto which you roll a wheelchair and clamp it down. It's a pretty precarious arrangement, though perfectly adequate for rolling down to the mailbox and back. 'Here. Let me show you,' says Wayne.

The entrance to his house has a covered portico, the driveway splitting into two around the outer pillars. It makes a pretty good oval track for a low-performance vehicle like a Yamaha Magic Carpet. Hold the throttle wide, heaving on the handlebars even while using them to support your tottering trunk, and you can even get the tyres sliding. Round and round he went, face set the way it was when he raced, faster and faster. My mind filled with dread. *Oh no. He's going to crash. Please no. Please stop now.*

Earlier that week, Wayne had told me of the days of black despair, the worst being his first night out of hospital. He just wanted a break, to sleep in a hotel room with his wife, away from the medical routine. But it had all gone wrong. He wasn't ready yet. He still needed almost constant professional care; the doctors had been right in their reluctance to let him go. And he'd ended up smashing himself against the wall in his wheelchair, trying to break his body even more to match the anguish that was threatening to overwhelm him. In all the many days and evenings I spent there, working and talking, acting (I often felt) as much as therapist or confessor as biographer, that was the only time I was pleased to get out back to my hotel, and to a reliably numbing line of tequila margaritas.

One more year passed before my next visit. In the meantime I'd seen Wayne regularly at the racetracks, but it was at his home that the change became obvious. Further surgery had eased some of his physical difficulties, and he'd become more accustomed to the huge 24-hour inconveniences of living with the lower half of your body in a state of troublesome if disconnected delinquency.

He'd refined the drug routine that keeps the worst excesses in some sort of check. And he'd proceeded several steps further along a road of spiritual comfort. Near to death at the trackside at Misano, he'd made a pact with God, who he'd never had any cause to trouble before. In that moment, it was perfectly clear to him. His life, in exchange for his faith. Confused at first, he'd been

19

conscientious in discharging this debt, and now draws great comfort from reading the Bible, and from the community of the Calvary Chapel.

Now came a counterpoint to the Magic Carpet ride. It was late winter, and California was trying hard to be balmy. We all went out for some fresh air, Wayne and Shae, myself, and Rex, now four years old and already an accomplished cyclist. He likes his father to commentate as he pretends to kickstart his kiddies' bike, then pedals off hard to the nearest patch of dirt where he locks the back brake to skid the back wheel, dirt-track style. His face is intent; his slides are of ever-increasing length and dramatic power. Dad, he says. Can I ride down that steep hill? OK Rexo, says Wayne. Then, as the tyke takes off: Hey, Rex. Not too fast! Shae smiles at him affectionately. Well, she says. That's a case of the pot calling the kettle black.

CHAPTER 1

THE HOUSE
THAT PO-PO BUILT

'You don't find it too much any more nowadays. Wayne, Renee and Rodney, I've drilled it into them: You've got to respect your elders, and never turn your back on somebody small.' Sandy Rainey, 1995

Today, it's just A big sprawl, almost endless. One suburb runs directly into the next, unified by freeways and a pall of visible air. Back in 1948, the sandy lane out east of downtown Los Angeles ran through open fields before it came to the house that Po-Po built. He started with the garage, then moved the family in there while he did the rest. The great swelling heave of expansion that would employ two generations of Raineys in the building trade was just around the corner. But as yet this place is undeveloped. The roads are waiting to be bulldozed, and the quarter-acre plots to be defined by picket, driveway and lawn. Which is why the phutt-phutt sound of a lone lawnmower engine is a little before its time.

Suddenly, with a puny roar, a soap-box car bursts out of the garage. A contraption of planks and nails, with a giant steering wheel vaguely roped to the wheels, it is a classic – made more so by the piping engine on the back and the wild-eyed kid stomping on a hinged plank accelerator. Down the driveway it bumps, a matter of a few yards. So far it's passed all the tests of self-propulsion. Then comes the first corner, 90 degrees, into the lane. One corner too many. The soap-box gets round all right, but the motor flies off at a tangent. Revving at full bore, lying on its side, it grinds its drive pulley to destruction. Oh oh.

The blond boy – of course – is a Rainey. Sandy Rainey, who will one day have sons of his own. The first one will be called Wayne, and he will conquer the world. The reasons why have already started. What's happening here bears upon what will happen, from Ascot Park in LA to Donington Park in England – to Suzuka,

Monza, Hockenheimring, Assen. And Misano. Things that in 40 years or so will seem very important to a great number of people.

Sandy was seven or eight, he recalls, when the family took root in Downey, a fledgling suburb between Southgate and Norwalk on the Firestone Boulevard. All this would soon become part of the greater gridlock of frame house neighbourhoods, but right now the Raineys had the place to themselves, so that sometimes Po-Po – as Wayne would later call his grandfather, John Rainey – could tow his son's wooden cart behind the family car.

When he bought a motor mower from Sears Roebuck, Po-Po realised he needed to lay down certain rules. 'He used to call me Joe,' says Sandy. 'He said: Joe, you leave that motor alone. OK dad. And I measured the motor up, and figured out a way how to get it on my wooden car – drilled holes for the four engine bolts.' Sandy wrangled a system 'with a hinged plank for a foot-pedal that would pull the whole motor forward, tighten the drive belt, and we'd go. Release the pedal, and an old bed-spring'd push the motor back. Kinda automatic declutch.'

Looking back, it is clear that the articulated engine mounting, while fine in a straight line, was not designed for corners. 'My dad beat me so I couldn't sit down.' Pick the ingredients, and the rest just follows: ingenuity, adventure, mischief, mechanical aptitude, speed madness and opportunity, underlaid by strict cause-and-effect discipline.

Sandy has more stories like that. About growing up in the West Coast, and about make-and-mend contraptions that would outperform the factory article. If he had a creed, it was to do it differently, then make that work. That was the satisfaction. Sandy didn't stop at fitting a Whizzer bolt-on motor to power his bicycle for the paper round. He bought his own welding torches, converted the pedals to footpegs, rigged up a footbrake. 'As far as I was concerned, I had a motorbike.'

Then there was the Soap-Box Derby. This American institution might have been made for Sandy. 'You went to your local Chevrolet dealer – it still goes on today. They sold the four wheels, the steering shaft, with the steering wheel. You built the rest. You had a weight limit, and you had rules on width, height and length, and ground clearance. They'd sit you on a wooden ramp, two cars butted up against a tongue. And when they'd put the tongue down, both cars'd roll off, and it's coasting and streamlining ability from then on. You ran in age groups, and if you won the combined final you'd get to go to Akron, Ohio, for the Grand Final.'

Sandy sounds a note of regret even today that he never did make Akron. Not quite. In spite of effort and ingenuity. 'The first year I got third in my class. Next year we modified the car. I got an old horse-machine motor, and made up a pulley system, and I'd oil the bearings and run the wheels for hours and hours to break them in, so it'd roll easier. Somebody told me if you put dry ice on your wheels, that'd make the tyres harder. So I was dry-icin', I was doing everything. I won my division, but not the final. Next year (1953), the new Corvette come out. That was the parade car. I won my division, and went to the last two eliminators. And I got beat by about four inches.'

Again, important things had happened. Sandy was bitten by the bug of organised competition. And he just loved the down-home high-tech – like this new space-age material, glassfibre, that defined the scoop-sided new 'Vette, instant style icon for the new American dream. All this exercised his teenage mind. He tried baseball, but as his own son later would observe 'you need too many people to win'. Then came the go-karts, offering scope for both self-reliance and technical inventiveness. They lasted through high school and into his early years learning the carpenter's trade. And he played at drag racing, and oval-track sprint cars. This after an inauspicious start: at 15, he was booked for street-racing in his $150 '49 Oldsmobile. 'The judge said I was the first one who'd had his learner's permit taken away for drag racing.'

Sandy's homebrewed metalworking got to the point when 'I could make almost anything, then modify it to go better.' Head first into the black art of two-stroke tuning, he admits he got lucky. He found out how to keep on raising the exhaust port with a rats-tail file. 'The more I raised it the faster it'd go – until I finally got it to slow down.' The motors came from post-hole drilling machines, at $12 apiece second-hand. The guys in the neighbourhood would meet up at an open lot and race each other until the machines were trashed.

When Ila Lewis met Sandy Rainey at high school, both aged 14, he was a full-on racer. Dating her when he was old enough to drive, 'there was usually a go-kart sticking out of the back of the car and I was racing somewhere.' Well, that was some kind of life for the self-possessed finely drawn blonde, and that's how it carried on when they married at 18. It was just natural that Sandy's young bride also should take the wheel on occasion; she only kicked racing when expecting their first child. 'That's what started Wayne's career – when I raced a go-kart when I was pregnant!' The well-worn joke has a wistful edge nowadays.

The sandy lane where Po-Po had built the first house was now officially named Sandy Lane: family legend has it that, having run short of poets, carpetbaggers, chiefs and civic dignitaries, the city authorities took up Po-Po's suggestion that it be named after his son. Sandy and Ila were living there still when Wayne was born, at 10am on Sunday 23 October 1960, at Downey Community Hospital. It was only after Renee and Rodney had followed, at two year intervals, that they moved across the street to Barland Avenue.

Wayne grew up around go-karts and gasoline and spanners and dusty racetracks. 'Some of my earliest memories are of my dad loading stuff up in the truck to go racing.' By the time Wayne was four, Sandy had graduated from outlaw races in the fields to national-level kart races. He got to be pretty good at it, for reasons beyond driving ability. Sandy was always looking for an advantage wherever it could be found, with constant technical experiments of course, but also lurking in the gaps and loopholes in the rule book. 'I believe in rules,' he insists, with the cheeky assurance of a man who studies them carefully as much for the omission as the commission. Thus when Sandy's great innovation, the world's first lay-down go-kart, saw daylight there were immediately three technical protests. All failed. 'It was within the rules. It was just that nobody had thought of doing it that way before.

'I'd gotten into two-hour endurance racing, and I was trying to figure out a way to get through the air better. I came up with the lay-down kart. It was 23 inches to the top of my head.

'I'd finished the thing after 1am the previous night, and I showed up at Riverside Raceway. Never driven it. I didn't know if it'd make the turns or not. But it had a fibreglass body in metalflake paint, so it really looked professional. Wayne was there, and the whole family. People just flocked. I couldn't pre-enter, so I started off 120th. There were two other guys behind me.

'It was a rolling start. I discovered the first time down the straightaway we were slick. Usually you could set up one guy to pass on the straightaway, maybe two. I was getting four at a time. Over the hill, I had to raise my head so I could see the track ahead. Took me about five laps to get my depth perception.

'In one hour and 15 minutes I worked my way from 120th to fourth. But an hour into the race, pushing the throttle had given me a charley-horse (cramp): my calf muscle had just locked. I was losing feeling on the throttle and brake. But I was going to stay there. Then I thought my leg was going to break off, but I was going to stay there. I was fourth and I knew I could go to the front. Then the damn thing broke a chain. I got out and I hobbled around. I was never so glad to break a chain in my life.'

The lay-down kart eventually got sold to a guy in Florida, who put a miniature rocket on it and did exhibition runs at the drag races. But the lesson had been learned. Nowadays the metalflake paint may be thankfully forgotten, but all endurance karts follow Sandy's lay-down original.

Motorcycles came along casually, it seems, when the guys Sandy used to hang around with said they were kinda fun to horse around on. No coincidence, however. The year was 1964, and the motorcycles in question were a new generation and a new nationality – fun bikes from Japan, with mettlesome little two-stroke motors and an affordable price tag. These machines would create a new recreational market, and an explosion of schoolboy competition. And then, stand back and see what happens when these kids grow up.

Sandy bought an 80cc Yamaha, but the factory-fresh technology cut no ice round the Rainey garage. 'Next thing I got an expansion chamber on it. I didn't like the rotary inlet valve, so I took it off, made an aluminium block. It was reeded and ducted, on alcohol, on Tillotson carburettors, on the street.' This was all two-stroke trickery he'd learned on go-karts; his personal cross-over was proceeding apace. The bikes got bigger, up to a 250cc. 'I let a friend of mine have the kart. He crashed it at Riverside, and was burned, up to 70 per cent of his body. An alcohol fire – you can't see it, and they couldn't get him put out. Even in the ambulance he caught fire twice again. He'd spun, hit the wall, fractured a fuel tank, and filled the belly-pan with alcohol, and it caught fire. Those days, you just wore a leather top, white pants and sneakers. I put the kart behind the garage. I never messed with a car after that.'

Sandy, along with a sizeable number of other So-Cal folk, had found bikes instead. Bruce Brown's milestone movie *On Any Sunday* later chronicled the explosion of motorcycle sport in the USA. Much of it was happening right here. LA had the population, and the weather. And it had the terrain for a hugely varied panoply of sport, from the hills and dunes beside the ocean to an ever-growing number of rough-and-ready dirt-tracks, to the vastness of the High Desert, the Mojave, just an hour and a bit inland, over the San Andreas fault into Joshua Tree country. Soon there was even a play area in LA, Saddleback Park, devoted entirely to motorcycling: trials, trails, motocross and oval-tracks, all just for fun.

Sandy started desert racing, hare and hound. 'That wasn't so much fun for the wife and kids though. You'd take off into the desert for an hour and a half, then come back and they'd say – how did you do? I don't know. They're gonna write and tell me.'

So he joined a high school buddy, who was running TT races, an unholy American mixture of the oval dirt-tracks and motocross, out at a big track at Corona, half-an-hour from Downey. By now Sandy was riding a Bultaco Metisse, heavily modified, of course. 'I was a pretty fair rider, but I could always get my bike so's it would make up for my riding with speed.' Sandy was no victim of the gumption trap. You don't like the cylinder head of your Bultaco? Why, make yourself another one.

Life was good for the young Rainey family. No barrel of money, but enough to keep things going, and a barrel of fun, doing things together. It was only natural that many of these would involve motorcycles. The whole motorcycle crowd seems to have spent their off weekends camping out in the desert, the guys'd be out fun-riding, the gels'd keep the kids'n'campfires burning, one way or another. And it was only natural that a born tinkerer like Sandy would build a bike for his first-born son.

Sandy's perspective: 'Wayne was six or seven, and I got him this little minibike to play in the yard. The wife was saying – man, don't you dare get him interested in racing. And I'd go – u-uh, no, not me. It was a Honda 50, the girls' kind (a step-thru, in Hondaspeak). I took the seat and the gas tank off, welded everything up smooth. Took the handlebars off and made some low bars. I made a little seat for him where the battery pad was. Because he wanted to go trail riding with us. It was supposed to be a piece of junk, but he rode the tar out of that thing.'

To Wayne, it was a towering monster of power and beauty. 'I remember my dad cleaning it up, and I remember the leather seat. It had dirt-track handlebars and a proper throttle and brake. Sandy is a real craftsman, real meticulous with his stuff, and when it got going it'd always work and it'd always look right.

'He'd make something the way it wasn't supposed to be made, and for me it always worked really well. We were in the little one-car garage, and he wanted to teach me how to use the shift pedal. It was like down at the back, then up at the front. If you held the shifter down it'd operate the clutch. When you let go, it goes. It had a straight pipe, so it was really loud, and I couldn't hear what he was saying and he couldn't hear me. So I let go and that thing did a wheelie and busted right through one of my dad's workbenches. It scared the crap out of me, and I leapt out of there crying. But it did something to me as well. It made me really excited. The danger of doing the wheelie and getting out of control gave me such a strong feeling inside. I can remember that feeling talking about it now.'

As for getting him interested in racing – well, when Sandy wasn't racing himself, he was helping other guys prepare their bikes, so by the age of seven Wayne was a Friday Night regular at Ascot Park, the LA district's most notable circuit. Ascot was a half-mile, enough for the big guys to raise some steam. Small for his age, Wayne would hang right up on the fence to watch the professionals. He used to like the spray of dirt when someone came through high on the cushion, sliding even more wildly than the rest as he abandoned the grippy groove to try to run round the outside, 750 Harley exhaust throbbing as he rattled a rooster-tail against the boards. 'I'd watch every race in every class, Novice,

27

Junior and Expert. I knew every guy's name – tell me a number, and I'd tell you the name, and the other way round. I really loved Dave Aldana. I didn't know anything about him except the way he rode. He was number 13. He was all over the place, and that excited me when I was 11 or 12. I also liked Mark Brelsford. I used to go to the Grand National race at Ascot, and see Gary Nixon and Bart Markel, and those guys you'd only see once in a while and I'd think like *wow these guys are really good*.

'After a race I couldn't wait to get home. The next day I'd get up on my old Schwinn bike. There was this one corner by my house on the smooth concrete sidewalk. And I'd go out there first thing in the morning and ride round that corner, that left-hand-turn, 300 corners a day right there – pedal your butt off, then flick it in, use a little bit of back brake, and you'd slide that thing. All day long. I'd wear out tyres. I did that for ever. I'd get kids – there were always a lotta kids round where I grew up – and line them up. Our race was that one turn. I remember how I'd want to see that groove slowly starting to form, marked up by the tyres, the way it did at Ascot. I'd make sure I'd always keep it on that groove, but I always went as fast as I could.' A compulsion, perhaps, to achieve surpassing excellence at one isolated element of technique. Just what an oval-track racer needs, come to think of it.

Then there were the giant culverts, flat-bottomed slant-sided channels of concrete that took the run-off from the San Gabriel and San Bernadino mountains to the Pacific. At times, they'd be strong deep rivers, but mostly they were almost dry. 'There was a lotta green moss there. On the bicycle you'd get in the green moss and you'd flick your kickstand down – and you'd slide for ever with your feet up on the pedals.'

These were settled years, of solid endeavour and stability. At work, layout-man Sandy would be the first at a building site, setting out the main frame layout of each new quick-up house; and then he'd be home in the garage on Barland, making something special for his bike. Or just painting and cleaning and polishing, because everything had to look good as well as work good. Wayne and his friends would hang around the garage and be pressed into service sweeping or washing or cleaning, the price to pay before getting to play with the machines.

When things started to go wrong, it seemed for a while as if they weren't going to stop going wrong. Sandy had won some trophies for TT racing, and was moving on to the pure oval-track American hard-core, going up to Ascot more often. He was working towards the full 750cc senior class. 'I was going to get me a Harley, and really go get 'em. Then I crashed at Ascot and busted my knee joint off.

'I had three kids now, and so my wife said that's it. That's all. I was off for about three months, my car insurance lapsed. My daughter got hit by a car right outside the house. Everything went bad. So I said, you're right.' But he wasn't quite done. Once he'd finished all the work on his left leg, and got it so the knee was working again, which the doctors had told him not to expect, 'I wanted to try it one more time. To see if I was scared or something. So I told the wife I was going trail riding, but I went short-tracking. And I'm checking my left leg to see if the steel shoe is going to make the knee pop out or whatever. Then I remember coming to, looking out of my new Bell Star helmet at all these people looking in. I'd highsided and knocked myself out. So I thought maybe she's right. That's when I quit racing.'

Renee's accident was a horror for a family who would have more than their share. With Sandy off work with his knee, Ila was cleaning houses to help make ends meet. Four-year-old Renee had wanted to go with her that day, but they'd left her with the men to get the work done quicker. It was all a freak combination of events: Renee sticking her head out between two parked cars just as an under-age driver swerved to avoid a van backing out across the street. She just missed the parked cars, but hit Renee. The car dragged the little girl 50 yards down the road, and she ended up wedged underneath it with serious head injuries. Wayne, aged eight, recalls: 'That really wiped my mom out – messed up my dad and mom. I don't remember a whole lot of goodness round then.'

Things came round, of course. Renee made a complete recovery, then set a new kindergarten fashion when she went in with her hair cropped short from all the operations: within a week a number of other little girls turned up crop-headed. The same thing happened many years later. After another serious injury she needed the support of leg-irons for a while, just in those teenage years when you don't want to look conspicuous. Then she tried a pair of Wayne's old racing boots, the heavy lace-ups worn by US dirt-trackers, and discovered an opportunity to mask her disability. 'Pretty soon, all the other girls were wearing race boots too.'

Having married young, Sandy and Ila were growing up along with their kids. It was now, as Renee was recovering, that they moved to Norwalk, to a house that Sandy would keep on and on extending, and where they still live today. Ila recalls the freedom their children enjoyed because of their own youth as parents. 'When we went to the playground my kids'd never play on the swings – they'd always be on top of the swings. We let them do a lot of things other people wouldn't.' Risky things, like getting into motorcycling. Of course she shudders now at the memories.

With hindsight Wayne realises what a close-knit family they were and what a good time they were having, mostly. But as a lad his great impression was of the authority exercised by Sandy. He was strict, and Wayne, Rodney and Renee were scared of him. If they stepped out of line they knew all about it.

Principally, this involved doing well at school. Not that Wayne had too much trouble. Good manners and respect for his elders were drilled into him, after all. This would distinguish him throughout his life. Anyway, there was lots of fun to be had for a competitive youngster in California. Wayne was tiny, but he was agile and feisty. He played a lot of baseball. Grandfather Po-Po liked the motorcycling, but he liked the baseball more. Wayne was a pretty good second baseman, and Po-Po dubbed him Hot-Dog as he yelled from the sidelines. The name stuck when Wayne was put up as a candidate for the presidency of his elementary school. His campaign manager built a big Hot Dog sign out of cardboard, and it did the trick. That was an early taste of politics, if you like, though Wayne recalls: 'At that age, they didn't really expect too much. Things got done because other people did them for you.'

Sandy had quit racing, but Ila gave the OK to preparing bikes for other people, so the family were still trackside regulars. And there was always the weekend play riding, with Wayne – and soon Rodney also – belting around the desert on a variety of homebrewed minibikes. When Wayne was nine, Sandy got him his first 'store-bought' machine, a Honda Z50. He was in at the birth of a recreational revolution. And it was organised: some of the other kids were already racing their minibikes, round dirt tracks that were springing up everywhere. Naturally enough, Sandy and Wayne ended up watching one, where a friend was racing.

'I asked him what he thought . . . if he'd like to try it? He says yeah. So I said, OK, but we don't tell your ma.' Next thing Sandy tells Ila he's taking the kid trail-bike riding at Saddleback Park. Instead, Wayne takes part in his first race.

CHAPTER 2

OUTLAWS
ON THE LOOSE

Little kids on noisy wheels are whizzing round like Hells Angels from Coast to Coast. With a puny engine, insignificant frame and tiny wheels, the minibike at rest does not look like much at all, but small boys and a few determined girls as young as age six see beyond surface trivialities.
Life Magazine, 1971

The 2 January 1971 issue of *Life Magazine* (price 50 cents) marked a trend. And photographed it. Under a heading 'Maxi craze for mini bikes' the magazine wrote:

'Minibikes . . . can go practically anywhere at speeds of from 12 to 40mph. Plenty fast enough to kill an inexperienced rider. At least two such deaths have been recorded. This sort of back-alley activity is hard to monitor. The problem increases with the bike population, which was zero a few years ago, and now is increasing by 250,000 each year.

'One solution . . . is to make facilities available for kids to ride safely under adequate supervision. In Mount Vernon, New York, this means a running track open to kids for two hours every Sunday, but in frisky Southern California where these pictures were taken it means day-long highly competitive racing meets, for different ages and classes of bikes every weekend.'

It is no surprise that among the frisky So-Cal faces they captured – little kids in big helmets, such big heads, such tiny bodies – was Wayne Rainey. Come to think of it, it wouldn't have mattered much which of the many tracks in the LA area he'd visited, the *Life* photographer could have hardly escaped without at least one picture of a future World Champion. This was where they were making them at the time.

Jeff Ward was one. He would become a distinguished motocrosser and leader of the twice-victorious US Motocross team.

The Moran brothers, Sean and Kelly, were also destined for greatness in speedway. Eddie Lawson was another, a couple of years ahead of Wayne all the way, and always a man of few, well-chosen words. Why does he – four times World Champion – think that his generation of schoolkid racers was so important? His answer is a laconic list of venues, conjuring a miasma of memories. 'Trojan, Ascot, Saddleback, Elsinore, Corona, Indian Dunes, Paris Raceway, Carlsbad. We could race seven nights a week if we wanted, and for years we almost did. When we weren't racing, we were on bikes anyway. And we got good.' Oh, yes.

They were not part of the AMA's (American Motorcyclists' Association) structure of officially sanctioned national racing. That official sporting ladder took in amateurs who, if they were good enough, could choose to become 'Professional' at the age of 16 (the title had more to do with proficiency than pay). Once there, a rider with a future could win points to climb to Novice to Junior to Expert, where the big guys fought it out for the Grand National Championship title. The Number One plate was awarded for a mixed series of 25 races or more nationwide, including TT events and some road-races like the classic Daytona 200, but concentrating mainly on oval dirt-tracking. The AMA, a member of the FIM (Federation Internationale Motocycliste) in Switzerland, is America's link to the far-off World Championship structure, embracing the road-racing grand prix as well as motocross, trials, speedway, ice-racing, and even the exotic sport of motoball, played (yes) on motorbikes on a football field. Not that America cared much. To the Southern Californians, 'back East' was almost a foreign country, the Grand National title was championship enough, and what took place in Europe hardly occupied the time of day.

Of course, the US being the way it is, rival sanctioning bodies flourished – still do today, running quite separately from the AMA. The one that matters here is the National Minibike Association, running informal and exuberant locally-based races for kids seven years old and upwards. Classes ran from one-to-three horsepower and four-to-six, and seven-and-over for nine-year-olds. The outlaw tracks, as they were known, varied from rough to ready. Corona, today submerged in suburban housing, was one of the better places, with a TT track, a half-mile and a short-track. It was all dirt-tracking, of a sort; sometimes on shrunken ovals like the big guys ran, usually with a touch of the TT tendency thrown in, with jumps and the occasional right-hand swerve. But it was not (and Wayne would like to emphasise this) motocross or scrambling. The kids wore steel shoes on their left feet, just like the Pros did at Ascot, to drag inside the turns while they urged their mini-motors to spin the rear wheel and slide out the tail. On a booming 750cc V-twin Harley-Davidson, the turn is completed in a wavering tripod of balance between the counter-steering front wheel, the skimming left foot and the rooster-tail of the rear, measured out by deceptively delicate body movement and throttle control. On a minibike, running on fat tyres out of the Sears catalogue, the slide tends to be short-lived, but remains an accomplishment for any nine-year-old to be proud of.

Wayne did not win his first race. He lined up, on his Honda four-stroke, with a football chin-piece on his open-face helmet. 'I was so scared and excited that I wet my pants on the line.' Afterwards, though, like a junkie, as soon as it was over he just wanted to do another one. And boy, had he come to the right place for that!

Sandy needed no persuading. One reason was the need to keep the kids off the streets. 'Where I live – anywhere in California – it's not nice. You've gotta have something to keep you out of trouble. And Wayne was a lot like me. Baseball didn't really ring his bell, and he was too little for football. So I had him try this.' He was careful never to push it. 'I hate that, to this day.' It was always Wayne asking, will the bike be ready for the weekend dad? For Corona. Or Indian Dunes? Or wherever. Sandy would say: How about school? Everything OK there? Then we're on for the weekend. It was a lever for his two boys. 'If they screwed up or got bad grades, she was parked.' As Wayne said later: 'I was kind of afraid of my dad, because he could get really mad. My folks made me appreciate what I had, and not abuse it.'

Pretty soon Rodney was racing too. Full on Rodney, who admits he 'didn't know nuthin' except how to wind the throttle open. Rodney was different from Wayne. He was more broad-based, and enjoyed a variety of sports, especially baseball. Which meant that he didn't eat, sleep and breathe motorcycling. And even then, when they'd all just started, that difference showed. Rodney remembers: 'At Trojan Raceway, I was on one to three horsepower, and he was on four to six, and there wasn't enough to make a class so they'd put us together. They got to start in the front row, and they had to go the whole way round and lap us to beat us. And by the third lap he'd already have gone by us once.'

Rodney – as an adult, dark and thickset – was then even littler and blonder than Wayne. His gung-ho style would make Ila 'laugh and cry at the same time'. Wayne's prowess did much the same to Rodney. 'He knew how to make the bike work. All I knew was wide open or nothing. Wayne knew how to roll it on, and get traction. I wanted to win. One time, the trophy was taller than me. We had to lie about my age. I wasn't seven yet. They'd just watered the track. I remember my dad was on the infield, and I think he was trying to tell me to stay on the inside, but I thought he meant to downshift. So I downshifted and the bike come around and I crashed. Wayne ended up winning. I remember him bringing that big trophy home and I was so mad.'

Soon the boys were racing three times a week. Renee recalls 'the most fun about growing up was packing and going racing somewhere. We could bring one friend – we took it in turns.' Wayne was winning and winning. Ila: 'When he was 10 or 11, people thought he was lying about his age, because he was so good. You couldn't help but notice Wayne. He'd be first off the line and he'd lead from start to finish.'

Wayne had natural, inborn finesse and, like his dad before him, a huge drive to win. He even won over Ila's initial doubts, so she was soon as partisan as any of the mothers who had to be fenced off from the trackside. 'Sandy told the kids, you do it on the track; your mother does it in the grandstands.' Sandy had bought her a scooter to get around on, 'but I was scared to ride it. Then when Wayne was nine he said, come on mom get on the back, I'll give you a ride on it. And he did. And after that I thought: Shoot, if that kid can ride it, so can I.'

It was Wayne's ability that reassured her on the track too. 'Wayne was so fast, but he always looked safe, and in control. I remember one time the bike slid and gripped and threw him up out of the seat so you could see the bottom of his boots. And it was like someone set him back down on the bike and he kept on going.'

Sandy was in heaven. His spare time was gone, just the way he liked it. He'd be home from work, a quick shower, and into the garage. They may only have been minibikes, but he was serious about trying to win, to beat the store-bought bikes with his own stuff. Because he wasn't riding, he couldn't tell how good or bad the engine was. 'Wayne made it look so easy, so it always looked like it had power. So I thought I gotta build a dyno so's I can measure what I'm doing.'

Sandy's garage dynamometer (a metered engine loading device to measure developed – or brake – horsepower: bhp) was a typical marvel of home-tech pragmatics. 'I got a 20-gallon drum, filled it with oil, used a go-kart axle and bought a used gear-drive pump, a lever arm, and a big fish-scale. I used to load the pump by metering the flow of oil to it.' Sandy would hook up a motor and run it up to full throttle against the load, to get a reading on just how hard it could pump that oil against the spring. 'The neighbours hated me, but that's how serious I got.'

Poor neighbours, poor Norwalk. Life was punctuated by the sound of blaring exhausts. Ila recalls how the Ascot bikes were particularly loud. One neighbour used to come out onto his porch with a Martini. Then Sandy'd start up a bike in the street outside, and he'd get such a fright he'd spill his drink. Over and over, it seems. Inevitably, the final assembly tended to get finished long gone midnight on the night before the race. Sandy rigged up a kind of silencer system, and learned to time it perfectly between running the motor long enough to check it out but switching it off before there was open warfare in the street.

Sandy would do anything to the motors. Fit twin carbs, completely change the induction. On Wayne's little Honda he fitted bigger valves and bored the carburettor oval, to flow more mixture while still remaining outwardly standard. He made transmission gears, and spool wheels. 'I liked to take off-the-wall stuff.' The minibike chassis had rudimentary telescopic front forks, but no rear suspension. Until Sandy got involved. Wayne's bike was the first on the block to get a rear swing-arm. A bit later, the 100cc Yamaha was the thing to have. 'So I got a 90cc Suzuki, and changed everything. I liked to try to win with something different. The oddball stuff was a challenge – to make something and catch these other guys.'

Then there was the fuel. Back in the one-to-three class, Wayne's Honda (nominally 1.9 horsepower) was having problems with the 120cc sidevalve motor (a full three horsepower) used by the Moran brothers. 'On a long track we just couldn't run 'em down,' says Sandy. 'So I wondered what to do. I read the rule book over and over. I couldn't do anything more to the motor. Fuel? Let's check what it says about that. The rule book says yes, you must have fuel. But it didn't say what kind. In go-karting we always ran methanol and a hint of nitro. So I bought five gallons of each. I made new needles and jets, because everything has to be 60 per cent bigger. I started trying to get it to carburate on a 50/50 mix.

'I took Wayne out of school one day and we went to Saddleback and I got her dialled in. And Wayne was pretty hard to beat from then on. I built a 70cc just like that for the four-to-six horsepower class, running 60 to 70 per cent nitro. Wayne could really put up a show on that bike – feet up, sideways. It had more horsepower than it could use, than we could ever hook up. And he had the natural talent so he could ride that thing right around anybody, feet up, including Jeff Ward. That thing was awesome.'

Anyone following on behind would have a hard time. Nitromethane stings the eyes and nose. Wayne remembers: 'It really increased the horsepower a lot. Back then everyone would line up to go onto the track single file. And my bike . . . it puts out an odour, and it burns your eyes really bad. So I'm in the group and all of a sudden everyone starts going nuts. They didn't know whose bike was making this smell. Everyone's eyes were watering, even my eyes were watering, and nobody knows whose bike it was. We just killed those guys out there and nobody could figure out what we were doing. We never cheated – we always got accused of it, because my dad worked harder than anybody else.' It was Steve McQueen who gave the game away. The movie star was part of the movement, and his son Chad was one of the Indian Dunes kids. It was through mutual friend Joe Hamilton that Sandy got to help Chad McQueen, but with such a high profile effort it wasn't long before the secret of his special brew got out. Not much later, special fuels were banned.

Where once Wayne had gathered the neighbourhood kids to race bicycles, now they would hang around the little one-car garage, with its array of tools and technical wonders. There was always a crowd. One regular was a quiet little red-headed kid, Mike Minnig, from down the road in Southgate. Minnig was a racing friend, another of the minibike mob. They first met at Trojan Raceway; pretty soon he and Wayne were always round at each other's houses. They built their own version of the powered soap-box car, to run around in the race paddocks. Sandy recalls: 'They'd go in the garage first thing in the morning and by noon they'd be covered with grease.' Mike remembers the down side to that. 'We always had to clean the workshop and the bikes before we were allowed to do anything.'

If racing was for fun, desert riding was for recreation. Or was it the other way round? The desert gang was growing. The Minnigs were a regular part of it, a nucleus even, with their camper-van. The kids would ride all day, reappearing at intervals only to refuel, or to get a scrape dealt with. At night they'd collapse round the campfire, righteously tuckered out. Mainly they went into the Mojave Desert round Dove Springs, where there was endless room to ride and ride. Wayne remembers chasing jackrabbits. You'd try and follow its every move as it jinked across the desert floor. Sometimes they'd drop dead in their tracks.

Wayne, all the while, was moving his way up towards high school. Academically he specialised in doing OK. He jokes now, 'I was good at metalwork' but his grades show he was better than that. Keeping them up to scratch was a major achievement for somebody whose mind was full of racing. It's a tribute to Sandy's work-ethic discipline that he was able to do well at both. He was popular too. Why not? Apart from being bright, friendly and well-mannered, he was a motorcycle racer. That made him a little different from the ball players – especially when they would come back from a big match with legs or arms in plaster casts, and bike racer Wayne never seemed to get hurt.

But even the best behaved child becomes a teenager. Especially, one might say, in Southern California, where the bratty breed was invented. Wayne's bad influence was his cousin Mike Lane, son of Ila's sister Joyce. Mike was a little bit older and a whole lot badder. He taught Wayne to smoke cigarettes when he went with them on holiday to Arkansas. Mike's preacher father Lloyd drove the family

Dodge window-van at glacial speed, halting at every state border (which might be days to reach) to take a snapshot at the signpost, also stopping several times a day, levelling up the caravan, so Aunt Joyce could make tea or lunch. They'd travel for days and barely notch up 1,000 miles. At night when the adults up front would light up, then Mike would duck behind the seats and light up too. 'Pretty soon I was down there with him. I remember turning green the first time and coughing my brain out. I never did take to smoking: it was just getting away with something my folks didn't know I was doing.'

Kids stuff. Like another time they were both staying with their grandmother at Newhall, just out of town on the road north. Wayne was 14, Mike 16 and a licensed driver. 'We decided to go out. So we fetched this other guy, and we took his mom's car, rolled it down the driveway and down the street. It had no gas so we syphoned gas out of other cars. A car came and I jumped into some rose bushes – I looked like a cat scratched me. We got the car going, so we're running these stoplights and signs and sliding round corners and stuff.

'Then all of a sudden the cops are behind us and there's this red light flashing. This guy goes: Mike, you take over. And he says no, I ain't driving. We ended up spinning out and landed up in some guy's front yard. We were surrounded by cops, and one of them has a Colt pistol pointed at us. I thought we were gonna die. But my cousin talked them out of taking us in, so they took us back to my grandma's house at 4:30 in the morning. So she says: Wayne you're supposed to be in bed. So I said yeah grandma, I snuck out. You're not gonna tell dad, are you? And she said, yeah I'm gonna have to tell your dad.'

Sandy never found out about another escapade with Mike Lane. 'I was staying round his house when we snuck out and broke into a school. We took Rodney with us – he was about 11. Is this funny coming from me?' The gang wore masks and dark heavy overcoats. They smashed a window, then ran and hid to see if the cops would come. After half-an-hour, no-one came. So they were in. Quick, where's the safe? Eventually they found it. How to open it, to reveal the riches within? Er – well. 'Eventually, I guess we thought we had enough pencils and erasers and stuff, so we could go.' That was the start and finish of Wayne's career as cat-burglar.

His role as terror of the highways was just beginning though, and would last rather longer. The family had a VW Beetle, notorious for its tendency to spin out of control under the pendulum effect of its rear engine. Yippee! Wayne as a kid had the incurable habit of yanking on the handbrake to provoke exactly that. From the passenger seat. It was somehow even worse when he took the controls a few years later. Rodney: 'He used to love it when it rained. On the freeways you could make circles out of the on-off ramps, and he'd go round sideways all the way.' And only hit the guardrail once.

The family bike trophy collection was growing apace. Wayne used to give away the little silvered plastic cups as prizes in games with the kids – Renee's birthday party guests would go home loaded with silverware. He'd organise bicycle contests for Rodney's friends, though Rodney recalls that when the school bus came by with the girls on board he'd make sure it didn't look as if he was playing with the little guys. Not this racing dude, no way.

Wayne was moving up through the classes, 60cc to 80cc to 100cc. He was about 13 when he reached the 125cc class. A couple of years before he'd met a gangling kid from Upland, a more distant LA satellite some 30 miles to the north-east. Eddie Lawson, two years older, had made a big impression that night at Trojan Raceway. He was clearly someone special. Must be. Rides a Tarbo, a motorcycle nobody's ever hardly heard of. And just look at that steel shoe. It's chrome-plated! It glitters when he walks, but better still when he drags it in the turns, it leaves a trail of sparks. Cool! So little 11-year-old Wayne Rainey walks right up to 13-year-old Eddie Lawson and asks him straight out: 'Where can I get one of them shoes?' It took only a little longer for each to recognise something else in the other, something shared. They were both deadly serious about winning.

Mainly this was because whenever Rainey moved up a class, Lawson was moving on to the next one. He was to remain one step ahead of his fellow Los Angelino right until they both reached the pinnacle, the World Championships, except for this teenage overlap in the mid-seventies. 'I raced him from Trojan Speedway to the 500cc GP World Championship,' says Lawson. 'He'd catch up just about as I was ready to move to the next stage.' Until there was no place left to hide? He laughs his dry laugh. 'Exactly.'

Getting serious had to come naturally. Wayne had been doing so all along, with considerable help from Sandy, who was an excellent and experienced coach. Minnig recalls how the two would 'pow-wow in the pits. His dad taught him a lot at the crucial time. Back in the Corona days. Everybody else was just riding, and he was talking about loading the back wheel. He always kept it secret from the other guys what they were talking about. He'd usually talk to me a bit, but even in those days we were competition as well as good friends.'

Lawson also acknowledges a debt to Sandy, who was to build him one bike and prepare several others. 'He was real good at not only working with the bikes but psychologically. He'd tell us to breathe a lot, and relax. My dad pushed me real hard. But Wayne's dad thought about it a lot more.'

The Sandy Factor didn't always go Wayne's way, at least in the short-term. It was all very well trying to beat the class-choice Yamahas on a Suzuki, but they were popular because they were competitive. Furthermore, the new generation of Japanese bikes had started out pretty good, and had continued to improve. It was getting harder for home-tech to compete. Wayne's bike started life as a 90, bored out to 100cc, tuned to the hilt. It would rev, Sandy recalls, to 14,000rpm, close to double its design speed, and went like a rocket. 'Ungodly fast, but we could not keep the rods in it. We called it the Checkered Flag Blues, because it'd never get there.' Wayne remembers being able to race against 250cc and even 360cc Bultacos on it. 'I could kick their butts for eight laps, but it was a nine-lap race. We had a connecting rod made up out of a special alloy – it cost $50. I couldn't believe anything could be that expensive. That lasted 16 laps.'

Sandy's garage already had a rogues gallery of broken parts. The Suzuki contributed so many broken connecting rods he needed an extra row of hooks. Po-Po was appalled, and told Sandy: 'You're gonna kill that kid. One day that thing's gonna blow up and just tear him apart.' No dad, Sandy would explain, that's not the way it happens. What did happen was that Wayne would power away into a magnificent lead, then the whole damn thing would rattle to a stop. 'I got to watch Lawson, Minnig and Tidwell a whole lot. We went to a lot of these AMA Point Runs (non-championship races), and while they were getting points to become Juniors, I was missing out.' The family had a black cat at the time, named Suzuki. When it died, they buried it out in the backyard with the old Suzuki engine alongside it. It probably took the cat's soul almost all the way to the afterworld, then blew up.

This may all seem like smooth progress. Sounds as easy as little Wayne made it look. But there was turmoil aplenty. Ila may have joined the mothers in the paddock, but she was never comfortable with Wayne racing. He says now: 'I hated to see my mom and dad argue over my racing, yet they always did. I was always stuck in the middle. It was really a troubled time for me. I'd hang out with a lotta other kids, and they'd all party it up after the races, and I couldn't because my mom and dad were with me. I always wondered what that was like. My dad liked for me to have short hair. He had long hair, but I had to have short hair. I really respected him, and I didn't want to get into trouble with him because it wasn't good when I got in trouble.'

Ila's disquiet was part of a pattern of trauma that was driven by a second ghastly accident to Renee. She was eight, Wayne rising 11, and Ila had taken all three to the Marine Stadium at Long Beach. 'We used to go there skiing and stuff during the week when my dad was at work,' recalls Wayne. Rodney and Renee were playing on the shore when the accident began some way off.

A waterskier had fallen, and his partner in the boat began hauling him in, rather than following the procedure of raising the warning flag and circling. Another boat hit the fallen skier, injuring him severely, and pulling the guy in the boat over so that he fell onto the controls. The boat took off at full throttle, circled once, then the second time round it came right up onshore directly where Renee was standing. It felled her in front of her mother's eyes. She was grievously hurt, gashed across her lower back so deeply that the sciatic nerve was cut. 'She would have died right there, but there were some trained paramedics right next to us and they saved her from bleeding to death.' It was the start of years of surgery for Renee. She has never recovered full use of her leg, although the only sign now is a slight limp for the pretty, breezy blonde who taught herself to tap-dance and to roller-skate in spite of it all.

Ila now hardly remembers the time after that, how she coped with Wayne carrying on racing. But one simple memory speaks volumes. 'Sandy just sat around.' She'd sure never seen him do that before. 'Then Wayne talked him into going racing again. I said: Wayne isn't ready for that kind of racing. He's not old enough to tell us. But when Wayne made up his mind nothing would make any difference. That's what Sandy wanted to do too.'

CHAPTER 3

THE KID
FROM NORWAY

'How different it might all have been if Yamaha's
headquarters had been on the East Coast.'
John Reed, guardian angel to the LA Crucible Kids

It is clear that during the 1970s Los Angeles was a forcing house of racing talent. What is less clear is why. Yes, they had plenty of tracks and lots of action. But the heartland of dirt-track racing was the Mid-West, while out on the West Coast the big fields and lots of rivals were in northern California – the spawning ground of the likes of Kenny Roberts. That was the cream of the racing. But the cream of the riders was down south among the city boys. The LA Crucible.

In fact, there were four of them, the cream of the Crucible. Rainey and Minnig from around Norwalk, Lawson and Tidwell from Upland, further out of town near Riverside Raceway. Intriguingly both Lawson and Minnig rate Mike Tidwell as the most talented of all. Which is, in the light of subsequent events, saying something. (Sandy, typically, insists: 'To me, that was just money. He always had really good equipment, while I'd be horsetrading. Of course he had talent too. He was like a works team to us – that's who I wanted to beat.') But Tidwell was not to be part of these events. After two consecutive back injuries his parents put a stop to it before anything worse happened. Lawson ran into him a year or two back. He's a pharmacist, happily married, with his own shop. A rather different set of career choices would grip the other three.

There might have been more, but for the sobering reality of a pair of fatalities in the group. Albert 'Junior' Turner, a little older and very talented, hit the wall at Ascot. All the survivors of that late teenage group go quiet at the mention of his name. Wayne carried a deep impression after attending his funeral: Albert's body lay in an open casket, dressed in his racing leathers. A little later, close companion Don Tortarelli – better at keeping the gas open than at actual finesse – fell off at Tulare, under the wheels of a full pack of AMA Juniors. He didn't get up again. Wayne: 'I was the last person to talk to him. I was riding the Yamaha by then, and he said to me, you be listenin' out for my Harley coming up. I said OK. He was killed on the third corner of the first lap. That year I realised that this might be fun, but it could be real dangerous.'

This was a shadow for the future. But right now it was just racing, whenever they could, two or three times a week. And when they couldn't race? Why, go out and practice.

Dirt-track racing is akin to European speedway, but rougher and faster. The art is all in the slide. First you must have the courage, on a bike with no front brake, to pitch it in to the turn so that it broadsides, scrubbing off speed. Then you must have the strength of mind and the delicacy of balance and throttle control to set the rear wheel spinning under power, sustaining the slide to complete the corner in a crescendo of stone-spattering acceleration. It's a repetitive skill, and sounds simple. Yet it is so full of subtleties that achieving full mastery can occupy half a lifetime.

Rainey and his cronies didn't want to spend that long, and the solution was to practise and practise, with a ferocity that still leaves them wondering at it all. Suburban LA had places enough to do it – mainly oil fields. Rainey and Mike Minnig would be out there every afternoon after school and for years to come – round and round and round. Once Wayne came flying over a jump to see a helicopter 'hoovering away about 10 feet off the ground. I got such a fright I laid the bike down.' It was a CHiPS highway patrol man, come to see who was raising such a dust storm that drivers on the adjacent road had to slow down. Better get out of here, boys. Then they'd take 500 or 1,000 feet of hose along to keep the dust down. They already had drag-along graders to clear the oval of bumps and bushes. Sometimes other guys would join in: Rob 'Burn-Out' Salerno or his brother, or others of the local bike set, recalls Minnig. 'They'd ride a little bit, then stop and watch us. But for me and Wayne it was just a wide-open grind. See how fast you could go, for as long as you had.' When Minnig started working and could only ride in the afternoons, Wayne and Eddie would get together to do it the whole day. 'We'd find a paved parking lot and set up an oval, then we'd push each other like you wouldn't believe,' remembers Eddie, 'sliding motocross bikes on motocross tyres on the pavement, all day long until we were out of gas. Anything anywhere, it was always a contest. And he'd beat me often as not, practising or racing. I was working on being smooth. He was much more aggressive.'

The four were soon in control back home. Tidwell and Lawson took most of the wins in the 125cc class. Wayne could race them, but his 98cc 14,000rpm Suzuki just wouldn't make the final lap. The tracks were mainly quarter-miles or even shorter, 12 or 14 seconds a lap. 'We'd also do these District 37 Point Runs out in the desert, with 400 or 500 guys; and while Eddie and Minnig and Tidwell moved up the classes by adding up points for finishes, I was always stuck in the 100cc novice class. I'd be riding with them, but I'd never finish.'

These were official AMA races. The association's structure divided California into three zones: District 37 was Southern California, where the Crucible Kids held sway; District 35 was Central California; and District 36 Northern California. This was the hot-bed, comprising not only the San Francisco Bay area, but also the farmlands of California's fertile Central Valley – towns like Bakersfield, Modesto, Sacramento, where a motorcycle crazy kid, without the distractions of the ocean, mountains, city life or almost anything, come to think of it, really could concentrate. Sandy recalls: 'What made Southern California great was the professional racing at Ascot Park, but when it came to our stuff it was always the same 25 guys. Up north, they'd have five heat races of 25 riders just to qualify for the semi. That was real racing.'

And that was where Wayne was bound. With the Suzuki dead and buried, he recalls an improvement in fortunes. 'We'd finally gotten some Yamahas, and I'd started winning down south. We were the first to go up to these different districts to race against different guys.' First it was a trip to Tulare, between Bakersfield and Fresno. 'I was just 15, and nobody had ever heard of me; but my bike had the number 82, black on white, like an AMA professional rider. I won both races, and they thought I was an Expert.' This felt pretty good.

Then it was up to the San Jose Half-Mile. 'That was a real cool place to be. It was one of the big-time race-tracks, like Ascot. And I got there and won my race. Just blitzed them. And everybody's going: who's this Wayne Rainey guy?' A question that was answered in a novel way the very next night at the Oakdale short-track, at the other end of the San Francisco bay. The commentator mis-read the address on the entry, taking Norwalk for Norway. Oh, so that's where this little blond kid's come from, who's so fast but we've never heard of him. He's Norwegian. Must be the Norwegian champion probably, because he's a real fighter. Fell off in his heat race, started from the back row for the final, and ended up passing everybody. So a big hand please, for Wayne Rainey, who came here tonight all the way from Norway (wherever that is).

Pretty soon there was a little So-Cal gang, three or four vans, sticking together in the paddock, a small invasion force spearheaded by the Crucible Kids. They had to stick together, because, in Minnig's words, 'it was kind of a grudgy thing. The guys up there didn't like us coming and beating them. We were the enemy.'

Notoriety is a valuable commodity in the renegade world of bike racing, and Wayne was getting noticed enough so pretty soon he and Sandy were getting outside help from racing insiders. This is where the key figure of Kenny Roberts starts to touch on the story. Not directly, but in an oblique kind of way. It is significant, for Kenny was many things to Wayne through his career, and he started like this, by paving the way.

Kenny, from Modesto, was then engaged on his meteoric rise through the American Grand National ranks towards world domination. On the way, he had mobilised Yamaha's American wing, on the crucial dirt-tracks as well as the road-race tracks where they were already so prominent. Yamaha's Pete Schick had in turn hooked up with one of American racing's living legends, the grizzled and gruff West Coast tuner Shell Thuet. The spearhead of an early and highly significant Japanese task force into US racing was established in Los Angeles.

Thuet was and is a remarkable man. In 1995, aged 82, he still attended the Grand National races, and didn't dream of retirement. 'There's too much to be done.' His self-appointed task is to beat the Harley-Davidson factory, and when Kenny and then Wayne came into his life he'd already been engaged in this for almost 40 years. First it was with Indians, preparing a factory bike for Jimmy Kelly in 1939. But 'if I got a good rider the Harley factory team would buy him away'. When the Indian factory died, Shell switched to Royal Enfields. Then Triumphs. Now it was Yamahas – the quest was the same.

Thuet's shop, Shell Racing, was close to Norwalk, and with all the race-bikes and whatever, it was a cycle-stop haunt for the pre-teenage Wayne and Mike Minnig. Shell recalls the kid Wayne bugging him. 'He always said he was going to ride for me. Ended up he did.'

That was a big deal, for with Kenny Roberts riding Thuet's bike they had been able to transcend not only the workaday origins of the parallel-twin XS650 Yamaha street-bike engine but also the power unit's fundamental unsuitability compared with the specialised developed-for-dirt V-twin racing Harley-Davidsons. Kenny's mountainous talent and determination had blazed him to two Grand National titles, in 1974 and 1975, defeating Gary Scott and all the other factory Harleys. The renegades had won.

The consequences of this impinged directly on Wayne because racing success had opened a new line of business for Thuet, selling hop-up kits to Yamaha riders to convert their 650 road engines into 750 race units. He prospered in partnership with machine-shop owner, engineer and racing enthusiast John Reed. 'He did all the calculations, and I did all the machining,' explains the taciturn Thuet.

Now John Reed was a serious man-about-the-tracks. His own children were part of the pack racing round Trojan and the desert-riding weekend gang; Reed Senior, who had his own precision gear machining business, was an urbane sophisticate at the top end of the adult hierarchy. He even had a couple of walk-on appearances in the landmark movie *On Any Sunday*. 'When Keith Mashburn went through the fence at San Jose, I was the guy who drug him out.' John had followed the Minnig and Rainey kids closely, the families were friendly, the kids used to stay over at each other's houses. He watched Mike and Wayne riding, the fastest of the bunch, increasingly impressed as they worked on imitating the feet-up full two-wheel slide style of hero Kenny Roberts. There was not much to choose between them on speed; if Wayne had anything, he was smoother. And with Eddie Lawson already on the books – another to pave the way as he climbed the AMA ladder a rung or two ahead – it was only natural that Wayne would follow into the Shell Racing Specialties stable.

Sadly, this was at the expense of Mike Minnig. 'I was 13, and Wayne was 14, and I'd always had sponsorship from Shell Motors. I'd just got my 250 Yamaha and we were at Elsinore Raceway, getting ready to race, in the burn-out area where you'd go and do your thing. I flipped it over. The exhaust pipe went right through my foot.' Mike was out for 18 months. When he came back – 'What's Wayne riding?' One of the nice new Shell Racing Specialties bikes. This was a key passage between the friends and rivals. Rainey would go on to national and world glory riding works bikes for factory teams, Minnig would remain a struggling privateer until the finish of his racing career some years later after a heavy road-racing crash, never having got beyond the USA. But the little flame-haired guy, who still lives in Southgate near where he grew up, has no resentment. 'Wayne had the upper hand right there. That's when things started really going his way. Even though it didn't really matter. I always knew somehow, even when we were kids, that he was going to be World Champion one day.'

Wayne turned 16 in October 1976. He was now old enough to become a Professional as far as the AMA were concerned, and to embark on the road towards his dream of a Grand National title. This entailed climbing the ladder, class by class, to reach Expert status, where the big guys rode the 750s for the Grand National title on the Mile and Half-Mile ovals and TT tracks, switching to 360cc single-cylinder two-strokes for short-tracks. It took one year as a Novice, riding a relatively tame 250cc single-cylinder two-stroke; and one as a Junior, up against fellow-beginners on full 750cc four-strokes. Complete those successfully and you were a Rookie Expert, and on your way.

He still had one year of high school to go – by the time he graduated in 1978 he was already an AMA Junior, racing a full 750 Shell Racing Specialties Yamaha.

He was still really riding for Sandy, in their own colours. Shell

Racing Specialties provided a Yamaha 250 two-stroke and all the parts he needed, but Sandy was in charge of preparation and tuning. Just as he liked. Sandy was also enough of a visionary to keep widening the horizons. Wayne was driving at 16, of course, a 440 cubic inch Dodge van, and Sandy'd give him a couple of hundred dollars and send him further and further afield. Mechanically simple, the bikes needed little maintenance, just a new piston ring now and then, and the gearing adjusted with sprocket changes. Wayne could handle that easy enough. And the rest. 'Took his homework with him: that was part of the deal. He had to graduate or I'd cut her off.' Wayne recalls that his classmates – especially the girls – had a kind of favourable way of looking at a guy who went racing weekends instead of playing football with the other guys, especially when the jocks would break their arms or sprain their ankles, and he'd never have a scratch. His teachers were not so impressed, but that had been going on for a while.

It started with sport – baseball, where as he grew up, and in spite of his tiny stature, Wayne got to be 'a pretty good second base man.' Without knowing it, he was already veering away from team sports. 'We'd play for a title game, and I'd get some big hits and big plays and we'd still lose. That upset me, because I'd feel I'd played well.' He was racing every weekend anyway. There 'I could try to win by just beating the next guy. And you blamed yourself if you lost. Racing's pretty much cut and dried.' So when the coaches put it to him that he would have to make a choice between racing and getting better at baseball, the decision was easy.

'I had to get good grades, and I had to get good citizenship. Which meant I couldn't get in any trouble at school. All day long, I'd be dreaming about racing, about the feeling it was to win, and sliding the bike and my style, and how it looked to other people. And what I needed to do to make it look more like my heroes. From 12 to 15 I really worked on my style a lot without even knowing it. Because I thought only about racing.'

In his final year, a long-hanging threat was verbalised. Norwalk teachers were no different from those anywhere else in the world in their opinion that there was no future in this racing foolishness. And if he missed any more school to go racing, he'd be kept back to repeat his Senior year. Wayne was not a bad scholar, just preoccupied, having already started another life. He kind-of agreed about the future, had brief thoughts of becoming a dentist which didn't last beyond lunchbreak, then decided not to worry any more. And to upgrade his travel arrangements, now he was going to Grand National races countrywide. Like the Louisville Half Mile, on 4 June in Kentucky. 'Friday after school I took my first plane trip. They had the Grand National race Saturday night, with guys like Jay Springsteen, Steve Morehead, Ted 'Too-Tall' Boody, Corkie Keener – all the guys Kenny used to race. I really liked to watch those guys, they were so fast. Springsteen won, and I was gonna try to ride like he did the next day, when they had a programme for the Juniors.'

This weekend out of school was to be a pivotal race: his first meeting with the rider who beat him for AMA Junior of the Year, and who in the 1990s would become one of dirt-track racing's biggest-scoring multi champions, Scott Parker. He rode a Harley, Wayne the Yamaha. The American bike with its pulsing power delivery was much better suited to the pea gravel of the Kentucky horse track. 'The Yamaha didn't hook up too good on that kind of stuff, but in qualifying I went quicker than Springsteen had on the Harley the night before. They were quite impressed.' In the race, on a one-line follow-the-leader track, Wayne did that, conceding the win to the new rival from Michigan.

Then Sunday night he flew back, in time for school Monday morning. The only mistake was telling one of the teachers. 'He hated it. But it was my last year and I guess they wanted me out of there.'

Not winning that first encounter was fairly typical. As a novice, he'd been second in the nation on points, but drew satisfaction from the fact that the guy who beat him had done '15 or 16 more races, and the only times I raced against him I beat him.'

He was working between times to support his racing habit. Mainly it was with Sandy, hefting tools around and driving the fork lift loaded with timber. 'I never did use the Skil saw (the standard power plank-ripper – or finger-slicer – from which novices were kept clear), but I could hammer the heck out of them nails.' He did workshop odd-jobs for John Reed as well, and later on also worked for a motorcycle shop, Hyperkinetics, then for the firm which made his own special racing exhausts, Bill's Pipes, welding up headers and expansion chambers. 'But I got worried that the welding might hurt my eyesight. I'd always worked on improving my peripheral vision, and when we were driving to races we'd have a family competition to see who could read the road signs first.' Wayne always won.

As a Junior, Wayne had already begun travelling out of California, to the lands beyond the mountains that the far-west Americans call Back East, in the tone of voice that implies a foreign country. His first such trip was to Sturgis in South Dakota. He and Vince Mead took the Shell bikes. They spent too long goofing off that time at a Macdonalds in Vegas, and Wayne missed his Amateur event on Saturday. So he stripped off his numbers and lined up for qualifying next day with Eddie and the Novice Professionals, his little 250 among the 360s, fast enough not to get noticed. The next big run was all the way to Daytona in Florida with his school buddy Stacey Berry, taking in some races in North Carolina, then the State Fair series in Kansas. A long way from home, albeit closer at least to Norway. For the next year or two he'd do the long-haul runs with Eddie Lawson, who recalls, 'I did most of the driving while he slept a lot.' (But Eddie, that's what Wayne said about you. 'No shit!' The Lawson humour strikes again from behind.)

On the way, Wayne would stop off at non-championship races – 'po-dock races' – to pick up $20 or $30 gas money. It was the first taste of what was to become a way of life. And a sweet taste. 'I ran 52 races that year, and won 50 of them.' Races for which you would first have to qualify. 'With up to 20 heats, they'd only take the winners of the fastest 10 for the final.'

The Daytona visit at 16 was Wayne's first encounter with the Florida speed bowl, one of America's – the world's – cathedrals of racing, with its soaring banking and hoary traditions. Wayne was dirt-tracking there, of course, in a series at local tracks that was a different part of Speed Week. But he did get a chance to see the pavement stuff for the first time. The word 'road' refers to origins rather than actuality: this is closed-circuit racing on tarmac, European style, and until 1979 was still one of the elements of the mixed-discipline AMA Grand National series.

The Camel Pro-sponsored title of 1976 comprised 28 events: five quarter-mile 'short-tracks' (on 360s), five TT events over twisty tracks with jumps, seven Half-Miles, six Miles (on 750s), and four road races, run under FIM F750 rules. Daytona was also a round of the FIM F750 title, and this year the likes of Barry Sheene and race winner Johnny Cecotto (a GP World Champion from Venezuela) joined top US riders including Roberts and Gary Nixon. Wayne watched in desultory fashion. The speeds of the 750cc two-strokes on the banking were impressive, but Daytona did not act as Damascus, and there was no blinding revelation of the future. Wayne was to remain a pure dirt-tracker for several more years.

Wayne was still small for his age, but he was already a grizzled veteran of racing at 17. 'After turning professional at 16, my first race was at Ascot. There was an eight-race series, and I won every one of them. By the time I became a Junior, I must have done more than 1,000 races already.' They'd all been on two-strokes, while Lawson – one step ahead – was already riding the 750 Shell machine. John Reed still remembers the day when they put Wayne on the 750 for the first time. It was at a practice session, at Corona, 'this wisp of a thing. He was so little. I told him: don't bust the fence. Don't bust your future. He went out there – he looked like he was just made for it. Lawson held the track record, and Wayne beat it first time out.'

The 750 was certainly a step up, but in retrospect it was a somewhat slippery step. Roberts had worked miracles on the Yamaha, while even in 1976 Alex Jorgensen had won a few races on a bike with a Norton engine, with a basically similar configuration to the more technically advanced overhead camshaft Japanese motor. But these vertical twins, with their evenly spaced firing order, had a basic disadvantage on the dirt tracks because of their smooth power delivery, making them prone to runaway wheelspin. The 60-degree V-twin Harleys, which could trace their ancestry directly back to the 1920s, had a lolloping beat that gave the tyre time to recover some grip before the next two-fisted boo-boom (or even, in the case of the simultaneously firing 'Twingle' just Boo-oom). It was a phenomenon that took GP racing many years to cotton on to, with the arrival in 1992 of Honda's 'Big Bang' close-firing-order V4 motor. By the time Wayne got on the Yamaha, however, it was seriously outpaced by the Harleys.

This effect was not so pronounced in the Junior class. Wayne won a lot of races as a Junior, ending up second overall to Scott Parker, his major rival, who had the benefit of more races on his doorstep: from Michigan, he had the choice of East Coast and mid-West tracks. 'When we met up, I'd beat him more often than he beat me. I remember my first Mile, at San Jose. I had about a straightaway lead when the clutch lever vibrated round and ended up against the engine kill switch. I thought the engine had broke, but it was only the lever shorting out the switch. So we lost that race. But to be number one in the points wasn't the main thing with me then. Just to get the points to go on and become an Expert.'

This was the big time, and it got tough. Until now, Wayne was used to winning pretty much as he pleased, most of the time. If not winning, finishing right up there. Even as the only Yamaha, that had been the case in his Junior year. Up with the experts, on the factory bikes, against tough riders with years of experience – well, this was where he wanted to be, but he had no idea just how much it all meant. 'My first Grand National was at the Houston Astrodome. I qualified for the final, and finished eighth. And I remember how tired I was after only 10 laps, and thinking wow, I'm really gonna have to shape up. I never rode that hard in my life. Until now races would be over in three or four minutes. The nationals were 25 laps, 15 minutes or more, and that was a long time. My arms were getting pumped up, my tongue was hanging out, and I was dead beat. It was a whole new experience for me.'

He also faced his Rookie season without one familiar support system. Sandy was relegated to the background. 'Shell told me OK, you can prepare a bike as a spare if you want, but he rides for me now. I said OK, good.' There was no rancour; even today Thuet talks of the hugely popular Sandy as 'a peach of a guy'. To his riders, Shell was rough, gruff and tough; John Reed acted as moderator. Reed remembers: 'These young kids – Eddie and Wayne – would say: well, Shell, d'you think we could change the gearing? And he'd say: What's that! Being around motorcycles and the dyno all his life, he was hard of hearing. Then he'd say: You ain't goin' fast enough to change the gearing. So they'd come to me and then I'd ask Shell, and he'd say OK. He was like an old junkyard dog. His growl was always worse than his bite.' But money was tight this particular year, and while Thuet had gone with Eddie to every race the year before, Wayne was on his own. It was a sobering experience for a sportsman who until now had never had to think about trying hard. Then, just to underline it all, the year ended with his first serious injury.

'At the end of that year I ended up going to the San Jose Mile. I showed up, but I didn't have a bike. The Yamahas weren't ready. I had all my racing gear but I forgot my boot and steel shoe. Then a guy named Tex Peel offered me a ride on his bike – his Harley. I'd never ridden one before, and I qualified in the top ten. But I had a funny feeling that day. The whole thing didn't feel right. I'd had to borrow a steel shoe. I didn't like that. All through my career, I liked to have my own stuff, and look after it myself. At the GPs, I would have six helmets and five pairs of leathers. I'd spent one and a half hours just getting the helmets ready. When I had to borrow stuff I knew right away I wasn't properly prepared for the race. It was as though I wasn't meant to be racing.

'In the final, I went into the corner – we're going into there at about 120mph. And this guy in front of me just parked it. I locked it up to avoid hitting him, and that caused the back tyre to blow right off the rim. That used to happen now and then back when they started using the bigger tyres.

'I hit the fence head on. I woke up on the race-track, and my dad was there, and I said: what's going on. He said: you crashed. And that was the first feeling I ever had in my whole life that doing something I loved could hurt me badly.'

He had two crushed vertebrae, and the heavy impact had caused his heart to shift inside his body. A potentially traumatic, even fatal, injury. As it was, Wayne was laid out for more than a month recuperating, back home with the family. Ila had Rodney and Renee home as well, which would have been just fine – but they too were bedridden. Rodney had broken his neck while out desert-riding; had to be helicoptered out and was similarly immobilised on his back, while Renee was recovering from yet more surgery on her injured leg. The little house in Norwalk was a hospital again.

Not surprisingly, this was a crucial time for the 19-year-old eldest patient. Having swept all before him on the way to becoming an Expert, he'd run into a wall. And only narrowly come through bouncing off it.

'I'd thought I could do good, and now I started losing confidence in myself. It went down a whole bunch. I used to line up at the start and look to see who I was racing against, and I'd think heck I can't beat these guys. So I was already beaten before I started. Being so young, I just wasn't smart enough to figure out the circumstances – that I was on a Yamaha against these Harleys. Even Kenny couldn't do it at the end. And I was on my own.

'I was questioning my dedication then, because I was chasing girls more and partying more. I was just a kid, and I was out driving around. Seemed like racing was the least of my worries. I'd gone from being the best to not even being sure I could run with these guys again. Yet I was still good enough to make the Grand National finals that year – the best I finished was sixth or seventh in a final. But it was nothing compared with what I was used to.

'After it got hard for me, I just didn't have that much fun. I wasn't nearly as strong mentally as I became later. It took me about three years to get out of that slump.'

That eventual recovery was marvellous, and took Wayne to the pinnacle of motorcycle racing – where he found Eddie Lawson, his long time fellow of the LA Crucible. And if the reasons for the Crucible Syndrome remain too diverse to be singled out, one thing is clear. This marvel was not created by opportunity alone. It was something else that took Wayne and Eddie all the way. A determination, a focus, an obsession, each in his own manner. Something that started so young that they retained a childish view of racing, where winning was the only achievement, and there was no such thing as a noble second place. It was an attitude that would prove devastating.

CHAPTER 4

THE
BARNSTORMERS

'You hate those missed opportunities. Looking back now, we really
weren't true professionals. We were like amateur professionals,
compared withwhat we could have made it.'
Itchy Armstrong, itinerant dirt-track entrant

Stale smoke and socks, beer-cans and damp towels, sour
adrenalin, leather, and a motel room full of feathers. This is
Kansas, the day after a dirt-track race, and about ten of them had
all pitched in for a room, to share the shower. Then they'd drunk
some beer, had a pillow fight, generally trashed the place until the
small hours. 'When we woke up,' said Wayne, then aged 16, 'it was
pretty late. There were feathers everywhere, and we were all
laughing, then somebody says, where's Jeff?'

Jeff was Wayne's girlfriend's brother, who'd come along to help
out with the driving. Some time in the after-race chaos he seemed
to have disappeared. Along with Wayne's vehicle.

About seven that evening, the county police come knocking on
the door. 'Anybody here own a grey Dodge van, with California
plates?' Well, yeah. It's mine. We've been looking for it. 'Well then,
sonny, you'd better come and take a look.'

Wayne's Dodge is half on the road, and half off it, wheels in the
ditch. Two sheepish faces at the window. One is Wayne's buddy
and travelling companion. The other is a girl. Not, Wayne
remembers, a pretty girl, by any stretch of the imagination. No sir.

Jeff'd been driving, she'd been hitch-hiking, and the two of them
came to the decision to park up for a little while. Get to know each
other. These were free and easy times. You couldn't behave like that
now. 'I'm glad I had this part of my life before Aids and that stuff.'
Wayne's attitude has shifted over the years, in a more complicated
way than the usual journey from wild oats to baby's oatmeal.

So there they were, parked up, doin' a spot of get-to-know-you wrestling. That was when the van eased itself over into the ditch and got stuck. That's about when the police came by.

They all pulled the van out again, and all went back to the motel. Including the girl. There they proceeded to do what motorcycle racers (all racers, it seems, or almost all) do to willing girls. If she'll take turns, then they'll take turns . . .

There are so many stories, kiss and tell stories. Some are hard to believe. There were girls everywhere they went. And they were willing. Especially when they met this cute little guy from California, dreamland, like they'd seen on TV. Wayne surfed a bit, and looked like it, with his sharp-cut good looks and long fair hair; and his hot-rod van was all-Californian, from the plates to the paint job. It was so easy for him. And so now Wayne, remembering, talks about them in his private moments. About how they used to swop back and forth; how he urged Eddie Lawson on ('Go, team-mate, go'); how he'd pass on the spare girls to his mechanics and helpers; or let them climb on the balcony, then put on a show. Girls, girls, girls. So many of them. And so badly behaved. Like 'Tag-Team' Tammie, and a hundred others. Even Shae, his wife, smiles indulgently along with the old stories now.

Wayne had been part of the loose-knit, loose-living dirt-track community from 16. 'This was freedom. For the first time I was at races without being with my parents.' The kid riders'd stay at each others houses. Then it was your turn. 'When they came to California, the kids would come and stay with us,' recalls Ila. 'All of them.'

Right through the dirt years, the racers from out west would set up temporary base. One spot was the Larsens' house in Indianapolis; then there was the Strube family in Peoria – Chuck and Boodie. And a bunch of vans from out West in the yard. Minnig remembers Wayne as a natural leader. Distinguished by his courteous manners (they continue to distinguish him to this day), good looking and full of fun. 'The thing with Wayne was every time he walked in a room, everybody liked him. Always have done. And he was so funny. People who only met him later in his career never knew this, because he got serious. He could make a roomful of people roll on the floor. And he did this, time after time, state after state. Everywhere we went, people would say: Hey, Wayne's here. The party would start. I was going on his coat tails, tell you the truth. I've never really thought about it, but I did.'

The charm worked every way. One night, at Boodie's place, Wayne asked Mike if he could borrow his van for a little while. He called the next day. From Ohio. 'This girl there had called him and he just had to see her. Two days later, he shows up again with my van, and a big smile on his face.'

The wild nights were symptomatic of wild days, and a wild lifestyle. This was the American dirt-track circus – a gang of guys who'd drive back and forth across the country, pitching up at Peoria or Louisville or Syracuse or Somewheresville out in the cornfields. The focus was the Grand National series, with a bunch of other money races in between. Oftentimes the races would be linked in with some larger event, like a State Fair, or the Daytona road-races. Town would be full already. Then the dirt-trackers would arrive . . .

Just getting there was an adventure. More dangerous, Wayne is quite sure, than the racing. 'We would drive down the road at 100mph, me and a group of these guys, all going to the same racetrack, on these two-lane roads in Kansas or wherever. We had fuzz-buster radar detectors, but we were still always getting stopped for speeding violations. There were so many times I should have been dead. We'd pass cars and there'd be someone coming the other way, so there'd be nowhere to go except his emergency lane. Or you'd be right up behind another van and it'd look like you were drafting him. But you were pushing him. Then all of a sudden your buddy would swerve, and right there would be a horse pulling a cart in your lane. We'd just miss it, then laugh about it.'

Often they were laughing anyway. There was plenty of marijuana wafting round the dirt-track paddocks, and Wayne is no Clinton: he inhaled, and now admits it with characteristic honesty. 'I guess I did it because everybody else did it. When you're travelling and all you can see is 500 miles of road and you smoke some dope – then everything's funny. It's nothing I'm proud of now, but being kids we did it.'

When he did end up in jail, back home in LA some years later, it wasn't for that. 'One night we got a bit wild, and I took my van round to Shae's school, and we were doing handbrake turns and stuff on the playing fields.' He was arrested, but when he was still inside almost 24 hours later he began to feel it a bit excessive. Turns out he wasn't the only Wayne Rainey in the USA, and the other one was a wanted man in Florida. Took a bit of time to be sure which one was which.

Dirt-trackers, along with rodeo professionals and the NASCAR (National Association of Stock Car Racing) oval-track car racers, are America's modern barn-stormers. The flying circus. Hard-living, hard-drinking, hard-riding, fast and dangerous. Wayne recalls the first time he got drunk – with Eddie, at the Bartonville race. They were technically under-age, not yet 18, but the guys at the Bartonville Fish Fry at the fairground weren't too fussy and they loaded up on big takeaway cartons of beer. It didn't take much. 'Eddie's never been much of a drinker. A bit like me.' Rainey was glad to be on the swing in front of Eddie on one of the rides when the whole bucket of beer came up again the same way it went down, spraying the line of would-be merrymakers awaiting their turn. 'I think because of the fact you couldn't drink until you were 21 meant that Americans partied it up a bit harder when they did get the chance.'

Rainey was a full Expert dirt-track racer for two years. On a Harley. One thing he had learned as a Rookie Expert, apart from how hard it was to win a Grand National, was that you're never going to do it on a Yamaha. Over the next two years he was to learn that he would never do it on a Harley either. The slump continued, though he hardly noticed. It was such fun. The most he had in his whole life. Questions about dedication were easily deflected.

The Harley days taught Wayne about plenty of things. Including how hard it is to win. Never again would he be unimpressed by the achievement that had seemed so easy in his early racing years.

Looking back now, he knows what he did wrong, and why he failed to rise far enough above the privateer Harley gang. His bike was one of scores of production-racer XR750s. But it was a good one, right enough, good as any of the others running on a tight budget. Thanks to Itchy Armstrong.

Now Itch is a languid kind of guy. He talks things through real slow and gentle, as if there's all the time and all the patience in the world. Even his nickname is redolent of a dogged acceptance. 'I was working with my father in a door factory. They had a pipe system running above where I worked, taking away the sawdust from the big ripper saws. There was a leak there, so there was always sawdust trickling down on me.' Itchy.

Itchy's settled down now, with children, and lives in the hills overlooking the city in an amiable sort of house that is probably almost always in the throes of some sort of rebuild. If not that, it'll be a machine of some sort. Itchy was born to tinker. People like Itchy are the backbone of the barnstorming crowd. These Harleys are roaring beasts, certainly. But they are also simple things, closer to biplanes than the jet age, perfectly scaled for a one-man engineering enterprise.

The XR750, still winning dirt-track races in the 1990s, marries a simple bicycle-tube frame to an old-fashioned push-rod V-twin engine. This is a time-honoured piece of Americana, honed and developed to the extent that for 20 years or more would-be tuners have been working on the minutest details. Hand-finishing bearings, trying different tolerances, working to the most obsessive detail in an effort to cut friction and maximise efficiency and power, to find that extra 100rpm. Sandy built a Harley motor, using the skills as he knew them. In other words, build it tight and accurate. Damn thing never would run like it should, remembers Wayne. The XR750 motor had long passed from normal engineering into a realm of wizardry. And this is where Itchy came in. He loved the devil in the detail, the nourishment in the nuances. It was something you could worry away at for painstaking hours on end. Itchy recalls taking the Harley's pressed-together roller-bearing crankshaft, setting it up on the lathe – then fiddle and fiddle so the big flywheel halves were set parallel to one another to within ten thousandths of an inch. Then you tack-weld, so they don't creep apart again when it's running.

'Those Harleys, you couldn't just buy them and race them. You had to do everything. You'd be grinding half-a-thou off a shim, cutting pistons to get valve clearances. And the cams. The Harley had four, with number two – the rear exhaust – running off the crank, driving the other three. That had a key, so you could remove it, pull the gears then refit it slightly moved. You'd change the valve timing that way – press it apart, move it a little bit, then press it together and measure it. If you liked the numbers you'd put a spot weld on it. If you didn't you moved it again. There was a lot of moving and checking, moving and checking. That's what would make those Harleys run good. They were meant to turn 7,000rpm, and we ran them to 8,000. I liked that kinda meticulous fussing over things. That's probably why my bikes ran as good as other people's. Sometimes they ran better – but just not all in one race.'

In 1979 Itchy was running Rick Hocking, and they were part of the Boodie Strube gang at Peoria. He noticed Wayne – you could hardly not – and felt his talent was not getting what it deserved. He was so young and so keen and he tried so hard, 'but he was having a hard time on that Yamaha. It was tough enough trying to ride the dirt tracks without that kind of handicap. Even so he was beating some big names. But nobody was offering him a ride.'

So slow-talking Itchy showed up at Norwalk at the Rainey house where, funnily enough, Sandy had already acquired a Harley. The deal was simple. Itchy would supply the bike ready to race, Wayne the van and the gas money to get it there. Wayne ended up going to a friend, Jim Headley, at a place called H&H Workshop, 'and he gave me a credit card.' The first trip was to the 1980 season-opening dirt tracks at Daytona Speed week. Pretty soon, the Union 76 credit card company was calling Headley. 'We're getting all these charges from back East on your card. Is that right? Has it been stolen?' And after six weeks of this, he regretfully called Wayne. I'm going to have to take that thing back. It's way too much money for me. So Wayne called Itchy. 'We're gonna have to stay home, Itch; because I can't afford to pay for the gas.'

Well, they didn't stay home, but the scale of the financial difficulties made it tough. Gas, even at US prices, added up to maybe $5,000 a year. The Grand Nationals paid little if you didn't win. Wayne was generally running sixth or eighth or thereabouts, and walking out with maybe $50. The only chance of a reasonable payout – around $500 for a win – was in Trophy Races ('Duck Races'), because not all the top guys going for the Grand National went in for them. They were only for money, not for points. Itchy and Wayne split the money, and had a kitty envelope to run the van and keep them in junk food and sodas on the road, each putting in $50 to top it up when it ran dry. 'But I still tease Wayne that he owes me gas money. Because he was supposed to find a sponsor.'

There was so much else to pay for. The bikes came first – new tyres and so on. The tyres were $50, and you'd tear up two rears at a race meeting. Then the gas. And if there was anything left, you'd sleep in a motel instead of the van. 'We wouldn't come home with any money left,' says Wayne. 'You just paid for your habit.'

It could get to be an expensive habit too. Itchy: 'After the 1980 season, my Mert Lawill frame was getting old and cracking. I had a stock Harley frame – some guys liked the way they worked. So I said, let's try the stock frame and these different steering clamps that I'd made up. The first race we were going to, back east, was Knoxville, Tennessee. It was a high banked dirt track. We made the main event – he was like the last guy to qualify, and the race started and Wayne got off in last place, I think it was. On the first lap somebody fell, and there was a big cloud of dust, and Wayne came upon that and he couldn't tell where anybody was. So he laid the bike down. And he virtually destroyed it. That just kinda broke my heart. All this effort, and the only thing that was usable on it was the engine. The bike slid up the banking and hit the haybales, went 10 feet in the air and came back down. I was kinda proud of the fact that nothing fell off.' Itchy promptly came down with shingles, from the nerves. The rider's perspective on these sort of things is kind of different. 'We tore some machines up, but that was all part of it, I guess,' says Wayne

The pair travelled the country back and forth in Wayne's prized Dodge van. It had a 440 cubic inch (7.2-litre) V8, a Harley and a Kawasaki short-tracker in the back, with sleeping accommodation behind the seats. It was powerful enough to rip its own transmission to pieces. 'It'd just whip the U-joints out of the drive shaft, and the engine mounts would break.' Wayne's job was to fix the van: Itch the bikes. And it chewed gas. Wayne recalls attempting to travel the furthest they could on the dollar. 'We'd pull into a gas station and reverse one wheel onto a wooden block, to jack up that side and get a bit more gas in the tank.'

Peoria was the main base. 'We'd do about 20 races at a stretch, and Illinois was pretty central. You could get to New York, to Maryland, Indiana, Kentucky.' The little team was often in the running, but they never did win a National. It was tough, but as Itchy told Wayne recently: 'I always wanted you to win, but I took

63

some satisfaction knowing you didn't win a national on anybody else's stuff either.' (Wayne later rode a special Mert Lawill Harley, and Bubba Shobert's factory Honda.)

Wayne still has that regret. 'The only thing in my life I'd wish to do over would be my dirt-track career. The talent I had I should have been winning, but I just didn't have it figured out then. I remember the Peoria TT, some left and right turns with a jump. We'd take the Harley and put some front brakes on it, and I'd race this big heavy thing. I won my heat race, got fastest heat, and everybody thought I was going to win. They didn't know that anything over ten laps, I was junk. Physically wore out. The race was 25 laps, so I was never going to win. I just relied on my talent. I didn't know enough about making the most of it, and I didn't train at all. I know I could have done a lot better. Itch prepared a good bike, and I thought the problem was me. When you start doubting yourself you go down real quick.'

Nor was luck on his side. Itchy recalls how their second year promised more than it delivered. 'We went to Sacramento for the first race of the season. The Mile. I felt this had some kind of impact on the rest of the season too. In the main event, it was Wayne and Alex Jorgensen racing for the lead, changing back and forth. These other riders were back ten bike lengths. You'd see some of the veterans would start to make a move, then drop back.

'It happens that Jorgensen's Harley, the fitting on the sump, where they pull the oil out of the bottom end back to the top, was cracked and it was spraying oil out the back in a fine mist. When these guys would get that oil on them, that's why they'd slow up again.'

Wayne had it on his shield too. He was out of tear-offs (disposable visor covers you rip off one by one as they get dirty) so he tried to wipe it clean down the back straightaway, and he smeared it. He said he might as well have shut his eyes. Couldn't see nothing. He sat up on the bike, and let off the gas, and guys went whoo whoo whoo by him. He got a little spot cleared so he could see, got going again, and finished eighth that day. After the race, he found he did have a tear-off left after all.

'You know, when you get that first win, you open up that door of confidence, or whatever it might be. If he would have found that tear-off, you never know, he might have won that race. And that whole year, we didn't finish better than eighth in the main event until the last race of the year. It hurts when they get away from you. You hate those missed opportunities. It's hard enough to win as it is. And I wanted to win a race with my bike so bad. I thought I worked hard at it. Maybe looking back now, I could have worked harder. We really weren't true professionals. We were like amateur professionals.'

Now rising 21, Wayne had been racing for 11 years, and it almost seemed the best was behind him. Sure he was good. To Itchy, potentially one of the best. 'Wayne was a deep-thinking rider.' The wins weren't coming, but all the same there didn't seem to be any choice but to keep going. Out to all those dust-bowls and pea-gravel ovals – show up, practice, qualify and race, all in a day, ride round and round as hard as you can, get beat again. Then go to the Burger King or wherever to look for some girls. And in the winter, carpentry work to pay some of those accumulating bills. There were generations of other dirt-trackers who'd been doing something similar for years. But the Crucible didn't cook these guys up for nothing, and Lawson had already found an escape, one step ahead. He'd been recruited by Kawasaki two years before.

It wasn't actually a works contract at first: just a little deal paid for by the importers, put together by Dave Dewey, heading their parts and accessories division. It was separate from the official motorsport division, where they were involved in road racing – Kawasaki never made a real 750 dirt-tracker. This was just a little finger in the pie, showing the flag to customers who short-tracked their 250 dirt bike, to have some fun, and to scout new riders. Which they did rather well, Dewey remembers with some pride. Two of them won seven World Championships between them.

By the time Wayne was hooking up with Itchy, Eddie was fighting hard for the newly instituted Superbike road-racing championship, that was gaining importance rapidly. Dewey wanted a dirt-track rider now, and naturally enough Lawson suggested his Crucible companion and riding mate from the Ontario Raceway car-park. And so, in 1980, Wayne first rode an official green bike – the 'unlucky colour' (Sandy insisted) that was to prove so important.

Dewey: 'We already had Eddie, then he broke his leg. It was

Shell Thuet originally suggested Wayne. I'd never heard of him at that time. He was about 17 – a real nice kid. If I had another son, I wish it'd been him.' With Eddie's encouragement, the crucial choice was made. 'Sandy signed the contract for him, and we put him on a short-tracker at San Jose, Houston, Daytona . . .'

This was a step up and no mistake. They gave Wayne the bike, to load up alongside Itchy's 750, and gave him tyres and some expenses. 'My first race for them was at the Houston short-track, and I got second. They were really pumped.'

Indeed so. It was Chuck Larsen, head of Kawasaki in America and Dewey's boss, who made the first suggestion to Dewey. Eddie was doing real good after making the switch to road-racing. Why not let Wayne give it a try too?

CHAPTER 5

LEARNER-WINNER

*I've done some road-racing work, but I don't like it. There's
more skill on the dirt. On asphalt you have to be more brave,
and be prepared to be skinned up.'*
Shell Thuet, dirt-track technician to the GP stars

Deep into his fantasy, the would-be racer sighted through Turn
Six at Riverside Raceway. The corner entry is blind, you swoop
in over a rise. Aim right, the track swims into place in front of you.
Miss the line and the kerbs go under your front wheel instead. So
you crash.

Our hero, lips pursed, has his markers all in place, his
concentration fully focused, his ducks in a row. Perhaps he can
even see in his mind's eye Kenny Roberts or Stevie Baker about to
fall victim to his superb technique. Close the throttle, kiss the
brakes and smoothly heel it . . . when suddenly a freight train
comes by! Feels like one, anyhow: two bikes nose to tail, travelling
so much faster that it's ridiculous. Fascinated, our hero is sucked
along after them. Until the rude awakening – hey, they've gone,
but I'm not going to make it. He grabs the front brake, stands on
the rear, and goes flying through the dirt. 'When he came back to
the pits, he told me the transmission had locked up. That's why
he'd totalled the bike. I just said: I don't think so.'

Keith Code had recently opened his California Superbike School,
after retiring as a rider himself. Kawasaki – Chuck Larsen in
particular – had been very supportive, including using the facility
for their own riders. Which was why this particular freight train
was out among the learner-racers in 1980. It comprised Eddie
Lawson and Wayne Rainey, the former helping the latter to get up
to professional racing speed.

Who was in front? A moot point. For Wayne had demonstrated
an instant aptitude for road-racing, even while still learning the
basic, let alone finer, points of technique. He'd often beat Eddie

during these sessions, he remembers, much to the older rider's dismay and the interest of the handful of people watching. 'Certainly got my attention,' recalls Code. Eddie was a very fine road-racer, soon to win his first national title. He was the latest ex-dirt-track prodigy, but for every one like him, scores more didn't make the switch successfully. There was no particular reason at this stage for the road-race fraternity to know that Rainey would be another from the same mould.

Like Roberts, Mamola, Spencer, Lawson and others, Wayne brought with him the aggression and adaptability of the dirt-tracks, plus a formidable streak of determination that was all his own. He soon adjusted to the increase in speeds. But he wasn't accustomed to all the gear-shifting and braking. You did a bit of that on the dirt, especially in TT events, but your main element of control (including slowing down) was to slide the bike.

On tarmac, it was a different matter. By tradition sliding was to be avoided, except perhaps momentarily. Fast times were achieved by keeping the wheels in line but by venturing closer to the point of breakaway than the next man. Braking was especially crucial – the major moment of overtaking, and an exercise in carefully measured brinkmanship, flirting with the front-wheel lock-up, and accomplished above all with maximum smoothness.

It was to be Wayne's great strength as a Grand Prix racer that he, along with a handful of others, combined these techniques. But this was only later. Now, with precisely zero experience of riding on tarmac, he found he had a lot to learn. It is a measure of his talent that he won club races as a rank beginner, while Code recalls that in his second full season Wayne was still entering the corners in a series of jerks, because he hadn't mastered the technique of blipping the twist-grip on the downshifts while still squeezing the front brake lever (all operated by the right hand). He was letting go the brake every time, unsettling the bike and making the front tyre's job harder. 'He'd never ridden a road bike, so he just didn't have the technique.' This story, however, is hard to take at face value. Wayne says gruffly: 'I don't remember that.'

There is no doubt that Code, author of a trilogy of books analysing race-track techniques, did help Wayne, especially in his first year, though Wayne believes that later on the roles were reversed, and that he was teaching Code. The Californian racing guru just smiles. 'When I first read he'd said that, I was upset. Then I thought about it, and it was a compliment. My method of teaching was not to issue instructions, but to try and help people reach their own conclusions.' An ardent Scientologist, he had adapted much of that discipline's methodology, and worked on Wayne's technique by helping Wayne to analyse it for himself, prompting with occasional questions. 'He'd come over here once or twice a week for a couple of hours. I'd just ask him questions. What made it a two-way flow was I had to get smart enough to continue to ask questions. I paid an enormous amount of attention to figuring out what the right questions were. You have to understand what a person is about without inserting your own opinions.'

Code would be happy enough with Rainey's acknowledgement. 'What I really liked about Keith is I got my confidence restored. I was willing to do anything to get better, and he had some philosophies that at that time worked really well for me. Up until a certain point, when I got good. He would have me sit down and write stuff out – what I would do on the way through a corner, where I'd brake and how I'd turn in and get on the gas, and so on. I really started to understand riding again, how it all worked. It got to be fun again, and a challenge again.'

Given all that followed, this was an important development. The whole deal was initiated and paid for by Kawasaki – by Larsen, and by Dave Dewey, and his little offshoot race team's tuner and race-team manager Dennis Mayhan. With hindsight, it has the hallmarks of a brilliant master-plan.

The move to pavement came during 1980, Wayne's first year with Itchy, alongside the short-track deal. Again, it was Dewey at the helm, with another of his small-scale sub-works programmes. 'We had some spare bikes that had been used for photography, so we put Wayne out on a GPZ550 and a KZ750.' These were typical four-cylinder sports street bikes of the time, and there were thriving club-level classes for them at the local racetracks.

Wayne won and won – 15 out of 16 races at Willow Springs and Riverside, and all the track records. Dewey recalls: 'We were often accused of cheating, but as a matter of fact the bikes were so stock. Dennis just gave them a valve job and a personal massage.' Code remembers how the little guy in the dirt-track boots caught the imagination. 'Everyone who met him liked him, and he even had a fan club before anyone knew who he was. In his first races, the crowds would root for him. Maybe it was the boots.'

All this, and perks as well. Rainey remembers how much easier racing became in important respects. 'Dennis Mayhan would prepare the bikes at his house, and they'd pay for everything like tyres and fuel. I just paid my own entry fees, and I could make $300 racing two classes a weekend in Kawasaki contingency money.'

They were just local races in the Sportsman class, including one championship centred on Code's school. It was below the level this hugely talented rider should be riding – but he was only starting. And how he enjoyed it. 'To me, coming from dirt-track to asphalt was an easy transition. Keith couldn't believe how good I was first time on it. But to me it was just easy. The biggest problem I had was using too much back brake, from dirt-track habits. But what I really liked about it, though I didn't realise then, it was a whole new fresh experience, a whole new group of people. I felt like a fresh kid in racing.'

The experience was good compensation for the down-side of the concurrent dirt-tracking. Besides, there was the example of Lawson. Dewey was already making noises to the 'real' Kawasaki racing team, and found a memorandum he'd sent at the end of 1980 to Gary Mathers, head of the competition department. 'I'd like to recommend you consider Wayne Rainey if you decide to field a two-rider team.' The Californian was, the memo vouchsafed, 'a personable young man.' Dewey felt some resistance from Mathers. Naturally enough, 'he liked to find his own people. So we got one of Eddie's old 250s for the national race at Loudon on 21 June 1981.'

The KR250 was a real racing bike – no humble street-bike roots for this feisty hand-built two-stroke that had carried South African Kork Ballington to 250 and (in enlarged form) 350 World Championships back to back in 1978 and 1979. Straddling this thoroughbred, Wayne cut a fine figure, wearing his old dirt-track leathers and lace-up boots. Especially when he won the race. His first national win in his first-ever wet-weather race. And if it wasn't a Grand National, only a Novice 250 event, it was a grand feeling nonetheless.

Mathers could hardly ignore him now, though his memories are a little different. 'We knew who he was when Dewey put his name forward. We just put him on a bike straight away. He was personable (that word again), and all the other things that matter. I was always pretty sure about hiring dirt-trackers because of the way Roberts and now Lawson had made the switch. And Wayne was good right from the start. Just straightforward. Most dirt-trackers came up the tough way, and with road-racing they either liked it or they didn't. Wayne knew what he wanted from the bike right away.'

Mathers, as we shall see, is an important man in US road-racing. He was important in Wayne's career – far beyond the first 'works' contract for the 1982 season, that seemed so lavish it almost took his breath away. Enough for him to turn his back on dirt-track right away; enough for him to take Eddie Lawson's advice and hook up with Gary Howard as manager, joining the stable of International Racers Inc that already included Roberts and Eddie. 'I'd never signed anything in my life. I gave him the contract, and I think they redid it. They'd offered $25,000, they'd fly me to races, I'd get a rental car, they'd pay hotels . . . Jeez, that was heaven. Then Eddie told me I'd gotta talk to Howard. He was sharp, and he'd pay all the bills and take care of the contracts. That's when Gary and I got hooked up.' They've been hooked up ever since.

Real money, for the first time in his life. True independence. And air travel! For the Loudon race, Wayne and Itchy had driven almost coast to coast in 50 non-stop hours. Wayne bought a car, instead of the van, and moved out of home to an apartment in Downey. 'We called it The Dungeon.'

The ride was in the Superbike class, on the big green 1000cc monster that senior team-mate Eddie Lawson would ride to a second successive overall victory. Almost a third. He'd won in 1980, or so he thought, only to have the title stripped and awarded to Suzuki rider Wes Cooley after a flurry of protest and counterprotest on various technicalities. The 1981 season brought his first undisputed title, and he would do it again in 1982.

Road-racing was in a state of great flux in America at this time. The AMA's traditional Grand National Championship had included a handful of road races in its mainly dirt-track calendar, and would continue to do so until 1985. But in 1977 – acknowledging the growing gulf between the different skills as well as the increasing importance of European-style circuit racing – they had introduced a high-level pavement series for GP bikes and other specialised racing machines. This was grandiosely titled Formula One. It had auspicious beginnings, being won by GP World Champion Kenny Roberts. Evolution saw it now open not only to 500cc GP machines, but also the popular Yamaha TZ750 two-stroke – power cut back with intakes restricted to 23mm – as well as four-strokes up to 1025cc, allowing in purebred racers built for European endurance and road racing. These exotic factory bikes, and in particular the Honda, were now becoming dominant, at the expense of the privateers.

Formula One would linger on until 1986, but by 1981 it was already dying on its feet. There was a rag-tag entry which, according to *Motocourse*, 1981/2, mixed 'factory backed and serious privateer machinery with barely modified high-handlebar street bikes complete with tail lights and pilots so slow they are lapped by the leaders every four to six laps.'

The national spotlight had switched to a different class – the Superbikes, based around relatively mildly modified and race-kitted street bikes up to 1100cc. This class, one year older than Formula One, had originally been conceived as a low-cost alternative to the big-time. Close racing and the opportunity for factories to showcase lookalike 'street bikes' – by now the beneficiaries of increasingly expensive technical improvements – had made the Superbikes popular with the crowds and the principal entrants alike. The factory-backed importer teams were by now supporting the Superbikes with growing fervour. Of course, they took the best riders with them.

Once again, the Crucible Kids were team-mates. But it was all much more serious now. For example, there was no more shared information about bikes or riding techniques. 'Eddie was pretty sly as far as set-ups and stuff went,' says Wayne. 'Not so much in the beginning, because he was pretty much quicker than I was, and the factory was all around him. He always got the good stuff first, but that was OK. He was the established star. But I think he knew I was coming, because I was getting better and better. He wouldn't answer some questions, and wouldn't tell me what gears he was running in some places. Or he'd tell me he was running third instead of second gear somewhere. I was figuring out my own stuff anyway, but I just wanted to compare notes.'

Lawson happily agrees. 'I was secretive with Wayne, but I was secretive anyway, not just to him. If I could find something that worked I'd keep it to myself. And I always made it a point to tell everybody on the team to keep their mouths shut. To me that's correct thinking, though a lot of other riders didn't bother about it. I think Wayne in his later years was worse than I was, so he has no room to accuse me. That's what you need to be. Maybe he learned that from me – how to be a prick.'

Wayne has another way of putting it. 'I think what I learned from Eddie was how to be serious about racing. He was really dedicated. He wanted to win real bad. And it was big business, which I wasn't used to. I could see he was working hard on things like suspension and tyre choice, the stuff I wasn't aware of at that time. I could see that most of the team followed what he was doing, and not so much me. I wanted that; I wanted to be in that position more and more as time went by.'

This was Wayne's first experience of The Team-Mate Thing. And it was an instructive introduction, given who his team-mate was, and the fact that Wayne was a class rookie. The Team-Mate Thing depends on the simple fact that with other riders, you can never be sure if their strength or weakness is because of machine characteristics; but with a partner on the same machine, you know it's down to sheer skill. 'Beating my team-mate was always my prime target all through my career,' says Wayne. 1982, riding with Eddie, was the only time that his team-mate generally had the beating of him.

Both future superstars remember their friendship as good during that year of Superbikes. It all began with an escapade at Daytona. 'I was much more serious then than I'd ever been, but I wasn't quite serious enough,' remembers Rainey. 'I knew I had an image, and that people were paying me, writing press releases about me and taking my picture every week. I had a responsibility to them not to get in trouble. Not that I'd got in trouble before, but . . .'

It is a habit of racers to trash rental cars, usually at the post-race party. After Daytona, Wayne, his girlfriend Lori and Eddie went out razzling. Lori was the designated driver, Eddie and Wayne were out of control. The usual problem after only a little quantity of even mild American beer. 'Me and Eddie went skinny-dipping in the ocean, and we jumped back in the car naked, and she drove off.' After a quick call at a 24-Hour Do-Nut joint (skinny dunking?), they were back at the Indigo Hotel.

'I'd throw it in reverse, then Eddie would throw it in drive, and I'd throw it in reverse again. Well, she panicked out, lost control and ran head-on into a telegraph pole. Put me into the windshield, and knocked out all the lights at Daytona Beach airport.' By the time the police arrived, Wayne had his pants and his cowboy boots on. 'And they're looking at the skid marks back and forth going up to the telegraph pole and wondering just what's going on. I told them I was driving and somebody ran me off the road. They said the skid marks looked like something weird was going on. They never did work it out. But I thought after that I'd better be more careful.'

As for team seniority, it was obviously in Eddie's favour. 'It wasn't riding skill, just saddle time,' says Eddie. Mathers agrees: 'We always had a two-rider team, with one lead rider. The policy was that both riders could choose from the same pile of parts. If we'd developed something better and we had only one, we'd give it to the rider who was ahead on points.'

Wayne had plenty of enthusiasm, but still quite a lot to learn. He had deeply ingrained dirt-track habits to eliminate. 'I was still using way too much back brake, and coming into the turns with the bike hopping around all over the place.' And he was accustomed to wrestling with the handlebars, whereas on a road-racer they have to be handled with subtlety as well as strength. As he discovered at Daytona, the opening round of the Superbike season.

'I was getting this huge wobble coming onto the banking, a great 160mph tankslapper. As I was running onto the banking the back would start to wobble a little bit, and I'd grab the bars and try and stop it wobbling. That just magnified it – threw all the wobble back into the chassis, and it'd shake so bad I'd have to shut off. Then it'd shake real bad when I did that. So I came in and told the Kawasaki guys, and they said – Eddie's not wobbling. Let Eddie ride your bike. So he did it, and didn't wobble on my bike neither. I knew it had to be something I was doing. Then I overheard another rider who'd been talking to Wes Cooley, that he was wobbling because he was holding on to it too tight. Next day I went out and it started to wobble and I just let go of the bars a bit, and it never got any worse. But Eddie'd never have told me about that. I had to overhear it second-hand from someone else.'

Rob Muzzy, running the Kawasaki team, remembers it all a little differently. 'The bikes of course weren't very good then, and Wayne was having these stability problems, and Eddie wasn't. The Japanese engineers were running in circles. Then somebody went to watch him coming down the back straight. He'd be all tucked in, then he'd sit up to brake and the elbows'd go way out. At those speeds, any small thing will get the bike moving around. So after two days of worrying about the bike, we told him to keep his elbows in. And he went straight as an arrow. He was pretty green at that time. And fast. He was always incredibly determined, and he never gave up. Those were his strongest points.'

Both riders rode also in the Formula One championship, Rainey on his Superbike, Lawson on an obsolete 500cc Kawasaki GP bike, and Wayne finished fourth overall, ahead of Eddie in a series dominated by big-spending Honda's specialised V4 race machine, with a best finish of third at Loudon, New Hampshire. But for riders and for Kawasaki the major focus was the 11-round Superbike championship, which opened at Daytona with a support race for the (Formula One class) 200-mile classic in March, and finished on 10 October at Palm Beach, Florida.

The Superbikes of this year were unwieldy monsters with big flat handlebars and a sit-up-and-beg riding position, in line with the rule that Superbikes must look like street bikes upon which they were based. The link was valuable: after Lawson's 1981 and 1982 victories Kawasaki produced a lime-green Eddie Lawson replica which cosmetically echoed the small but distinctive changes from stock bike to racer. A decade later, the reverse had taken place, with street bikes aping hard-core racers, with drop-handlebars, high footrests and uncompromising riding positions.

Contemporary photographs show Wayne sitting upright like a

dirt-tracker on his Superbike, yet to develop the hunkered-down style, but looking as determined as he always would. The main opposition came from Honda, fielding Mike Baldwin and ex-motocrosser Steve Wise; with Wes Cooley on the relatively uncompetitive Suzuki. Baldwin took the opening round at Daytona, with Rainey fifth in his first Superbike race. He was third at the next round at Talladega, with Eddie winning, Wise second, and Baldwin crashing. This was a strong finish for Wayne: he and Baldwin had both started from the back of the grid on a jump start technicality. At Riverside, Lawson won from Baldwin, Rainey third; at Elkhart Lake, Lawson won from Cooley and Rainey.

Then came the race at Loudon, New Hampshire, on 19 June. A milestone. As team-mate Lawson lagged, to complain later about tyre problems, Wayne came of age. He fought with Wise until the Honda rider crashed (as Baldwin had before him), then powered on for his first win. 'Afterwards, Eddie couldn't understand why I was so happy. But I guess I was more excitable in them days.'

In fact, Wayne did have another reason for his elation – though it was only in future years that the full importance was revealed. For this win came as a direct result of his first contact with racing legend and triple World Champion Kenny Roberts.

Wayne's mechanic at Kawasaki was Sparky Edmonston, who'd worked for Kenny before. Sparky called Kenny and spoke about the problems Wayne was having, then Wayne and Kenny talked. The difficulty was familiar to the vastly experienced Roberts, who'd followed the same transition from dirt-tracks to road-racing. Wayne was trying too hard – rushing into the corners and losing the rhythm that would give him a faster and more effective exit. 'He couldn't get it stopped and turned. Everyone does it when they start. But his next race was at Loudon, and I told him the trouble he was having at Daytona (with flat infield corners), you can probably win at Loudon, so don't change anything right now. Loudon has real banked corners, so you have to run in a little hot and let it drift up high under brakes, and then bring it back down across the line. I figured he'd do well there, because I did well there before I knew how to road-race.'

Wayne: 'He told me, get in there, square it off, and come out. So I won the race the next day, and that impressed Kenny. He thought

I was a pretty good learner. Then the next race at Laguna I fell down three times.'

Something else happened at the Californian track, in the folds of the coastal foothills down within sight of Wayne's home. Eddie beat Baldwin in the Superbike race, then suffered a potentially ruinous injury in the next day's F1 round, breaking his seventh vertebra and escaping paralysis by a miracle. He still led the title on points but was not expected back that year. It was up to Wayne to take points away from Baldwin.

At Pocono, Pennsylvania, he led the Honda, dropping back to second after missing a gearchange on the banking. Then came Sears Point in Sonoma, California, which local observers counted as Wayne's race of the year. On the bumpiest and most technically difficult track, Rainey led Baldwin brilliantly for almost the full race. Then he fell. Contemporary reports blamed spilled oil. Rainey blamed himself. 'It was the last lap. Mike had been pushing me, but I had him beat. But I was just a little bit tired, and mentally I was just whipped. I gave it a little bit too much throttle over this rise, and it stepped out and highsided me. Broke my collarbone. I raced the next week, though.'

To the amazement of all, Lawson returned for the next race at Seattle, winning from Cooley, with Rainey third. And though Baldwin won the next two rounds at Daytona and Palm Beach, the title went to the Kawasaki rider, with Baldwin second and Rainey third. It had been an auspicious year.

CHAPTER 6

TO THE CHAMPIONSHIP
– AND BEYOND

'It was an old design, and the bike was quite slow at first. We kept
working to try to improve it, and he hung in there. Like I said,
his strong point was never giving up.' Rob Muzzy, Kawasaki
team boss, later World Superbike team owner

There was a fundamental change to the US Superbike class in 1983. In an alignment with proposals worldwide that eventually resulted in the World Superbike championship, engine size was cut to 750cc. This made all previous machinery redundant. Kawasaki (not to mention Suzuki), were at something of a disadvantage. Though a new street bike was available as a base, the GPz750, the motor it used was relatively old. In particular, it had but two valves per cylinder – technology that was soon to be left behind by multi-valve designs. Honda were the major beneficiaries of the timing of the rule change. They had a brand new V4 model, the VF750 Interceptor, with four valves per cylinder, and a whole generation of further development ahead of it while the rivals were already near the end of their possibilities. Honda, with Mike Baldwin leading the team, were expected to be impossible to beat.

There was another big change at the Kawasaki team. Eddie Lawson had moved on, into World Championship Grand Prix racing as team-mate to Kenny Roberts in his final year. Wayne's contract had been renewed, and after his race-winning third-placed debut he quite honestly expected to be head of the team. To his dismay, Mathers signed on former champion and seasoned veteran race-winner Wes Cooley as his running mate, and once again the 22-year-old was a natural junior. This acted as a considerable spur. The Team-Mate Thing.

Muzzy explains the position. 'I think most of us knew Wayne was going to come out on top. The reason for hiring Cooley was we had a new bike to work on. Wayne only had one year, and he was inexperienced. We knew Wayne could win, but we needed Wes to sort the bike out as quickly as possible. And the reality is that in first tests Cooley was faster. It didn't take long for Wayne to overcome that. Maybe he had to prove it to himself, but for me and Mathers there wasn't any doubt.'

Much work needed to be done. Muzzy continues: 'The 750 was a completely different machine from the 1000. It was an old design, and the bike was quite slow at first. We kept working to try to improve it, and he hung in there. Like I said, his strong point was never giving up. He did the best he could in the early races, then we figured out how to make the bike run well. It was just camshafts and some other things. We got it to go faster, but the trouble was it used to break valve springs. When we got that so it could go race distance, that was the beginning of the end for Honda. Wayne basically outrode Baldwin.'

That's it in a nutshell. But it was an unfolding story. Wayne: 'Muzzy was working on Cooley's cylinder heads and my crew chief Steve Johnson was getting my heads done at Vance and Hines. They did a great job for us. Then Muzzy found a way to run the big-lift camshaft without breaking springs – they improved the valve-spring material – and we started winning races.

'The Honda had a lot of torque, and our bike had to make a lot of rpm. It was our only way to make horsepower. At the start of the season, even the privateer Hondas were faster than the Kawasakis. Then I felt what I had to do was to beat Wes. That was when I really felt I had to always start by beating my team-mate. He was an established rider, and he'd beaten Eddie and Freddie (Spencer) in the past. I put a lot of effort into outqualifying him and beating him every time. Pretty soon, he was pretty easy to beat. But I still couldn't beat the Hondas.'

Wayne's fee had leapt to $65,000 the second year, and he thought that was pretty good. Until he found out what Eddie was earning in GP racing. 'More than six times that. It made me realise that the GPs were a lot bigger business. I remember at Daytona that year I was running round on the apron in practice to break in a new Kawasaki engine for 100 miles. Eddie was coming past so hard on that 680cc Yamaha (a special bored-out version of a 500cc

GP machine), just smoking by us. I wondered how he felt looking down at the team he used to be with. He came back a few times that year and we'd go out to dinner and stuff, because he knew all the guys in the Kawasaki team. He told me how difficult it was trying to race with Roberts and Spencer. What he told me was about all I knew about GP racing. Superbike racing was the biggest thing in my life, and I didn't think then that what he was doing was any bigger. I found out later it was quite a big difference.'

Wayne remained in touch with his roots. It is a key element among friends and family that he never got too big to remain himself. Minnig recalls how Wayne would help him with equipment. Even later when he was in Europe, Wayne would show up with some spare knee-sliders or whatever, and a voice of encouragement. (Minnig's own career soldiered on until ended by an accident a couple of years down the road. He never realised his potential as the last of the Crucible Kids.) Rodney Rainey meanwhile had given up motorsport in favour of baseball. He was an able player, and made it as far as the NY Yankees minor league team. 'Wayne was like a second dad to me. He used to come and watch me play, and if I needed a bat or a new glove or something, he'd always jump to get me the best there was. I really appreciated that he backed me in my sport. Once I was playing in Florida and he was at Daytona, and he flew me down from Fort Lauderdale so we could work out together. We did a lot of that.'

By now, Wayne was taking fitness seriously. He'd started running on a bet with Mike Minnig. Then with Itchy, who'd quit working on the bike every day at noon to watch the soap opera *All My Children*. Wayne used the down-time to run. It was the start of a crescendo of running – mile upon mile – that would be the cornerstone of a fitness programme of ever-increasing severity right up until the end of his racing career. Wayne ran as long as he could run, and in the last months, on six- or eight-mile loops on the steep roads of his hilltop estate outside Monterey. By then, driving himself to exhaustion, the 32-year-old triple World Champion found inspiration by imagining he could feel Kevin Schwantz breathing down his neck. It was enough to light the fire for that extra spurt to the gatepost.

The 1983 season spanned 14 rounds, and was always a two-man show. Baldwin had the advantage at first: second at Daytona behind soon-to-be 500cc World Champion Spencer. Rainey's thoroughly outgunned Kawasaki was a distant fourth. Talladega: Baldwin first, Rainey second. Riverside: same again. Mid-Ohio: both crashed out. Elkhart Lake: Baldwin then Rainey again. Loudon: worse still, with Rainey third behind Baldwin and Cooley with gearshifting problems. Baldwin led with 96 points to Rainey's 72, and his chances of repeating Lawson's giant-killing feat were shrinking. But the fresh-faced Rainey was to learn something important about the value of pressing on regardless when it comes to championships run over a long season.

The turnaround came at the next race, at Pocono. Practising for the Formula One race, Baldwin fell and broke his wrist – the critical scaphoid bone. In his absence, Rainey claimed his second-ever national Superbike win, and the crucial first of the year. Three weeks later, Rainey defeated the pinned-together Baldwin at Laguna Seca. Now they were equal on points. But problems in the two-leg race at Portland, Oregon, saw Rainey non-finish in one of them, and Baldwin moved ahead once more.

There were just five races left, and now Rainey was coming on strength, the bike up to speed. He took a fine win on sheer riding skill at Sears Point, with Baldwin only sixth after dropping back. Then came Brainerd, and the most important win of the year – the Minnesota track had a very long straight that should have favoured Baldwin's Honda. One more confrontation at Seattle saw another victory for Rainey, who clearly outrode the older man. There were two rounds left, and Rainey was five points in front.

'Baldwin was riding a 500 Honda in the Formula One class too, and trying to go to Europe as well (running a tight private Honda effort at some GPs). He had a lot on his plate. Our thing came down to Willow Springs. They told me that they were going to bring Freddie Spencer in to help Baldwin (Spencer was currently engaged in defeating Kenny Roberts in Europe). The way I was feeling, I just said – well, good. I felt I was ready to race Freddie. I wasn't, but I thought I could. In any case, he didn't show. It was just something Honda were saying to psyche me out. I outqualified Mike, had a faster heat race, but he was leading me in the final when he ran off the race track and crashed. So I won the championship.'

The last race at Daytona was a formality. Rainey was second to Fred Merkel's Honda, but the real work was already done. Rainey prepared for a well-earned celebration after his victorious season. The dirt-track doldrums were well behind him, and his career was on fast-forward. Surely it could only keep on getting better. Then came the bombshell.

'Two days after the final race, Kawasaki USA called and told me they'd pulled out of motorcycle racing. I was just totally devastated. Two years, we'd just won the championship. Everybody was really excited and I thought I had a great future with Kawasaki. Then they pulled the plug. They let the whole team go. All the mechanics. Everybody was done. I was champion, and I was unemployed.

'I was devastated. I got drunk a few times that winter. I put on weight. I'd gone from really regaining confidence to being really puzzled and confused. I had no direction, no plans. Nothing. I wasn't even answering the phone. I'd had a really good thing – I'd made a bunch of money, for those days, getting paid to do something that I loved. It was as though my world, my dream, had just stopped, and I couldn't figure out why, because I'd done everything right. There was nothing out there for me. Honda had Fred Merkel, and they were basically only racing against themselves anyway. I didn't want to go back to being a privateer. I'd had my future ahead of me, and now I just didn't know what I was going to do. And time was running out.'

His championship season ended with what should have been a celebration party with Kawasaki, that turned out to be a farewell party instead. Then came a memorable trip with Kenny Roberts – their first real meeting. Kenny recalls that part of the deal with Gary Howard was that he would help train up the younger riders, and 'I needed people to ride with myself anyways.' So he arranged one of his typically haphazard trips out to the trails in the Californian mountains on the way to Coalinga. The result was a story that has been told many times. 'Kenny tells it to everybody, and he always jazzes it up. He makes things that didn't happen really happen when he tells it.' Wayne's version is tinged with Kenny's appreciation and embellishment.

'He called and said come up and let's go riding. I had some dirt bikes so I loaded them up. I also took my disco clothes in case we'd go out dancing or anything. I couldn't believe I was going to KR's house. I drove six hours, and as soon as I get there he jumps straight in and says let's go. And we're driving and driving. And after about two hours I noticed there was a van behind us. It was Chuckie' (Chuck Aksland, nephew of Skip Aksland the rider, and part of a clan that has been involved with Kenny almost throughout his career as rider and manager). 'He was carrying all the camping stuff, and I didn't even know we were going camping.

'We were staying two nights, so we went to the store and got six steaks and six potatoes. Then we got bacardi and rum, and some milk and ice. And then we headed for the hills.

'I'd never done that kind of riding before. And I didn't know Kenny and Chuck, and I had no idea of the sense of humour he had. To me he was the great Kenny Roberts, and it took me time to find out he's just a huge kid a little bit older than Rex (four years old, at the time of speaking).

'So we're sitting round the campground getting a little tipsy, then Jimmy Filice (another Californian racer of note) and his girlfriend – now his wife – show up, and by this time we're real shit-faced. So we opened the passenger door and we're saying like: hey, we finally got a girl. So Jimbo just puts his foot down again and took off. So we're saying hey, what's wrong with him? Then we're back at the campfire and we kept drinking. Next thing I know I'm wrassling Kenny, and he goes in the fire. And his clothes caught on fire. We had to pull him out . . .

'When I drink, something happens. This guy called Buzzy comes out. And he proceeds to do whatever he wants, I guess. So we're looking at this mountain in the moon, and saying: I'm gonna climb that in the morning. And all of a sudden I just take off and go running through the woods. They didn't know why. And then I came back, and they said where have you been. Hell, I didn't know. Then Chuck asks me to get that Dainese bag out the van. So I go, how do you spell that? And he didn't know. So I said come here. I'm gonna fight you, because you don't know how to spell. He says, you'll have to fight Kenny too because he doesn't know how to spell neither.

'It was about 20 degrees, we were just freezing. And we threw the bikes out of the back of the van. It was so cold that the plastic fenders snapped off. We passed out in the back of the van, only I didn't have no blanket or sleeping bag. I woke up and my teeth were chattering. I was so cold. And I said hey, where's my sleeping bag. And they said it's outside. You threw it out with the bikes. So I said hey, Johnny (because I'd forgotten Chuck's name), let me into your sleeping bag. And he said, git outta here, go get your own. So I got out and found my bag, but I'd locked myself out of the van, and I was knocking to be let in again. Kenny was just laughing.

'Anyways, the next morning we woke up, so hung over. And we started talking about Johnny. A make-believe guy. And we talked about him on the ride. Like where's Johnny. Oh, he must be back there.

'After I went back home, Kenny and Chuck wrote me a letter, signed from Johnny, all about how he missed me so much, and how that night in the van was so wonderful, and he couldn't wait to see me again. And they put in a picture of Kenny mooning – just his butt. They sent it to Gary Howard's place, and his wife opens it up, and sees this picture of this butt and says woah, and seals it up and sends it on to my parents' house. So I got this, and I was cracking up, and I called Kenny and said that was pretty funny. But then I put the letter inside my desk, which was inside my sister's room. I just threw it in there and forgot about it. Two weeks later I came home one night, and my mom and dad and my brother and sister are all lined up on the couch. And the girls are crying and my dad is just pissed, and there's this letter and the picture lying on the table. So my dad says, real fierce: Who's Johnny? So I say well, it's kindofa long story. And he goes: Bullshit. I'm getting you a psychiatrist tomorrow. And my sister's going: Wayne's gay, Wayne's gay. So I said no, I'm not gay. And I explained how Kenny wrote it and so on. My dad said – Kenny's gay too! Three or four years it took him to get over that.'

CHAPTER 7

THE YEAR OF LIVING
UNCOMFORTABLY

'I hardly knew anything about GP racing. I thought since I was a champion I must be pretty good. But I had no idea. I was so green that I thought whatever Kenny said is what he would have done out there. Later I realised he was just having fun with me.'
Wayne Rainey, on his first year of GP racing

The atmosphere of a Grand Prix startline in the mid-1980s was the culmination of almost 80 years of tradition – unchanged in its elements, unchanging in its tension. It began with the bustle as 36 bikes assembled, mechanics making last-minute adjustments, umbrella girls pouting alongside the big stars up front, the riders looking absent, focused on something nobody else could see. The one-minute board cleared the last stragglers, the 30-second board would make the riders hunch a little harder, staring now towards the starter – usually some local dignitary – as he puffed himself up, preparing for his big moment with the national flag. By now, the silence was deafening.

The flag dropped. Then came the patter of feet pushing hard into a run. Almost simultaneously some 36 racing two-stroke engines would chime in, straight onto full throttle and full load in first gear as the riders leapt on and powered away. Sometimes, there'd be a rider left behind, still pushing, having timed the critical operation just slightly wrong. Sometimes he'd have been a fast qualifier, on the first or second row of the starting grid, and a whole bunch of slower riders would gladly have seized the chance to set off down the track ahead of him. Sometimes the safety car would already have left – following the riders round their first lap – before he got a cough or a kick off the bike. Then, eventually, he too would be tucking in behind the bubble and shifting up the gearbox, in headlong pursuit of the pack, his job made doubly difficult.

During 1984, often as not, that man would be Wayne Rainey.

When the American Superbike Champion showed up at the GPs, few realised just how little experience of road-racing he'd had, or that he'd never raced a two-stroke (except for that one outing at Loudon in 1981) anywhere except on the short-tracks, on converted single-cylinder motocross bikes. Few realised also that the bike he rode was a plain-and-simple production model, the same as the TZ250s that most of the 250-class riders campaigned. Surely this could not be true? After all, look at the team owner. None other than the great Kenny Roberts, freshly retired triple World Champion. It was surely inconceivable that Yamaha were not passing him special parts under the counter. The great man's obstinate denials were merely taken as further proof.

And Rainey's performance? On paper, eighth overall with a best finish of third was good for a GP rookie, learning new tracks in among the cream of the world's 250 riders – the second class down is traditionally a hotbed of close racing. But it fell short of Wayne's own ambitions, and the standards set by the likes of Kenny and Freddie, both 500-class World Champions at the first attempt; and also of Eddie, fourth in his first 500 season but first in 1984. Anybody who failed to be impressed however did not take account of several stirring rides, including one lap record and one pole position, by a two-stroke beginner who made a hard job all the harder by consistently letting everyone else gallop away into third or fourth gear as he flapped and faltered and fiddled to get that fiendish little fighter to fire.

Roberts today reiterates that the bike was as stock as could be – though he did what he could to make it better, including using special cylinders made in Europe. The team, basically, was a bodge-up, slapped together on a minimal budget at short notice. Kenny says he put it together for Wayne, but also of course for himself. After more than 20 years of racing, he now found himself as an ex-rider, with a great empty void. He and his new young friend were both at a loose end, and deciding to go GP racing was one of those schemes that only escape being hair-brained by a small margin. Yet both learned a lot – Kenny that if he was going to run a racing team it would have to be done properly, with the proper budget and top-level machinery; and Wayne that there was a whole lot more to racing in Europe than met the eye.

The friendship between the two men had grown since the camping trip and the Johnny affair. 'We just hit it off right from the start,' says Kenny. Though as Wayne had already discovered, friendship was no easy road with this gigantic personality with his endless capacity for mocking laughter in among the inspirational enthusiasm.

Kenny had surprised Wayne when he confided in him after losing the 1983 title to Spencer, in spite of his superhuman efforts on a relatively ill-handling Yamaha against Fast Freddie's nimble three-cylinder Honda. 'I couldn't believe he would be so upset talking to me,' remembers Wayne. 'He said Freddie was prepared to hang it out further than he was – he was talking about the Swedish GP. It meant a lot to me that he was talking to me like that. He was the best, and he was having problems accepting that it was time for him to retire because that kid was willing to go and do it further than he was. What he said made a big impression on me.

'Finally, about two weeks before Daytona, Kenny said: Let's try and put something together and go to Europe.' (This was in late February, barely a month before the first GP of the year.) The team, backed by Kenny's old sponsor Marlboro, would run a pair of stock 250 Yamahas, with British youngster Alan Carter, at that time the youngest ever GP winner, as the second rider.

Now they had to move fast. Kenny and Wayne went directly to Europe – Wayne's first trip out of the US – to tie up the loose ends. Wayne played the role of innocent abroad. 'I was falling asleep in the meetings with the jet lag. I was trying so hard to be polite, while Kenny was doing everything. But I was just like a little kid, wide-eyed at the way the people all talked funny.' In Amsterdam, Yamaha's European HQ, Kenny took the stunned Wayne to see the degenerate sights of that famously degenerate city; in England he took him out for a curry. 'I told him I'd buy him a hamburger, and he was pretty happy until he saw what came to the table,' recalls Roberts. 'People in America hadn't even heard of Indian food – he was just in awe the whole time.'

Wayne soon realised: 'Kenny was joking at me, making fun of me, and they all laughed. That's the way Kenny was. It didn't bother me at the time. We went to England, then Italy to see Dainese (leathers), Alpinestar (boots) and AGV (helmets). It was like a five-day tour of Europe. It seemed so far away from what I wanted to do, which was to race in America. But I had no choice. I had to go to Europe to race 250s.'

There was already a strong American presence in the top 500 class of GP racing, but at home the racing folk paid only scant attention – once they had left home – to the exploits of Kenny and Freddie, Lawson and Randy Mamola. American racing being just as parochial as baseball. Wayne followed the trend, in spite of his contacts with Kenny and Eddie: 'I'd never even thought about GP racing. The first I knew that there was a 250 class was when Kenny brought me a *Motocourse*. I remember him saying, look at this 250 thing. And there was an article saying: "250: No Longer Second Class". It was a world I couldn't imagine.'

Rainey's first time on the bike, at a special test at Daytona, started badly. He overslept after taking medicine to cure insomnia – his wake-up call was from the irate Kenny, already in the pits. Then he had to drill the plastic fairing screen, or bubble, to fit on the fairing. 'I started drilling and it starts cracking and breaking up. Then my mechanic Bruce Maus shows up, and I said – man, I don't know how to work on these things.'

The Daytona race was a first encounter with the people he'd read about in *Motocourse*. One of them, future World Champion Sito Pons, would later become a close friend. Another was German rider Martin Wimmer. 'I knew he was good because I'd heard of him. I just wanted to pass him anywhere. I got by at the end of the straight under brakes. I flicked it off into that turn so hard it was bouncing off the ground.

'In the race I'd come up and passed Sito and he raced with me. Man, I could get him through the corners, but that Rotax thing he was riding was just smoking us down the straights. I could get through the chicane really good. I seemed to have a natural instinct of where to go fast and where not to go fast. I think from all that dirt-track riding, making all the mistakes, and my dad saying: you're riding way too hard through the corners and you're all over the place. Sito jumped off chasing me through the chicane. He crashed. I remember talking to him after, years later. He remembered seeing this one guy out there in yellow. That was me. He didn't know who I was but he realised he'd have to race me. I didn't know who he was either, but we knew each other after that.'

The 1984 Grand Prix season proper began two weeks later. The South African round at Kyalami on 24 March launched a 12-race series running until September. It was an instructive outing, most especially concerning the sort of treatment Wayne would be getting from his new team boss. Like sending him out – a rider who had barely raced in the wet before – on untreaded slick tyres on a wet track. An invariable recipe for disaster.

'In practice I had trouble push-starting the bike, and by the time I got it going I was last out. It was on slicks but it was starting to rain. Kenny made me go out on slicks anyway. He said: you've got to learn to ride in the rain; and I didn't know any better. Later I remember Barry Sheene saying, I can't believe you let him do that to you. And I said, I really didn't know there was anything wrong with it. I was so green that I thought whatever Kenny said is what he would have done out there. I thought he was sincere. Later I realised he was just having fun with me. Eventually after about five laps he called me in for wet tyres. I thought – well, this feels a little better.

'Next thing I know I'm passing everybody. Then I caught up with Carlos Lavado and Ivan Palazzese – they were team-mates (in a Venezuelan factory-backed Yamaha team). I remember passing those guys, then they'd smoke me down the straightaway. And I'd pass them again, and they'd smoke me again. I didn't know who they were. I had no idea Lavado was a World Champion. And I'm just this American kid come over and I'm beating these guys.

'I didn't realise how wet it was. I flicked it off into this corner, and I crashed. But I took Palazzese down with me. Boy, I ripped my finger really bad. He got up and he was shouting and screaming, and I had no idea what he was saying, because he was speaking a language that wasn't English.' Someone else, at least, who would from now on know who Wayne Rainey was.

Wayne qualified fifth, with Carter fourth. He didn't like that – the Team-Mate Thing again. Carter led the race early on, so perhaps it was lucky for Rainey's equilibrium that he was way too far behind to notice. He'd got away at the back, as was to become his custom, 'but I'd worked up to sixth. It was wet, but a dry line was forming. I didn't know then to get off the dry line to cool the tyres down, so I was just staying on the dry, and when I came to pass guys I'd go out into the wet. I'd slide around, but I'd pass them. Wimmer came over and told Kenny after the race: That guy's pretty crazy. He's sideways everywhere out there.'

All the craziness came to nothing when the gearshift stiffened up because it had been lubricated with a non-waterproof grease – an error that shows the haphazard nature of the team. Rainey pulled in, Carter had meanwhile dropped back to 10th, his tyres shot to pieces on the drying track. Then came another lesson. 'Carter's front tyre was completely chewed up, and my rear tyre was completely chewed up. The front tyre looked brand new. I was riding with a lot of throttle, but Carter was riding with high corner speed. When I heard Kenny explaining that to somebody, I really thought about it. I realised it was because of the dirt-track way I ride. I'd never really understood that stuff, but now I could see exactly what was happening. So I knew that I was using a lot more throttle control than the other riders – so if the front wheel would start to slide, I'd get on the gas to get the weight off it, like you do on the dirt.'

The trip was an eye-opener in other respects. 'We were staying at the promoter's house, Roger McCleery. He had a daughter there, and a black maid. That was my first time I'd been around people who had black maids, and apartheid and all that stuff. I didn't know anything about it. I remember every day I'd come in and take my socks off and my pants off, and I'd wake up the next day and they'd be folded, clean, right next to my bed. Her name was Maria, and they told me she was a Zulu, and she had this religion: her bed was up on a pedestal so this evil spirit wouldn't get her. I peeked into Maria's room, and I was real serious, and I said well Maria, what if this guy has a ladder? She laughed, and said: no no no, that's not the way it happens.'

There was a big-money race at Imola in Italy before the next round: a final (and victorious) European race for Kenny and a 250 ride for Wayne. 'I'd fallen in practice in the rain, then in the race I took off – it was a clutch start, not a push-start – and I was smoking those guys. Then, when I put the brake on, all this brown liquid goes onto the screen. I thought I was losing brake fluid, so I pulled in to the pits. Turned out it was rusty water that was in the handlebar tube after the practice crash! I went out again and I was slamming that thing round breaking the lap record. Man – I didn't win again.'

Then the GP circus moved down to the Italian coast, to open the European season at the Misano racetrack near Rimini on the Adriatic coast. The scene of Rainey's European GP debut was to become his favourite circuit – and, nine years later, the place where disaster was waiting.

He ran straight into trouble. Delays with official insurance release paperwork (a legal requirement to indemnify track owners and race promoters) reaching the organisers from the AMA meant that when the team showed up for 'untimed' pre-practice on the Thursday, they wouldn't let him out. 'Paul Butler was the team manager, but didn't do much. I did all the calling back and forth to the AMA. My team was so slack.' He missed a full day of practice before the matter was resolved, with the help of riders' representative Martin Wimmer.

'My first day out was the Saturday. So I went out, I did six laps, and my bike blew up on the back straight. And it was starting to rain.' An entry didn't guarantee a start: Wayne had to set a lap time within a prescribed per cent of pole position, already set in the dry. This was now looking difficult. 'I ran all the way back to pit lane, and Alan Carter had already qualified, so they changed the fairing and gave me his bike. I qualified 19th. Then they tried to disqualify me because I didn't ride my own bike.' This second brush with officialdom in two days was rather puzzling: a jury meeting found there was no rule preventing a bike change at this point, but they decided to censure the team anyway, and told them to make sure it didn't happen again. Eh?

'I felt that the Italians or the FIM guys just hated me. They really tried to get me out. They ended up letting me race. I got one of my famous push-starts. By the time I passed the pace car he was half way down the back straight. Then I got down to it.' His ride was a spectacle – a demonstration of an original and powerful talent, underscored by his unique ability to treat a purebred 250cc GP bike like a rag-tag dirt-tracker. His race was distinguished by a lap record almost four seconds inside the previous best. That he also made the rostrum for the first time is almost by the way. It remains astonishing that after such a performance there could still at the end of the year be some observers who didn't realise the size of his talent.

Misano is a track with many U-turns. But there is a feature that lifts it from the ordinary – the back straight is approached through a trio of left-hand bends, each one a little faster than the one before, with the final one taken in fifth gear approaching top speed. It is important that they are left-handers. Dirt-tracks comprise only left-handers, and Wayne knew a thing or two about how to get around them.

'All those lefts, I was really digging them, because every lap I got to know them a little more. It was left, left, straight a little, then left again. Through the first two lefts was like a dirt track. Most of the guys were making two corners of it. I was just like squaring it off in the middle, and sliding it. And I was thinking, man this is so cool. I'd no idea what place I was in. I didn't even know where my pit board was. I was just out there going.

'I remember I stuffed a couple of guys through the last corner there.' This was another place where he was visibly sliding the bike's back wheel – a style completely alien to the usual 250 riders, who had come up through the European ranks, often via the 125 class, where to slide the rear wheel means you are wasting power.

'Then I saw the chequered flag. I just thought – damn. I came in, and they made me go someplace away from the pits. I wondered what I'd done wrong this time. For sure I was in trouble again. Then they told me I got third place, so they had to take my bike away with the first two for technical inspection. I just said – I did? That was a big surprise.'

In those days, GP riders would take part also in big-money international events. The one that came now was crucial in bringing this practice to a stop. Even Kenny Roberts had been tempted out of retirement for the Trans-Atlantic Challenge series – the Easter Match Races between the USA and Great Britain, to be held this year entirely at Donington Park, outside Derby. The star-studded American team surged to victory, but in the process defending 500 champion Freddie Spencer crashed his works Honda and suffered injuries that helped to ruin the rest of his season. It was the last year Honda would risk their lead rider at a non-championship round, and the other teams as usual followed suit.

It was crucial also for Wayne. Kenny had acquired a 500 GP bike for him as well – an old in-line four, a full generation behind the current works V4. Wayne was awestruck by the power and acceleration of by far the fastest motorcycle he had ever ridden. 'I couldn't believe how fast it was. I called my dad, and said: Wow – that thing is wheelying all the way down the straightaway. And that was an old bike. It had been modified for Jimmy Filice, who has real short legs, so the footpegs were high, and I was cramped up. It was cold, and the back tyre was like concrete. I was moving around trying to adjust my bodyweight on the left-hander after the Old Hairpin when it highsided me, got on top of me and chased me all the way into the fence. It broke my foot and gashed my back. I got back to the pit in a wheelchair, and I remember Kenny sticking my foot in a bucket of ice water and laughing about it. And I just said: I'm going home. Then when I got off the plane at LA my mom and dad and girlfriend couldn't believe it was me, because I'd gotten so skinny, in just a couple of months away.'

Wayne was just about fit enough to take tenth in Spain a fortnight later. Then came Austria, where the team had some special Bartol cylinders to try. 'Talking to Harald Bartol, the bike was going to be a missile,' recalls Rainey. 'First lap, I was breaking it in, and I ran up the straightaway, just idling. Then coming down to the right-hander I shut off, and the thing seized up and spat me off. I thought – oh, man. Then I heard a group of spectators up on the hillside, just cracking up at me. I flipped them the bird.' He fell again in the race. 'I fell off a few times that year, just not knowing what I was doing.'

In Germany, a good start for once saw Rainey a respectable sixth less than a second behind Lavado in a group chasing the leaders – he had qualified fourth on the brand new Nurburgring track. He was sixth again in France; a fighting fourth at Rijeka in Yugoslavia after qualifying in pole position then losing the advantage with another atrocious start. At Assen for the classic Dutch TT, he did get away well, only for the race to be stopped after a sudden rain squall on the first lap. In the restart, the old trouble again – compounded as he paddled along behind the pace car by hearing Roberts yelling obscenities from the pit wall: 'Push harder, you c*cks*cker.' Twelfth, after qualifying fourth, an impressive feat for a first-timer at the technically complex track. A non-finish followed a week later at Belgium's daunting Spa Francorchamps circuit in the Ardennes.

Then came another American interlude, a trip home for only the second time in the year. To do what? To race, of course – in the big international at Laguna Seca. The reigning Superbike champion was entered on a 250. It was a Yamaha, of course, but with a special frame Kenny had built, doing most of the work himself. This was an echo of the 500cc GP Yamaha's frame, built in aluminium. It proved so flexible that it required massive gussetting so it ended up about five kilos heavier than the stock steel frame; but it offered one tangible improvement – a proper rising-rate rear suspension linkage, in place of the by-now primitive Yamaha monoshock system. And with Rainey on board it was good enough to win the race.

The incident that mattered happened after the flag. 'I was slowing down for the winner's circle, which in those days was before the end of the lap, when a guy coming up behind fell off trying to stop in time, and his bike hit mine from underneath me – just popped me up in the air. We got to the winner's circle without a motorcycle.' The crash left the new chassis somewhat bent, but nobody noticed.

It was Kenny's idea to bring it to the next GP, the British round at Silverstone. 'It was no better than anything else I'd ever ridden, but it was Kenny, so I said OK. I felt if he was willing to make me a chassis, he's trying hard. So I was prepared to try too.

'Silverstone is mainly right-handers, and I had the attitude I could win there. Then when we went out it just wouldn't turn right. But boy it'd go through them lefts. I told Kenny, and we're changing the front, and raising the back, and the Japanese guys and everyone's laughing at Kenny because this chassis's just a pile. He wasn't laughing about it, and I wasn't laughing either.' Wayne finished 14th, a long way short of his expectations. 'After the race we found out it was about two inches out of line. Other riders told me they could see the front wheel coming down the straight behind me. That's why it turned in only one direction. After that we couldn't use it no more.'

Just two races left. In Sweden, Wayne was with the leaders when he ran off the track, recovering for a glum 13th place. Up front, Christian Sarron secured the World Championship. All a long way from where Wayne was sitting, as the pressure continued to tell.

The final round was at Mugello, in the Tuscan hills outside Florence. Officially, Wayne retired after burning out his clutch at the start. Now he has no time for face-saving excuses. 'I'm gonna say what actually happened. I pulled in because I was scared. I woke up that day, and I didn't feel right. I had that feeling once before, at the San Jose Mile in my rookie year. I rode a borrowed bike with borrowed riding gear, and I had a real bad feeling about doing that. And I ended up having the worst crash of my career. Now I woke up with the same feeling, and I couldn't get rid of it. So I pulled in. The way the season was going I didn't want to end up being hurt, so I deliberately fried the clutch, then pulled in after the first lap. That's the only two times I've had that feeling. I've never had it since.'

Wayne made a good impression in the GP world. Although the international make-up and the size of the stakes means there isn't the same degree of camaraderie as in US (or any other national) racing, the Rainey smile and easy good manners worked their usual magic. The living was anything but easy. His fee was $40,000, a significant drop in earnings; less indeed than Kawasaki's bonus for winning the championship; and he leased an ex-Kenny motorhome to follow the trail round Europe.

Motorhomes do not age gracefully. The best thing about this one was that Wayne would find piles of money slipped into odd corners. 'Kenny'd do invitation races, and get paid in cash. He'd put the bundle down somewhere and forget about it. I'd keep finding bags of money, and I'd tell Kenny, and he'd say: Shit, I forgot about that. Most I ever found was seven grand.' The worst thing was that the lavatory leaked. 'In those days, you'd pitch up at a GP and just park anywhere you'd find a space. At Spa, these Italian guys pitched next to me, and put out all these little tables and things. There was this foul stream coming from my thing and running right under where they were sitting. Wasn't much I could do. They told me I had a leak, and I said – well, I know. But they carried right on sitting there drinking wine and stuff. Jeez . . . Italians!'

Among the culture shock, there came the discovery that one thing was the same as in American racing. The girls. The old Californian glamour and the Rainey smile worked its magic every time and every place, it seemed.

The living was tough enough. 'I'd show up at the racetrack, then go straight to the outdoor sink and wash my clothes. I was cooking for myself, there was no such thing as a team cook back then. Between races I hung out near Kel (Carruthers – former World Champion and now team engineer for Agostini's works Yamaha squad). I'd go and park up at Bergamo. I'd run in the daytime, I started really hard training that year, and watch a video at night. I was alone most of the time. Kenny would fly to and from the races. I helped Kel instal a washing machine in his motorhome. After that his wife Jan'd wash my clothes for me.' He went home only twice during the year: each time his family would be more shocked at how thin he was looking. Sandy would reassure Ila. 'She was fretting, but I knew he was growing up. He came back from that year a lot tougher, and more of a man.'

Then there was the results problem. The riding was fine, though Wayne's aggressive dirt-track style was better suited to bigger machinery than the fine-edge 250s, and he learned little about riding technique that was of much value later on. It was the start-line problems that cost him good finishes. He'd practise and practise so he could get the bike chiming every time after just a couple of steps. But do it in anger, in among a grid-full of exploding noise and action, and it'd go wrong time and again. 'Starting's a feel thing. It's not something you can be taught. Kenny'd go on and on at me. Finally, I said: you start this thing. Show me how. He jumped on and pushed it down the pit, and pushed and pushed, and turned down the paddock road and he was still pushing. Right at the end of the season Martin Wimmer showed me how to blip the throttle then hit the kill button with the throttle open, to load the crankcase full of fuel.'

But the hardest thing of all was Kenny. He rode Wayne harder than Wayne rode the bike.

'Basically Kenny put the team together for me, but I've never been on a team that bad. It was a mess. That year helped me. I probably learned more that year than I had in my whole career. It really matured me. But at the time I just wanted to forget. I wanted never to go back there under those circumstances. And I was really gun-shy about riding for Kenny again.' Even then, Wayne understood why. Kenny was having a hard time adjusting to not being a rider. 'He was pissed off that he wasn't racing, and because he was upset he didn't really care about how bad he made people feel. And he really could make you feel terrible. Most of the time he was joking, but you wouldn't know it.' The jibes were constant. 'Every time he'd come in he'd go: man you're fat. You're too fat to ride a 250. I think I weighed 148lbs – later my racing weight was always 132 to 135. I heard that all year long.'

Then there was the Brother Wayne episode. 'On my first trip home, my girlfriend of many years suddenly wouldn't sleep with me any more. She'd become a Christian while I was in Europe. When I got back I told Kenny about this, and he just cracks up laughing and goes and tells everyone about it. I was so embarrassed. At dinner after the race, in this steak house opposite the hotel, after a few drinks he stands up all serious and starts calling me Brother Wayne. Eddie and Randy and some other guys used that nickname for a while. By that time I had figured out a bit of what it was all about, so I went along with the jokes.' Wayne was the principal victim, but not the only one. 'After races we'd always have a big dinner, and Peter Ingley was our Dunlop tyre technician. Seems he'd always pass out, then we'd write 'Michelin' across his forehead in felt-tip pen. Don't know how many times he woke up in the morning and saw that in the mirror.'

For Wayne, matters came to a head during another interruption to the GP season, the big-money invitation race at Imola.

'After that we were having dinner, and I said to Kenny: I want to go home. I want to quit. I can't win anything, I'm really homesick. And you think I'm no good. He went real quiet, and after that it wasn't so bad.'

Kenny, looking back, admits he may have been heavy going. 'He was very young. He was a real homebody, and he'd left it all to travel round Europe. Some of the things, I'd try to explain something and he thought I was attacking him, because of the way I'd say it. It's a sharpness in my tone of voice. I find it with my kids too. I think he just got used to it eventually. But at that time, I was still very very competitive. I didn't really mellow out for years after that. From going to just killing everybody in sight to trying to run a team was hard for me. And when I get short, I'm real hard to get along with. When someone's not doing what I think they ought to be doing, it's not easy for me to walk away from it and say never mind. It's getting easier now, but at that time it was probably impossible.

'I thought he did really well that year, learning new tracks and a new type of racing. We'd done the whole thing on a whim, under-funded. And he matured a lot.'

The two men didn't part on bad terms. The strength of the friendship would grow. But they split, each knowing that they had other things to do before they would get back on the GP trail. Kenny would be back in 1986, after a highly beneficial year off. Wayne would take just a little longer.

CHAPTER 8

FROM A
JACK TO A KING
– CHAMPION AGAIN

'He was the only guy I'd deliberately run into throughout my racing career,
and he was the only guy who ever deliberately ran into me.
We raced so hard that we didn't know there were people watching us.
It was just meand him on the track.'
Wayne Rainey on his 1987 rivalry with Kevin Schwantz

Wayne spent the next three years in America, and during that time he formed two crucial relationships. Both were to mould him, and to give him the strength he would need for his later achievements. All of them.

Tell the truth, he already knew Shae Grigsby. Her father, a lovable gruff bear of a man, was also a carpenter, and he and Sandy were sometimes on site together, driving out to Corona or wherever before dawn and working in the truck headlights, so as to get a day in before the smog got too bad.

Shae was special, Wayne realised that from the start. She still is. A cool blonde with fine firm features, Shae carries her own oasis of calm; a centre of gravity, sheathed in reserve. Those whom she allows behind the reserve find her company wonderfully reassuring. All this and much more Wayne had known since even before their bow-tie and party-frock date when she was 15 and he was 18 – a Christmas high school dance, where the girls invited the boys. Shae called Wayne. 'I'd always known Shae. I'd raced against her brother. She was only 12, about the same age as my sister. I always thought she was cute, and I knew she liked me, but she was just too young. I could imagine what it took for her to call me, and I decided if I say no, it'll break her heart. So I went.' The picture of the teenagers at the hop now has pride of place in their living room.

That was it for a couple of years, with Wayne off racing and Shae growing up and graduating. Then they got together again for a few months. 'Then we broke up for five years – I had my girlfriend and she had a boyfriend. But we still dated sometimes.' (Shae, listening in, interjects: 'We'd sneak out.') 'On the quiet. There was something about Shae that really excited me and drew me to her. I'd always feel nervous when I went to pick her up, and I never was for anybody else. I'd get sweaty palms, then after I'd drop her off, on the way home, I'd think: Man, you really screwed up tonight, you shouldn't have said this or done that – she'll never go out with me again. I worked hard on that girl, like I worked on that World Championship.

'She gave off this aura, like she was so positive about herself. And she was smart, and quiet. She would never just talk for the sake of it, to say something stupid. Not like most of the airhead girls I knew.

'I remember in '84 I was in Europe, actually on the beach at Monaco with Eddie, and I was thinking about Shae. So I wrote her a letter, to say we should have lunch.' She takes over the story. 'You borrowed your mom's Corvette, so I was real impressed.' Wayne: 'Yeah, and I let you drive it.'

It wasn't long before Wayne knew this was the girl he would marry. He remembers telling Kenny as much, when he was up at the ranch with Bubba Shobert. Of course, they all laughed at him. But he was right. 'During 1985, Shae became my full-on girlfriend,' Wayne remembers happily. Love grew and grew between the likeable though increasingly thoughtful and serious racer and the calm, mature, sensible Shae, so that in March 1987 they were married in Long Beach, California – a typical racer's wedding, squeezed in between fixtures, honeymoon on the road and in the pits.

The other important relationship was by then already taking shape. It was with a man – a bitter rival who would inspire Wayne's entire forthcoming glorious drive towards perfection, and would in turn be inspired to marvellous feats of daring of his own. His name was Kevin Schwantz. He was the other half in grand prix racing's forthcoming great double act.

Fittingly, the seeds were sown not only in America but on the world stage, in Britain for the 1987 Trans-Atlantic series. Or, as contemporary observers put it, the Schwantz and Rainey Show.

Kenny had contemplated another year in the 250 class. Wayne must be considered a potential champion, after all. 'Wayne wanted a Rotax – they were getting pretty fast. I spoke to Phillip Morris (Marlboro), but they weren't interested in 250 racing, not with us or with Yamaha, anyway. I was still working for Yamaha then. He had a good offer from Bob MacLean to race in the US. I took a year off, so I could start to get normal again. As normal as I can be.'

The 1985 offer was as good as was going for a rider in Wayne's position in a rather thin year, but it continued the downward trend in earnings. 'They didn't pay me anything, and we split the prize money. I wore white leathers, with Honda on them, but not MacLean's name. He wasn't happy about that, but it was a deal arranged by Gary Howard.' The deal was to ride a three-cylinder RS500 Honda GP bike in the AMA Formula One series and a 250 in the Formula Two class. Formula One, still a separate entity from the Superbikes, was showing one last spark of life, thanks to the availability of the new generation of GP 500s. The Honda RS500 was something like a replica of Freddie Spencer's NS500 World Championship-winning machine of 1983, and could be had for $26,000. It was expensive, but good value nonetheless for a machine only just short of the full works entries, and was already the privateer's weapon of choice in GP racing.

MacLean is a wealthy fan of motorcycle racing and a long-time sponsor, still involved as a 500-class GP entrant in the mid-Nineties. His 1985 team was started with high hopes: the redoubtable Rainey backed by GP-seasoned Rich Schlachter on a pair of the shiny new Hondas, with every hope of winning the title. Might easily have done so, especially since the eventual victor Mike Baldwin didn't even run all the races. Already three times champion, the New England rider's priority was a tight-budget near-solo assault as a 500 GP privateer, with European races taking precedence over domestic rounds in case of a clash. If Baldwin's season was fragmented, Rainey's was more so, through a combination of bad luck and circumstance. At the same time MacLean failed to attract the big sponsorship budget he had hoped for, not only to cushion the costs of the first year, but to go on to greater things.

Rainey's year was to have begun with a one-off ride for the in-house Yamaha importers team (as distinct from the official squad) on the new FZR750 Superbike at Daytona. The outing set some sort of tone for things to come. 'I did one lap of practice then on the second the exhaust burned through the oil line – it was rubber instead of braided steel. It spilled all over the rear tyre and highsided me coming out of the second corner. Broke my collarbone. I was supposed to race Bob's bikes in the F-One and F-Two classes as well.'

Rainey's Honda debut was deferred to the next race, Sears Point. Victory in both classes. On to Elkhart Lake, and another double win. Then Loudon, and straight into two different kinds of trouble. The first was with officials. 'Some of the haybales had trees growing in them. They were like concrete.' Wayne tried to organise the riders to some sort of action. 'I was suggesting that we shouldn't ride, but the other guys didn't seem to care. Then I got in a big fight with the track owner Don Brymer. I just wanted them to move some haybales, but the attitude was: Shut-up and ride.' It was an early attempt at rider politics, and was overtaken by part two of his misfortune. Practising the 500, Wayne fell off. Missed them haybales, but found a big rock in the grass of the run-off area with his elbow, and smashed it good and proper.

Baldwin won that and the next race at Pocono. Wayne came back to race four weeks later in the worst condition he'd ever come to the line. Dean Miller – long-time physiotherapist/fitness guru/ nurse to Kenny Roberts and his riders – had made him up a special articulated plaster cast. It was hinged at the elbow, allowing only just so much movement, so that as his weight was thrown onto his arms under braking it would take the strain and prevent his weakened arm from folding up. The scene was set for an epic comeback at Laguna Seca. Instead, a batch of racing gasoline the team had specially purchased was transported in tins of industrial solvent that hadn't been properly cleaned. The resulting tainted brew seized up all their engines – 500 and 250 – one by one, and Wayne didn't even make the start.

Yet more misfortune followed at Mid-Ohio. Still screwed and pinned and suffering pain and weakness, Rainey was losing touch with the lead when team-mate Schlachter came by and then crashed in front of him. Emergency action to avoid involvement wrenched Wayne's elbow painfully. Fourth, while Baldwin took the race and the title with one round to spare. The East Coast rider then departed for the rest of the GP season, but there was to be no compensatory Rainey win at the final round at Brainerd, Minnesota, as yet another breakdown meant one more non-finish.

'I don't have a lot of fond memories of that year,' recalls Wayne now. 'I had a good time with Bob and Tim (O'Sullivan – then a MacLean partner, later a close friend and right-hand man to Rainey after the accident). I tried hard and I won some races. Most times I was the fastest guy out there, if I didn't crash or break down. I won my first AMA national. But it wasn't a works team. Bob spent a lot of money, but our bike wouldn't run. I had a lot of bad results because of bike failures. It was kind of a half-assed deal. I had Chuck Aksland ("Johnny") looking after my 250, but he was also riding in the same class. So in practice I'd pull in and there'd be nobody to work on the bike. I'd have to lean over the pit rail and call Chuckie in.' His win rate on the 250 was good, however, with five wins out of 12 rounds, although the points system put him only third overall, with the title going to Californian one-race winner Don Greene. The penultimate race was won by a new name: John Kocinski. We'll be hearing a lot more of him.

There was a sort of opportunity to redress the dirt-track balance, that also came to little but frustration. 'Kenny came out of retirement for one dirt-track race that year – they paid him a bunch of money to race the Springfield Mile. Kenny gave some money to Mert Lawill to prepare a Harley for him, and I rode the bike to get it ready. Came close to winning a couple of races. But that was also half-assed. First time I showed up Mert was working on the bike. As I walked up to him, the battery shorted out and the bike caught fire. Then in qualifying I was sitting there idling, waiting to go, and the steering damper fell off. Came the one-lap qualifying run the left footpeg fell off.' Contemporary footage shows Wayne making a stirring start to grab an early lead on the blue-and-white Harley, only to be overwhelmed as the race wears on, his ill-sorted bike wobbling and almost throwing him off down the straight as he fights to exceed its possibilities. The sight is familiar to those who watched him doing similar things on his Yamaha in his last GP years.

Wayne also enjoyed being at home. After he'd moved on, Sandy had gotten himself hooked up with a dirt-tracker named Bubba Shobert, a smiling, drawling Texan who trusted Sandy so much that he even drafted him in to his dirt-track team. Bubba and Wayne became the greatest of friends, two goofers-off who also happened to be very talented motorcyclists. Bubba took the hybrid Honda dirt-tracker to three straight Grand National titles from 1985 to 1987, while making his own ultimately ill-fated switch to road-racing. 'We had a lot of fun together at that time,' recalls Wayne rather wistfully. The two old friends lived near each other in California until recently, when Bubba moved back to Texas. Both were by then in very changed circumstances.

The title may have been elusive, and MacLean's team ill-starred, but Rainey had put himself back on the US racing map, at a time when new opportunities were opening up. This came about with a restructuring of the championships for 1986, with the AMA instigating a rather extraordinary combined Camel Pro Series which totted up points from the dying Formula One class as well as the growing Superbike series. This year, the two classes survived, but with just one champion. Eight rounds would feature races for each class. A rider could compete in both, but not on the same motorcycle (although Superbikes were eligible and increasingly competitive in F-One). Points were taken from a rider's better finish of the weekend. Just to make it more labyrinthine, some races were run over two legs, overall results being computed on an aggregate system. For some reason, there were only eight F-One rounds, but a ninth Superbike round came at the season-opener at Daytona, skewing the new championship in favour of the four-stroke class.

This attempt to please everybody ended up merely confusing most of them. Be that as it may, it revived the interest of the manufacturers, in particular Honda, who had downsized somewhat the previous year, fielding just a one-rider team that took Fred Merkel to a second Superbike championship. With Kawasaki out and Suzuki lacking a competitive machine, they were largely racing against their own customers. Now Suzuki had a new bike and Yamaha were coming into Superbikes, and they decided to expand once again. And who should be running the

Honda Motorcycle Sports racing department? Why, none other than Gary Mathers, Wayne's old boss at Kawasaki.

'Honda had a much bigger programme than Kawasaki: road-race, dirt-track and motocross. Udo Geitl was managing the road-race team, and he had another rider in mind for the open slot, John Kocinski, who was kind of a friend who was just starting out. I told him to look at Wayne Rainey, but he wouldn't. So I went over his head and hired him anyway.'

The offer was to be number one rider on a three-year deal. In 1986 he would race the still-dominant V4 VFR Superbike, and an F-One class RS500. Nor was it the only thing on the table. Kenny Roberts had not been idle in his year off. Now he was back for the 1986 season heading a properly financed and equipped team: with Lucky Strike backing, running in the 500 class with works Yamahas. And one of them was for Wayne. 'He offered me the same money as Honda, but I just didn't feel ready mentally to go and race against Eddie and Freddie. The 1984 catastrophe was still too fresh in my mind. I knew I had a better chance to get back on my feet financially if I raced in America, because it would be easier. And I could work on my riding and training, to get ready to go to Europe. I might never get that chance again, but . . .'

The Honda deal was highly political, through no fault of Wayne's. The main issue concerned the fall from favour of Flying Fred Merkel. The fashion-plate racer and future World Superbike Champion had displeased his American bosses in spite of winning two titles so far, and they had not planned to renew his contract. An appeal direct to Japan got him reinstated but very much as the junior rider: Rainey was top dog with the fullest technical support, while Merkel's much smaller team operated more or less independently. Rainey also contested both classes, giving him almost twice as many chances at gaining top points scores, though the task of racing two such different machines back to back was not easy. In one way, the results reflected this status. Wayne won seven times, Merkel only twice. But – partly due to the weird points structure and partly due to his own better consistency – the irony was that Merkel won the title.

Rainey was back on familiar ground. His crew was run by Rob Muzzy, and he had another Kawasaki crewman, Sparky Edmonston.

Looking back, Wayne recalls that they never did recapture the family atmosphere of the lower-key Kawasaki squad – those internal politics again. Plus the Team-Mate Thing, which even came between him and best buddy Bubba to a degree. Shobert was Honda's contracted dirt-tracker, but had occasional outings on the Superbike in 1986, and full on in place of Merkel in 1987.

'That was when my friendship with Bubba got a little thin. It was the first time we were racing against each other at a professional level, both going for the same money, and one of us was going to win. I beat him every time, but he tried hard. There was a lot of friction between my crew and his. Muzzy ended up just hating those guys. At the time I didn't understand what the bad atmosphere was about. I was thinking it was me they didn't like. Honda was never a good home for me, even though we did a lot of PR, and built up a good rapport.'

The formerly green gang had another year of highs and lows, often caused by a variety of tyre problems. At Daytona, Rainey was disputing the lead with Lawson when he was forced to pit twice with his Michelin tyres starting to break up on the high-speed banking. He finished fourth, Merkel (who crucially was running on Dunlops all year) was third. At Sears Point Schwantz led the F-One race until his new Suzuki blew up, Rainey faded to third after a bad tyre choice; in the Superbike race the win was awarded to Merkel, even though both Schwantz and Rainey finished ahead. This was pivotal, and one of two things that Wayne would later blame for losing the title. It happened after the pair of leaders passed lapped riders under a yellow caution flag (under which no overtaking is permitted). They argued that it would have been dangerous not to have passed these much slower riders: Wayne blames a power play within the AMA for the fact that the decision went against them.

Rainey broke down while leading the F-One race, and beat Merkel in the Superbike round at Brainerd, Schwantz out with a broken collarbone. Rainey beat Merkel again at Road America, Elkhart Lake, and took the F-One race too; Rainey beat Merkel once more at Loudon, New Hampshire (third in the F-One). And at Pocono, Pennsylvania, Rainey beat Merkel again, Schwantz returning with a third place.

At this point, with three rounds left, Rainey had a 17-point advantage over Merkel. He extended it still further at Laguna Seca with yet another Superbike win: in the F-One race, Wayne had some fun hanging with guesting GP stars Lawson, Mamola and Baldwin on their full works 500s for a while, but crashed out, breaking his collarbone.

Clearly the title was to be decided on the Superbikes (even if Wayne did get a 20-point maximum on the two-stroke, he wanted to stop Merkel doing the same in the other class). Still in some pain, Wayne elected to concentrate on the VFR for the race at Mid-Ohio. This was the other pivotal event, for the wrong reasons. However, Wayne had nobody to blame but himself.

The two Honda riders' different tyres were crucial. The slippery track favoured Merkel's Dunlops over Rainey's Michelins (largely a matter of having the right combination of construction and tread compound available in the range). Wayne scorched away in the lead, but as the race wore on his too-soft tyre choice went bad on him, and he was obliged to slacken the pace. This allowed Merkel to catch up and overtake. It should not have mattered. Second place would still have secured the title. But Wayne succumbed to the Team-Mate Thing, pushed too hard to get back in front, and fell. 'It was the first time all year he was really racing me, and I made a mistake,' he ruefully admits.

This shifted the climax to Road Atlanta in Georgia. Rainey must win, and he needed Merkel to finish third. Then he would be champion. Wayne duly did win, after fending off a strong challenge from Schwantz. His rival crashed in the attempt, leaving second place to Merkel, who had rather a hard time fending off the coming man Kocinski. And so Merkel was champion: the new combined title was his. Not to mention the substantial bonus money. Defeat by just two points cost Rainey plenty, both financially and in terms of his peace of mind.

Not that there was too much of the latter, with Kevin Schwantz around.

Wayne had first noticed the gangling, fun-loving Texan back in 1985, in the ex-motocrosser's first full road-race season. 'I was racing the 250 in Kent, Washington, and I saw him go through an ess-bend real sideways, and I thought: that guy's got some talent.

I'd done the same thing a few times, so I knew it was something most riders didn't get away with. And he was getting away with it. But I didn't talk to him, and I didn't tell anybody else either. I was trying to get my own deal going, so I didn't want to talk about any other rider.'

The next year, Schwantz and Rainey ran across one another regularly in the Superbike class. But although Schwantz – younger by almost four years – was fast and sometimes in front on the new GSX-R oil-cooled Suzuki, he either fell off or blew up too often to be much of a threat. It was in 1987 that their rivalry became epic. Rainey was top dog on the top Honda in a championship now devoted exclusively to the big Superbikes; Schwantz was the brash new kid on the screaming new Suzuki, with the benefit of a full year's racing development behind it.

Schwantz was a problem for Rainey right from the start. 'I just didn't like him. He was probably the only guy in racing that I never really liked. Besides Fred Merkel – and they were big buddies. I just didn't hang around with those guys. It seemed to me that Kevin had everything pretty easy. He always had his mom and dad around with him, looking after him, while I'd been racing on my own for years. He had a big motorhome even back then – the way they like to do it, and seemingly everything he wanted. I thought he never knew what it was like to have it tough, where I felt I'd really had to work for what I'd got. It just didn't set well with me. Plus I really wanted that championship in 1987. It'd had cost me so much losing it in 1986. And I was liking the money by then.'

Schwantz, speaking in 1995, responds a little surprisingly. 'I'd be the first to admit it all came pretty quick. I've seen a picture of Wayne when he was just an itty-bitty kid going up through dirt-track on stuff his father built. I didn't even get on a road-racer until '84, and at the end of that year I got the Yoshimura Suzuki trial. At the end of '84 my parents had sold their motorcycle business, so they were semi-retired and had the ability to go with me.' (They stayed with him throughout the GP years.) 'I don't think I'd have been able to do any of it without their help, because it would have been too big a step. But to me, Wayne was the one who had everything. Honda had given him by far the best Superbike out there. Y'know, you're just getting it thrown in your hand. You ought to be able to win. So at that point, I disliked him for what he had.'

Mutual dislike is the one thing upon which Schwantz does agree. 'Fred (Merkel) and I had got to be buddies when we raced Superbikes in '85. Of course, he hated Wayne, who had come into the Honda team and got all the good stuff. My initial opinion of Wayne was that I wasn't supposed to like him. I was friends with Fred, and Wayne was the enemy.' Fred and Kevin were also still in the party mode that Wayne had left behind some years before. Schwantz: 'Racing on Sunday had nothing to do with Saturday night. I think I learned the hardest way possible. On Saturday at one race we all went out to the lake, skiing. I had a bit too much to drink. And on Sunday morning I crashed on cold tyres and broke my collarbone. I heard about that for quite a long time.'

The early animosity played to the full throughout the US season, on the track and in the press. Riders frequently bad-mouthed each other in public. It was known as 'flapping their lips'. The Rainey–Schwantz hostilities led to some epic racing that people still talk about today. Especially as during 1987 Suzuki had found reliability, and their GSX-R was giving Honda a hard time. What happened in England in mid-April was only a preview. Yet Wayne recalls it as pivotal.

'I'd gotten married after Daytona, and we went straight to Britain for the Trans-Atlantic Challenge series. Bubba was my best man; now I was going on honeymoon with him. He didn't last long. I think it was the first corner of the first lap of practice and he crashed, and went straight home again.'

Rainey took a satisfying win over Schwantz in the first-ever Camel Challenge at Daytona – a five-lap sprint for $10,000 – then won the 200-miler after Schwantz crashed out of a convincing lead at about three-quarter distance. Each took their own comfort from this. And sniped at the other in the press. Rainey had been closing slowly, but as Schwantz points out: 'I had 13 seconds, and on the banking at Daytona, that's forever. I saw in the press Rainey said I'd fallen because I was feeling the pressure. My response was: It's Monday today. It'd probably be Tuesday before he'd have passed me, the rate he was catching up.'

The mood was fragile as they rejoined battle at Brands Hatch.

And what a battle. Team tactics were forgotten as the pair broke away ahead of the pack from the first race onwards, and fought tooth and nail. Looking back now, Wayne shakes his head at their stupidity at not cutting a deal – that whichever won the first race should win all the rest. This would put him in line for a £100,000 bonus, which the whole US team could have shared. But that was way too rational a solution for the crescendo of circumstances. 'The team spoke to me about that, and I said I'd talk to him about it. But it was never ever said, because there was no way I was going to let him think he could win all the races.' Schwantz had exactly the same attitude.

In fact it was Schwantz who took the first one, after narrowly surviving a clash of fairings when Rainey showed him some of the old dirt-track elbow. Rainey was in front for the next round, and Schwantz was riding as aggressively. He had a desperate last lap pass-and-block manoeuvre planned, but hesitated slightly putting it into action. 'I left tyre rubber all over his leg and his fairing. Man, I thought he was gonna get unglued when we come in. He says: What the f*** are you doing? You could have killed us both. I said: What d'ya mean? Just paying you back for what you did in the first race.'

Just like traffic arguments, this sort of discussion has no winner when both parties believe they're right. This is one of the prime reasons for the development of that malady of the 1990s, Road Rage. It makes for fraught commuting – but leads to unforgettable motorcycle racing.

For the record, Rainey had won that second race at Brands, and he ended up with more victories in the Easter series that took the US and British teams to Donington Park for two more days after opening at the Kent circuit. With three races each day, Rainey won five times, and Schwantz four, but Schwantz emerged as the higher points scorer by virtue of one poor result in the rain from Wayne. Naturally enough, the American team trounced the British. But none of this mattered as much as what the confrontation meant – the birth of a phenomenon.

For Wayne: 'That's where it all really started, in England. At Donington I remember I'd suck him into a slow turn, and that cowboy'd be sideways so's all I could see was Suzuki written down the side of his bike. We left our mark there, and we boned each other for the rest of the year, and after that.' Schwantz also has vivid memories of the grey English spring weekend. 'There were a couple of times at Brands where I saw my life go before my eyes. It was brutal.'

The atmosphere of seething hostility lasted the rest of the year. They avoided speaking and even meeting if possible. Press conference photos show them always at opposite ends of the table. On the rostrum their eyes would never meet – each was gazing firmly off in a different direction. Schwantz recalls how the glacial temperature would always drop a few degrees more when he took his occasional visits to Europe, the Suzuki GP team's star guest rider at three GPs each year. 'Seemed to me when I'd get back, the animosity was greater.'

The racing was always red hot. Kevin won more of the nine-round Superbike series than Wayne, five races to three. But this time Rainey got the championship. 'He was tough, but he was making mistakes and I was getting points. It seemed that year I pulled back a little bit, because I knew from the year before that falling down wasn't a good way to win a championship. It was a good way to lose one.' This judgement represents a somewhat narrow line, because Wayne was prepared to go to extraordinary limits.

'It was one of those rivalries where you race so hard that you never leave the other guy any room, and you're always running into them. I never did that with anyone except Kevin Schwantz. He was the only guy I'd run into, and he was the only guy to run into me. We raced so hard that we didn't know there were people watching us. It was just me and him on the track. Like two fighters in the ring, and there's only one winner. We just hated each other, and we would ride each other right into the grandstands. I just didn't care. And he didn't care if he rode into me going into the pits.

'It was always just the two of us. I was trying to beat him, and also hold back because I needed that championship. He was just like in a bull ring. Just nuts. I could sucker him into these corners, and watch him buck and turn right off the race-track. And I'd beat him. And I'd think, when this guy gets smart one day, he's gonna be tough.

111

'At the end of the year, I won the championship but Kevin won more races – and it seemed I heard more about him winning than about my title. Maybe that was because I read everything Kevin said about me. That he could beat me. That when we got to Europe he was going to smoke me. All this stuff. Then the press would ask me what I thought, and I'd say: Well, he's always said that stuff, but he can't stay on the motorcycle. He might be fast, but he's not fast for very long.'

There were other complicating factors. One was Honda's switch to Dunlop tyres. This turned out to be badly timed, while Schwantz was striking up a career-long preference for the new improved generation of radial Michelins. At the same time, Honda's previously dominant V4 was being pushed into obsolescence by the newer and nimbler Suzuki, now reliable as well as fast.

With the AMA finally abandoning the F-One two-strokes, the all-Superbike championship season went like this. Daytona: Schwantz crashes out of a strong lead, Rainey wins. Road Atlanta: Rainey defeats the Suzuki in a fierce pitched battle. Brainerd: Rainey wins after Schwantz escapes with bruises from a 160mph crash in practice. Then the pattern changed, and Wayne did not win another round. Loudon, New Hampshire: Schwantz, transformed, runs away to a lap-record win; Rainey is demoralised in second. Elkhart Lake: Schwantz does it again.

The next two-leg race at Laguna Seca was pivotal. Wayne and team-mate Bubba had both been penalised for jumping the start in their heat race – to settle a private one-dollar bet as to who would get through Turn One first. Starting from the back of the grid, Wayne fought through and closed remorselessly on leader Schwantz, only to have to pit when a rear tyre blistered yet again. In the second leg, he put the pressure on even harder. Schwantz crashed shortly after losing the lead to Rainey on the last corner of the Californian course, right at the start of the pit lane. (He would do the same thing, even more ruinously, at a GP several years later.) Shobert was credited with overall victory; Rainey was fifth, Kevin down in 13th.

Then the Schwantz express resumed business. The shrill in-line four Suzuki not only looked more businesslike than the slabby V4 Honda, with its gruff engine note, it was now also going a lot better, in the hands of this fast-improving road-racer. Mid-Ohio: Schwantz won confidently, Rainey second. And again at Memphis. And in the final round, Schwantz once again won going away. Rainey only needed one point, however, to be champion, and he cruised to sixth to win the year by a margin of nine.

Schwantz had definitely finished the stronger, and Wayne now felt a new sensation – that of underdog. 'I was the established guy, and he was trying to take over. He was fast, he was cocky, and he could beat me. I had dominated Fred Merkel the year before, just kicked everybody's butt. I think I still hold the record for the most Superbike wins in a row.' (This was equalled only in 1995, when Miguel Duhamel was romping to his title.) 'And Schwantz comes in there and he beats me. I won the championship, but he was the fast guy. I realised that now I was the underdog. I had to come back and prove myself.' Not for the last time in his career, Wayne would find this a powerful inducement to reach the next level of improvement.

'I didn't want to be known as just a consistent rider, racing for the championship the easiest way. Because I didn't. I raced the smartest way. I used my brain, and racing is using your brains and using your talent and using situations. I did the best with what I had, and I won. Because I was smarter.'

Wayne still had one year of his Honda contract to run, but it suited both parties to give it a miss instead. Honda were facing budget cuts, while Wayne had a much more attractive option. Kenny never had given up on the idea of running him in his top-league 500 team, and now he was pressing him again. This time, Wayne felt he was ready. And besides, that's where Kevin was heading too.

This one would run and run.

CHAPTER 9

OH
LUCKY MAN

'Wayne wasn't the type of rider who just learned it right away.
He had to apply himself, to figure things out. His improvement wasn't
overnight. It was step by step. He's like a little bulldog.
He grabs you by the ankle and won't let go. At first, he's not a real threat,
but he hangs on until he kills you.'
Kenny Roberts, speaking as a team owner

The opening round of the 1988 500cc Grand Prix series was a magnificent triumph for the latest new full-time works rider from America. In slippery conditions, riding the most challenging of all motorcycles, the class rookie humbled the establishment with a superb ride to victory. Sadly for Wayne Rainey, that rookie was Kevin Schwantz.

Given the way the previous season had finished, taking into account the amount of preparation work Wayne had put in, this was a serious blow. All that, just for his hated rival to start off looking like he was going to dominate. Oh boy. Especially in view of his own beginning, failing to complete his very first lap of practice. 'It was wet, and I fell off. That was a big moment for me, lying there in the mud, wondering what I'd gotten myself into. I decided that I had to get straight back on, go to the pits for the other bike, and go out again immediately and go as fast as I could.'

Wayne couldn't afford any self-doubt. A professional racer must eliminate this from his make-up, if he aspires to beat the world, lest it take seed and become the truth. But it wasn't as though everybody shared his and Kenny's confidence.

The Roberts team was now very different from the one-truck effort of 1984. In two years the Lucky Strike hospitality awnings and huge team transporters had become a major presence, adding prestige and glamour to the GP paddocks; their factory Yamahas had been regular rostrum finishers. Randy Mamola had even come second in the world in 1987 (to Australian Honda rider Wayne Gardner, and ahead of Eddie Lawson's rival Marlboro Yamaha) and had won four races during his two-year stint. Baldwin had come close, but had suffered an injury early in 1987 that pretty much ended his GP career.

Kenny had surprised everybody by dropping not only Baldwin for 1988 but also veteran clown-around superstar Mamola, who was still a serious championship contender. 'I wasn't sacked. We just failed to reach agreement,' Randy would later insist. Kenny was already complaining about his lack of dedication to pre-season training. 'And he wanted some things I couldn't live with – mainly to do with testing, and some non-GP races for Lucky Strike in Japan and Malaysia.'

Roberts signed Wayne. There had always been a place for him on the team, just as soon as he was ready. The previous season they had run two GPs with new Australian discovery Kevin Magee, who had distinguished himself at Assen by qualifying on the front row of the technically difficult track. Kenny continues: 'So I called Lucky Strike and explained the problems with Mamola. So they said, hey – sign up Kevin Magee. We liked his attitude. He really wanted to be a racer.' Thus Team Roberts was equipped with two GP learners for his works bikes.

Wayne had a good idea of what he would be up against. While he would still focus on his team-mate and on Schwantz, this thing was bigger than all of them. He threw himself into preparation directly after the end of the US season. 'I worked really hard. Bought a motorhome and moved up to Kenny's ranch. Me and Shae left LA to live there. I rode every day, and I trained every day for more than two months. I just lived motorcycles. I'd ride with anybody who'd come out. Kenny if he could. Bubba. Ricky Graham (a dirt-tracker from Salinas, not too far away near the coast). Magee was there for a while.

'I wanted to be in the best shape of my life, because I knew this year was going to be yes or no for the rest of my career. I knew I could make a lot of money. I was getting $60,000 to wear a helmet (a Shoei) in 1988; $400,000 from Kenny to ride the bike, $50,000 from the leathers company. I was making half-a-million dollars without even sitting on the motorcycle. And there was like a $200,000 bonus if you'd win the championship. There were some big numbers out there. Coming from where I'd been, with all the ups and downs, this was a dream to me. This was by far the most dedicated racer I'd ever been, up until that point.'

Kenny's ranch, in the soft Central Valley hills outside Hickman, not far from Modesto, was fast becoming something of a racing institution. He'd bulldozed an eighth-mile oval short-track there and shipped in a parcel of little-league 100cc dirt bikes – here, sliding the tail out, you could practise throttle control all day long, if you could put up with Kenny whooping at your heels trying to knock you off. Plus there was a motocross loop or two, to build up endurance. Team men, invited (privileged) riders, paying guests from the GP world and nominees from Yamaha came to practise. None of them did so with the determination of Rainey.

He and Magee had met at the back end of 1987, combining a first chance to test the V4 YZR500 Yamaha with one of those show-the-flag Lucky Strike races at the Johor Baru circuit in Malaysia. Rainey liked the uncomplicated Australian from the start. 'He wasn't like us city boys – he was from the woods. It used to crack me up the things he'd get off on. They were so, so simple.' It must have been nice to feel wise and sophisticated, compared with the adverse culture gap Americans usually find when first they come to Europe. The two men spent a fair bit of time together that winter, knocking back cold beers and satay in Malaysia, playing gin rummy in the control tower at Jarama while the wind raged outside, playing in the paddocks, travelling round Europe, at the ranch, or down far away in Brazil, testing.

And there was plenty of that too, circulating for hours a day, getting the feel of the two-stroke. Or at least getting a glimpse of its potential. Compared with a clumsy, friendly old Superbike, a grand prix bike does not yield up its full depth instantly. A works 500 is faster, more accelerative, lighter, harder braking, more agile – more mettlesome in every way. It is a single-minded racing machine, a purpose-built hand-made 'prototype'. Wayne believes it takes at least a year for even the most accomplished four-stroke rider to learn its full capabilities, and then only if he works very hard.

Kenny's big budget and full-on approach meant an arduous

schedule well suited to Wayne's own determination. Tyre testing alone during 1988 was a monumental task way beyond anything he'd experienced with Honda in America. 'We'd test twice a year. Now in the off-season I'd done more laps than I'd done all year with Honda.'

The programme was focused on tyres. Michelins were the popular GP choice; Kenny's choice of Dunlops was becoming increasingly eccentric, but made sense on the principle that to find an advantage over the rivals it often helps to start from a different place. 'We tested mainly in Brazil, and in Australia, 300 tyres in each place. Lap after lap. People who think racing's glamorous when they switch on the TV on Sunday just don't know the work that goes into it – the hours in the gym, the hours training on a motorcycle. Or leaving your family and going to Goiania, where they have snakes going across the track and grass growing up on the kerbs. It took something like 25 hours to get there, and we went several times that year. You have to test 300 tyres, and 299 of them are no good, but you have to test them all. If you let one slip by, that could be the one. I remember retesting tyres because I wasn't sure about them.

'I was sure tyres were going to be really important, and I wanted to be a really good tyre tester. So I got to learn how tyres felt when they were cold. How they felt when they went off. How they felt when they chattered. How they felt when they were out of round. How they felt when they gripped, when they stepped out. I learned all this.'

The schedule was tough. At first they'd run four-day tests, but later they cut it down to three, because 'by the fourth you were just in a rut.' Riding from nine until six, with an hour for lunch – '200 laps a day, sometimes (six or seven times GP distance). I got really good at testing. I could go out straight away and test a tyre, an engine part, or a chassis, and come back and give the engineers the feedback on what it was doing. I learned how to ride at 80 per cent of what I and the bike were capable of. Then every year I could bump that level up a bit. All the riding was making me physically stronger too, really using my muscles. Through my experience I knew how to push a tyre in a different way, how to go over a bump or through a corner differently. I was forcing down on the footpegs harder, doing stuff I'd never done before. And learning and remembering it because I was doing it so much. I started to get really good after the end of my first full season. In the pre-season tests for 1989 I was the fastest guy at Phillip Island.'

That was the year I started to get to know Wayne Rainey better, and it was enthralling listening to him talking through his discoveries, as the season progressed. Principally, they concerned exploring the potential grip of the front wheel, under braking and into the corner. Wayne already knew everything there was to know about using the rear wheel, playing with the power to make it spin and slide the bike. Dirt-trackers did that for breakfast. But to match the masters of the 500s he had to learn how to dally with front-wheel skids as well. Difficult territory, and very easy to fall off.

His first grand prix year was a period of intense education in every aspect of GP racing, and how to become the dominant figure. Kenny had faith he would do it. 'When I hired him for the 500, everybody thought I was nuts, because of his results on the 250. He rode good then, but he didn't set the world on fire. But the bike wasn't good, and we didn't get the help from Yamaha we'd expected. I think he could have been in the top three first time out had the motorcycle been better. I think he would have been successful at dirt-track too, had he continued.

'Wayne wasn't the type of rider who just learned it right away. There were sparks of natural talent, but it didn't flow out of him, like some riders. Like Freddie (Spencer), for example. He had to learn how to do it. But when he did learn it, he just kept getting better. He had to apply himself, to figure things out. His improvement wasn't overnight. It was step by step. But he never seemed to take a backward step.' Kenny readily agrees that this dogged side to his character played a vital part in what was to come. 'He's like a little bulldog. He grabs you by the ankle and he won't let go. At first, he's not a real threat, but he hangs on until he kills you.'

Wayne could turn the doubt felt by others to his advantage. A quote from journalist Alan Cathcart's *Cycle News* season preview became a particular icon. Wayne still has a copy in his desk drawer, though he hardly needs it, the whole thing being etched on his memory. "Rainey is a good rider, but he'll never be a great rider.

And he'll certainly never be a Randy Mamola." That made me so mad. He'd never even spoken to me, and I still have hardly spoken to him to this day. I'd think, if he writes that, how many other people are thinking it? Stuff like that really did get me motivated. I liked to have to prove myself.'

The GP world Wayne was rejoining had moved several steps ahead since 1984. One fundamental change made it a more comfortable place right away. No more push starts. In response to demands from American riders, the FIM had adopted clutch starts from 1986. A level playing field, so that Wayne could exploit the first-lap speed he'd worked on so carefully to try and build up a lead, rather than to pass the pace car.

Eddie Lawson had also moved on, winning the title in 1984 and 1986, and was now in his sixth year on a 500. Eddie's works Yamaha was basically identical to Wayne's, but for the Marlboro paint job that came with the Italy-based team run by former multiple champion Giacomo Agostini. His chief rival was the 1987 champion Wayne Gardner, the gritty Australian Honda rider. Others riding the V4 Yamahas were ex-250 champion Christian Sarron and Lawson's team-mate Didier de Radigues; while works Hondas went to Scotsman Niall Mackenzie, Italian Pier-Francesco Chili and Japan's Syunji Yatsushiro. The Suzuki team saw big Briton Rob McElnea alongside Schwantz; the French Elf-Honda was a curious experimental device sporting car-type suspension, ridden by Briton Ron Haslam; while Cagiva's red Italian bikes had a new-found American star on board – the displaced Randy Mamola.

The series ran over 15 races. The third one was in the USA. Here at Laguna Seca Wayne was on home ground. He qualified on pole for the first time, and came in fourth. Satisfactory, especially since he was 13 seconds ahead of fifth-placed Schwantz. But at Jarama in Spain, further inspiration by humiliation awaited. Another rookie winner: this time team-mate Magee.

Well, here was a target. From the start, without Magee realising it, Wayne had been working on him. In the nicest possible way, of course, but it had to be done. Like most team bosses, Kenny insisted that there was no number one rider: each had equal status. But there has to be a pecking order, and Wayne wanted it sorted out in his favour. 'At first, I think the team was leaning towards Magee because of the way he'd ridden for them the year before. He'd gotten right on it, and was going pretty good. I was trying to make sure that I would beat him every time. At racing and everything – training runs, playing pool, whatever. I started working on him real early.' Years later, Magee was still wondering at how upset Wayne used to get if beaten at the seemingly unimportant pursuit of racing the paddock runabout four-wheeler 'quads' around impromptu tracks. Magee was just having fun, but Wayne was losing a battle in a planned campaign. And Kevin didn't even realise there was a war on.

It didn't last too long. Wayne had observed that chief engineer Mike Sinclair always debriefed Magee first. At Assen, around the midpoint of the season, he was pulling ahead of Magee on points. 'I said to Mike: Hey, you'd better start coming to me now. Because I'm beating this guy. From then on, he came to me, and he stayed with me until I crashed at Misano.

'Magee was basically a real thrasher type of racer. Not much thought went into it. He just rode on ability, and at that stage of our careers that was OK. I kinda knew what was going on, and I gave the 500 a lot of respect, and he didn't. When he won that race at Jarama, it just devastated me. Everyone thought: Magee's the guy.'

The next race was at Jerez, new since 1984. 'At new tracks I'd look in the previous year's *Motocourse*, and study the layout. I'd arrive early and run around the track. I'd always watch the other classes in practice. After qualifying, we'd think about the track, and talk about it with Kenny. Go out on scooters after practice. It was a full-time job.'

At the Andalucian circuit, Wayne qualified second behind Lawson, with Magee third. Then came an epic race. Magee recalls it as his best ever with his team-mate: 'He had a few seconds from the first lap, then I caught him. Then we were just rocking. I'd take two tenths, then he'd break one tenth back. Then I'd take a tenth and he'd break two-tenths. Going for inches on each other for 20 laps.' Wayne recalls it from his own point of view: 'I had a really good race. I led most of it. It was close with Magee, then I started inching away. I got a three or four-second lead. Then the rear Dunlop just shredded. I had a pretty hard time just keeping it on the track. Eddie passed me with about two laps left, and won.' Magee was third, narrowly fending off Sarron.

From then on, Rainey watched and drew ahead on points as his team-mate gradually deteriorated. 'He was going down pretty quick mentally. He didn't have the experience I had, and he was a no-worries type of guy. He was much more laid back than me, and it was starting to show – as the season wears on it's not so exciting. Bringing him in for a couple of races like they had the previous year was a perfect Kevin Magee scenario, because he didn't have to put a lot of effort into it.

'We're racing a World Championship, and you're in there every week, and by the end of the year you're beat. You're whipped. It's the concentration. You have to keep pushing yourself to that peak, and learning the circuits, and going through tyres and chassis setups. And staying pumped up, to try and beat those other guys. Getting in your motorhome, travelling to the next race, trying to have fun between races. For the Americans and Australians, you wouldn't see your home or your family for months, unlike the Europeans. There's not much glamour in it. And he was whipped before the end of the season.'

Magee agrees. 'It was the travel and living in the motorhome that brought me undone the most. I was used to being home between races, and being able to ride bikes in the bush, like I'd always done.' The difficulties of life were complicated still further by the fact that he and his young wife Julie also had their baby son Jake with them. 'Julie and I were very naive kids, and running a season in Europe hit me pretty hard. Wayne had been there, so he was sussed and psyched up for it.'

They got on well though. Indeed it was quite difficult for anybody not to get on with them. Wayne had his ingrained courtesy and that winning smile; Magee had a perpetual grin as wide as the outback, full of innocent fun. Judge by his remark: 'You don't have to hate your rivals. Just race them.' It went much deeper than that for Wayne. They travelled round Europe together. The two couples did touristy things when there was the time, visiting cathedrals or camping out beside Alpine lakes. 'Shae video-taped everything,' says Wayne. 'The signs on the motorways, the cafes, gas stations . . .'

There was one other aspect where Wayne could be helpful. Dealing with Kenny. For one thing, he was a lot calmer now than in

1984; and when he and Wayne talked about racing, Wayne could understand a lot more of what he was talking about, as well as place his own interpretations on it all as he developed his own style. And he knew that the teasing, the put-downs, the in-your-faceness, was only joking. He could tell Kevin: You shouldn't take it too seriously. Even when he teaches your infant son to say Oh Shit! as almost his first words. Nonetheless, Magee found it hard. 'I had Kenny Roberts trying to get me to change my riding style, which obviously didn't work. Wayne would listen to Kenny, then go off and do his own thing anyway. I remember Wayne telling me he'd told Kenny to shut up in the past. I should have, but I was still Mr Kevin, the Nice Guy.' (Three years later, when Magee was racing for the Yamaha factory out of Kenny's pit in Malaysia, he did blow up at Kenny in the pit. Roberts disappeared for about 20 minutes, says Magee, then came back and gave him some really good advice about the starting problem he'd earlier been making fun of.)

After Jerez, the season proceeded apace. To Imola in Italy, where Rainey made third, eight seconds ahead of Schwantz, Magee fifth. Then to the Nurburgring, where Schwantz again showed wet-weather skills to win his second race of the year, speeding up in response to a dogged challenge from Rainey in second. An early demonstration from the double-act.

Rainey lay third in the world now, behind Lawson and Gardner, and comfortably clear of both Schwantz and Magee. In Austria, he was third in the race, his turn to fend off a late-charging Schwantz. Gardner crashed out, and this moved Wayne up to second on points. He was well on target for his hoped-for top-five finish, but part two of his pre-season plan – to win at least one race – was still elusive.

Assen, and he again held off Schwantz while nursing his tyre home, but only for seventh. Then came Spa-Francorchamps, second of the two traditional mid-season circuits, last and most majestic of the grand old road races. The classic track in the Ardennes valley was by modern standards long (4.3 miles), fast and dangerous, especially because of its propensity for bad weather; and it was dropped from the GP calendar after 1990.

There were no better tracks than Assen and Spa for demonstrating the grim and glorious realities of the World Championship. And it was at Spa that Sandy and Ila Rainey had an introduction to their son's latest occupation. The shock was so severe that Sandy fell ill (his turn to develop the nervous complaint of shingles), and Ila decided: 'You couldn't visit with him when he had his race face on. He was in another world and we had no business in it. Anyways – racing! Who wants to watch it!' I recall standing with Sandy beside the track at the daunting Eau Rouge corner. Riders brush the pit wall at 130mph-plus, then swerve left and right at barely abated speed through a profound dip, fighting the bike to clear a third apex for the full-throttle left-hander that follows. Desperately fast with the barriers hard by the trackside, in the misty drizzle, it is one of the scariest places in the world.

Sandy was in awe. Looking back, he recalls the moment. 'I'd never even seen racing in the rain. It really rocked my boat. I couldn't believe what he was doing. My last impression was him on Superbikes. And now these . . . these things that don't even want you sitting on them. You're racing them as hard as they'll go, and they don't even want you on their backs. After seeing what he was on, it made it worse waiting for the phone calls. I never went to another GP. Didn't even switch on the TV. Just waited for that phone call.'

Rainey – fifth at Spa – was in any case not the guy his parents or anyone else knew from US racing. He was even considered 'quiet' in contemporary reports. It was the start of the fierce concentration that was to intensify over the coming years.

Yugoslavia and Rijeka provided a welcome lightening of the mood. 'It's a real dirt-tracker's circuit – a lot of left-hand turns. I liked tracks where you could run it off into the corners real hard, and left-hand turns that come back on you, and you can use the throttle to slide it a bit. My riding now was at about 80 per cent of what I would reach when I was champion.' He was third again, then fifth in France, struggling with spinning Dunlops behind a classic four-bike battle won in the end by Lawson, when Gardner's bike went sick on the last lap. After Lawson came Christian Sarron, Schwantz, then Gardner.

Now came the annual interlude that top riders dreaded: the gruelling trip to the Suzuka Eight-Hour endurance race, where the factories depended on a strong performance from their GP stars in Japan's most prestigious race. Magee said later: 'I never forgave Wayne for spoiling that race. He stopped it being memorable. The year before I'd ridden almost single-handed. I rode the wheels off for five-and-a-half hours: two double sessions and two single sessions, and I only got a new tyre for the last two hours, and we were second. Winning it with Wayne made it just too easy.' Wayne's four-stroke interlude left him pumped up: race victory at his first attempt after pole position. The doubts of the early races were far behind him now.

The next GP vindicated everything. Victory at last, in the sun-baked acres of Britain's Donington Park. The new track surface clearly skewed the advantage away from the Michelins to Wayne's Dunlops, but (as they say) he still had to ride the thing; Magee on the same tyres was fifth. Wayne's own maiden win came after Schwantz recorded his most embarrassing moment in racing, knocking home hero Ron Haslam off on the first lap, and breaking his own knee in the process.

Wayne recalls everything about the day, including a relaxation of his usually strict self-imposed rules. 'The night before the race, I didn't eat pasta: We ate tacos.' This may not sound much, but understand that many racers set great store by some such combination of beneficial practices and almost superstitious ritual.

'I'd decided to use the carbon-fibre brakes. Some people had tested them, but nobody had raced them yet. They didn't work until they were hot, and on the warm-up lap, I just about took out Schwantz and Gardner because they were too cool. I always made sure they were hot after that.

'I led out of the first corner, and I was just racing at my speed, and pulling away two tenths every lap. When there were about five laps left I had six or seven seconds, and I was thinking, maybe I could win this thing, then saying, don't think about it, just get to the finish. It was my most special race until that time, but it was also one of the easiest. And it got that winning thing off my back. It was a tremendous boost.'

Wayne was fifth in Sweden, third and on the rostrum again at Brno, his first visit to the newly-built then-Communist track; then he retired from the final round in Brazil. His non-finish was the result of a puncture, prosaically enough, and spoiled a perfect finishing record for a top-level debut season. More importantly, he'd won his first race, stood on the rostrum seven times, finished third in the world. He'd defeated Schwantz on points, and left Magee trailing. Most importantly of all, he now knew he was ready to win the championship.

The year ended with a flag-showing race at Sugo in Japan, followed by a monumental party with Roberts, Paul Butler, Magee, Bubba Shobert and some other guys. Racers' year-end parties are dangerous affairs, involving the imbibing of alcohol by people who have been on a knife-edge for months. The release of tension is spectacular. So it was this time, with Butler falling off the top of the bus, then an incident in Tokyo with Bubba damaging a 'borrowed' taxi and the police called. 'We were all cocked up, and Kenny was trying to control us.' It was solved millionaire-style with Kenny paying everybody off; but Japan took revenge on at least one of the miscreant visitors.

'I got really bad diarrhoea from some sushi or something, and I went to a chemist and kinda mimed what the problem was. He gave me some medicine, which I took. Then we went on to Hawaii to meet our wives for a holiday, but by then my diarrhoea was so bad I could hardly leave the hotel. Eventually I was so sick I had to go to hospital and they ran some tests. Turned out the medicine was to loosen the bowels, not to stop them up.'

CHAPTER 10

KNOCK, KNOCK, KNOCKING ON HEAVEN'S DOOR

*The more successful Rainey became, the more desperate was his ambition,
to the point when it drove him to destruction. 'After that year, I promised
myself I'd never lose the championship that way again. I was starting
to become obsessed with being better than I ever was.'*
Wayne Rainey, on the end of the 1989 season

The racing equation has many elements, from mechanical to motivational, with much in between. That is why racers talk about 'the combination.' It's a very Kenny Roberts word, and he gives it wide application. It's what he aimed to give his riders in terms of machinery, equipment and attitude, and it's also what he and Wayne were. The combination.

'Kenny has a very dominant personality,' says Wayne. 'Especially if you looked up to him. I really believed in a lot of things he did. He had me bluffed on a lot of stuff, but at that stage of my career I needed somebody I could draw from. I'd never had nobody like that before. He was three times World Champion, and he was very outspoken and clear on his ideas. He was the guy in charge, but it was all benefiting me. He had the background and the profile to demand all kinds of things, and I was happy to go along with the show. There was no friction between us. Never was. He seemed willing to do anything to go and race – and so was I. He liked the commitment I made. We were good for each other, and we had a lot of good times together. There's not too many people who got on like me and Kenny.'

Lucky Strike and Kenny Roberts were now well established together, going into their fourth year. The American brand was a big sponsor whose annual spend was close to $10 million. Riders' fees were beginning to move up fast. Eddie led the way and passed $1 million for the basic sign-on. Wayne was very close to the million-a-year mark, with bonuses and side deals. He was in the big-time, with a manager who knew how to make the most of it. The result was to skew the emphasis. Now that he no longer had to worry about money, the reason for racing reverted to a purer past. He wanted to win, just as on the little dirt bikes as a kid. The child-like attitude then was that first place is everything: there's no such thing as a noble second place. And this feeling was growing stronger with maturity rather than weaker.

Wayne and Kenny's joint motivation at this pre-championship stage was inspiring. Wayne had no doubts about where he was heading. He'd just turned 28, and he was on the ascendant, reaching the age at which racers customarily peak, though few of them have by then already accumulated 20 hard years of experience. Motorbike racing is a more artful business than it might appear, as well as risky. Time maximises the former, while experience helps to reduce the risk. In the space of a year on a 500, Wayne was already one of the best, and his position reflected it. He was the number one rider (in all but name) with a team of consummate professionals. He was returning to familiar tracks on a familiar machine. He was a very serious 500 racer.

At the same time, his V4 YZR500 Yamaha was settling into design maturity; Suzuki's close-echo machine paid tribute to the rightness of the conception. It was state of the art, while Honda would take another three years before their powerful but hard-to-handle V4 NSR would reach the same evolutionary stage.

Honda did have something different for 1989, however. It was newly crowned triple World Champion Eddie Lawson. Playing his cards typically close to his chest, Eddie had unexpectedly switched from Yamaha during the winter. He would be the sole rider in a new team sharing Rothmans sponsorship and works equipment with the rather miffed Wayne Gardner and his new team-mate Michael Doohan, but operating separately under the wing of ex-Spencer tuning guru Erv Kanemoto. Schwantz was with Suzuki again, now with Ron Haslam as his team-mate; formerly Fast Freddie Spencer was making an ill-starred come-back on a Yamaha, with Mackenzie as his team-mate. As it turned out, this meant that Team Roberts was very definitely the senior Yamaha team. It only remained to sort out which of the above would put together the strongest season to vie for the title.

One other rider change made Wayne pretty pleased. Bubba Shobert had arrived in GP racing after adding the 1988 US Superbike title to his three dirt-track Grand National crowns. He was riding a Honda for one of the handful of offshoot semi-works teams, and it was good to have him around.

The tyre question was once again crucial. In spite of a number of problems in 1988, the Roberts team stuck with Dunlops. One reason was the Anglo-Japanese firm's commitment to testing and development; another was the desire to be different. A third was the discovery in post-season testing at Goiania that a simple switch in rear wheel size from 18-inch to 17-inch made a huge improvement. Plus, Wayne liked the feel of the slip-slidey Dunlops, when they did hold together. They didn't have the same grip as the Michelins, but though they would spin and slide earlier, they were much more manageable in a slide. Just right for a dirt-tracker. Wayne's ability to stay in command of a bucking and slithering motorcycle that looked out of control (this in the middle of the era of the dreaded highsider crash), his aptitude for blinding fast starts and early-lap speed, and his near-perfect finishing record were triple themes of the year; so sadly was a tendency for the tyres to blister and 'go off' towards the end of the race.

Wayne typically made it look easier than it was. 'The Michelin guys could get to their race tyre quick. We had so many tyres to test that sometimes I'd still have two to try on race-morning warm-up. I could tell in two or three laps if they were going to be OK, because we'd done so much testing.' Even so, unless it was wet, and especially if it was hot, the Michelins had an edge. 'Their biggest advantage was when they first cracked the throttle open. The Dunlop was prone to stepping out, while the Michelin was strong on initial side-grip. I ended up losing a lot of races because I wanted to stay on the bike. I knew if I would have tried to go with them, I'd have crashed.' Something he knew with even more devastating clarity after falling off the top of the world in Sweden. Another problem was a lack of consistency with the tyres, painstakingly built by hand at Fort Dunlop in Birmingham. 'You

EARLY DAYS

ABOVE LEFT *The right hat lends a man distinction – and an orange balloon doesn't hurt either, when it matches your shirt.* (Rainey Family Collection)

ABOVE RIGHT *Proud parents Sandy and Ila in 1967. Wayne, Renee and Rodney range in age from seven to three.* (Rainey Family Collection)

BELOW *Wayne, aged two, shows cousin John Lane how he'd drive Sandy's go-kart – if only he could reach the pedals.* (Rainey Family Collection)

ABOVE *Nine years old, and the set of the jaw is already familiar.*
(Rainey Family Collection)

BELOW LEFT *Pre-teenage Wayne drifts his 50cc Honda.*
(Rainey Family Collection)

BELOW RIGHT *Sandy made the bikes look good and work good. Wayne's 80cc Yamaha had a home-engineered rear disc brake as well as twirly-whirly 1973-style paintwork.* (Dennis Greene Photography)

DIRT TRACK DAYS

ABOVE *Rainey takes the low line inside Danny Perkins: the year is 1976, the bike a Shell Racing 250 Yamaha.* (Wizard Racing Photography)

BELOW LEFT *Stone-spattered number plate, battered boots, and a grin as fresh as the future: Wayne in 1978 aboard the Shell Racing 750 Yamaha, with Shell Thuet's nephew Veryl.* (Rainey Family Collection)

BELOW RIGHT *The Crucible Kids show their trophies: Mike Minnig (left) and Wayne Rainey glower with toughness.* (Dan Mahony Photography)

ABOVE *Five feet (and a couple of years) ahead, Eddie Lawson leads Shell Racing team-mate Wayne Rainey on the Yamaha 750 dirt-trackers in 1978. 'He chased me all the way to the World Championships.'*
(Wizard Racing Photography)

BELOW LEFT *Wayne and Eddie started going green in 1980, on dirt bikes at the Houston Astrodome. Eddie was already road-racing Kawasaki Superbikes; Wayne would follow. They flank Kawasaki racing stalwart Steve Johnson.*
(Dan Mahony, Wizard Racing Photography)

BELOW RIGHT *'The cutest boy I ever did see.' Teenage Shae bucked up the courage to invite Wayne to her high school Christmas Dance.*
(Rainey Family Collection)

GOODBYE TO GRAVEL

ABOVE *Wayne's first 'factory' ride was on the official Kawasaki Superbike in 1982. The new road-racer poses with lead mechanic Sparky Edmonston and (left) dirt-track companion Chris 'Itchy' Armstrong.*
(Kawasaki News Bureau)

BELOW *The lap record and a rostrum finish at Misano in only his second 250cc GP. Fausto Ricci (centre) and Martin Wimmer were his 1984 companions.* (Malcolm Bryan)

ABOVE *Wayne chases 1987 Honda Superbike team-mate Bubba Shobert at Mid-Ohio. He will pass him, but the race-winner was Kevin Schwantz (left).* (Rainey Family Collection)

WAYNE AND KENNY – THE COMBINATION

BELOW *First GP, 1984 at Kyalami. Wayne and British team-mate Alan Carter are on the pit wall; newly retired Kenny Roberts talks to his ex-tuner Kel Carruthers (white shirt). In the foreground mechanic Bruce Maus fettles Wayne's very standard Yamaha TZ250.* (Malcolm Bryan)

ABOVE *Wayne and Kenny listen to team technical man Warren Willing in 1988, his first 500cc GP season.* (Gold & Goose)

BELOW *At Kenny's ranch, dirt-bike training was frequent, from 1987 until the very end. Wayne (left), Kenny (centre) and a companion pause for breath in the Californian hills.* (M. Watanabe)

ABOVE LEFT *Fixing the bike with a steely glare: Kenny and Wayne in 1993.* (Gold & Goose)

ABOVE RIGHT *In 1995, a long-standing friendship was complicated by new business rivalry, among all the other things. The friendship survived.* (Gold & Goose)

SCHWANTZ AND RAINEY – THE DOUBLE ACT

'When we raced each other, it was fierce.' TOP RIGHT *1987 Trans-Atlantic,* RIGHT *1989 Brazilian GP,* BELOW *1991 German GP.* BELOW RIGHT *1993 European GP. 'It went right on to the end.'* (Malcolm Bryan)

ABOVE *1987: Rainey and Schwantz were thrown together a lot in those days, but their eyes seldom met. 'I felt like I was meant to hate him,' said Schwantz.* (Gold & Goose)

BELOW *But by 1993, 'it got so we were pretty friendly.' Walking back after practice.* (Gold & Goose)

CHANGING FACES

ABOVE LEFT *1987: Champion of the USA, ready to take on the world.* (Gold & Goose)

ABOVE RIGHT *1989: In the Dunlop truck, making that crucial tyre choice. Or just having fun.* (Lou Martin)

BELOW *At the end of 1992, Wayne moved into his newly-built house outside Monterey.* (Paul Carruthers)

ABOVE LEFT *1993: the strain of the compulsive battle to win is starting to show.* (Malcolm Bryan)

ABOVE RIGHT *1994: Wayne's first public appearance, barely four months after the crash, was with Shae and Rex, just one year old.* (Paul Carruthers)

BELOW *Seven months after the crash, Rainey was back as a team manager. Here he debriefs stand-in rider Jimmy Filice.* (Gold & Goose)

GRAND PRIX GALLERY

ABOVE *Rainey was running away with his fourth 500 GP at Jerez in 1988 when his tyre let him down. Lawson (a distant dayglo blur in fourth) won the race.* (Gold & Goose)

BELOW LEFT *Spa in the rain was always sobering, especially for any loved ones watching.* (Lou Martin)

BELOW RIGHT *1989: Triumph in front of the packed grandstands at Hockenheim – team manager Paul Butler greets German GP winner Rainey.* (Malcolm Bryan)

ABOVE *1990: 'It felt great –*
for about two-tenths of a second.'
Rainey celebrates his first World
Championship win with Shae at Brno.
(Gold & Goose)

LEFT *'So I just steered round him like*
this.' Wayne's only win at Assen came
after Schwantz broke down ahead of
him. A win is a win is a win.
(Lou Martin)

RIGHT *Rainey's ascendancy came at a*
time of grand prix greatness. Here
Eddie Lawson and Kevin Schwantz
chase him in Austria through the
short-cut at the chicane.
(Malcolm Bryan)

ABOVE *Assen, 1991, and the full drama of a Grand Prix start. Pictured are Rainey (1), de Radigues (27), Schwantz (34), Doohan (3), Gardner (5), Garriga (6) and Lawson (extreme left, 7).* (Malcolm Bryan)

BELOW *The 1993 British GP. Concussed and in trouble, Rainey leads through, unaware of the mayhem behind. Doohan (on the ground) has skittled Barros (9), sent Schwantz looping. Cadalora (7) managed to get through unscathed.* (Wout Meppelink)

ABOVE *For the rest of the race, Cadalora shadowed his slow-paced team-mate, before nipping past to win.* (Malcolm Bryan)

BELOW *Wayne never liked riding this close with Alex Criville or others of the new generation, but by 1993 it was getting hard to avoid it.* (Gold & Goose)

THE STYLE OF WAYNE RAINEY

ABOVE *Pushing on during testing, Rainey still has the time for a gesture showing his friendship and respect for photographer Lou Martin, who has a large collection of similar shots.* (Lou Martin)

BELOW LEFT *On Dunlops, Wayne could slide a 500 as if it was a dirt-tracker. He sometimes used this as a tool to intimidate other riders.* (Lou Martin)

BELOW RIGHT *Wet weather demands the utmost precision. Spray shows how only half the tyre is used to transmit more power (cc for cc) than a Formula 1 car.* (Malcolm Bryan)

RACING PEOPLE

ABOVE *The Evil Empire: At its peak, Team Roberts was a formidable presence. This 1992 picture puts King Kenny between warring partners Kocinski and Rainey. Note also Chuck Aksland, between Kocinski and Kenny, Warren Willing and Mike Sinclair (glasses) between him and Rainey, and Wayne's mechanics Bernard Ansiau and Howard Gregory next to him.* (M. Watanabe)

BELOW *Americans in Europe: team boss Rob Muzzy, Rainey, and teamster Gary Goodfellow at the 1987 Trans-Atlantic Series.* (Malcolm Bryan)

ABOVE *Wayne's first 500cc team-mate was Kevin Magee: he was dismayed when the Australian won the third GP of 1988, particularly after deadly rival Schwantz had already won the first.* (Lou Martin)

BELOW *Waynes' World: Gardner, the 1987 World Champion, was stubby and determined to the point of recklessness.* (Lou Martin)

ABOVE *There always seemed to be another Australian ready to pop up. Michael Doohan was the most successful, but the Rainey/Doohan dream team foundered.* (Gold & Goose)

BELOW *Behind every great rider . . . pit crew led by (from left) Mike Sinclair, with Howard Gregory and Bernard Ansiau.* (Malcolm Bryan)

ABOVE *Sharing in the glory: Marlboro's man Leo de Graffenried (red jersey) with Wayne, and Dean Miller and team manager Paul Butler at Brno in 1990.* (Lou Martin)

BELOW *Dunlop tyre man Jim Murphy (left), Sinclair and Rainey on the start-line in Austria.* (Lou Martin)

ABOVE *With John Kocinski, 1991. 'He was talking big before the season. I just listened to him. I knew by the end of it one of our Grand Prix careers would be ruined.'* (Gold & Goose)

BELOW LEFT *Hands-on team physio Dean Miller supervises Rainey's diet. He patched him up throughout his GP career.* (Gold & Goose)

BELOW RIGHT *Bubba Shobert: best friend, best man, sad victim – with Wayne at home in Monterey early in 1993.* (Paul Carruthers)

Shae Rainey – two moods: sunny in Spain, worried in Italy.
(Malcolm Bryan and Lou Martin)

ABOVE LEFT *Austria, 1993. 'After the race, I was so happy I stayed in my leathers for ages, hugging Rex and celebrating third place.'* (Lou Martin)

ABOVE RIGHT *After the crash, Kenny was promoting the US GP, then flying back to be with Wayne in hospital. And he looked like a ghost.* (Malcolm Bryan)

BELOW *Randy Mamola and Wayne at that last GP weekend at Misano in 1993.* (Gold & Goose)

THE CRASH

Six steps to disaster: Wayne and his Yamaha leave the track together. As they hit the gravel trap, they both start flipping end over end, the bike shedding its bodywork. It is not clear whether Wayne was injured being struck by his bike, or in his final head-first backward plunge into the gravel. The fight for life started directly. (Heimo Kernmayer Photography)

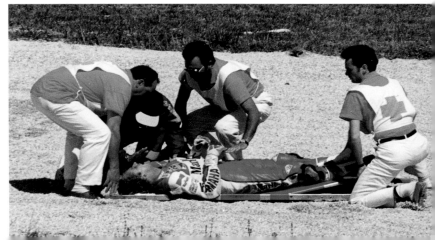

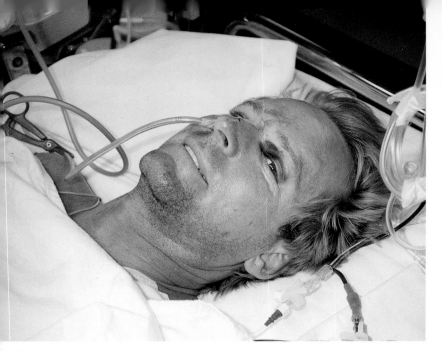

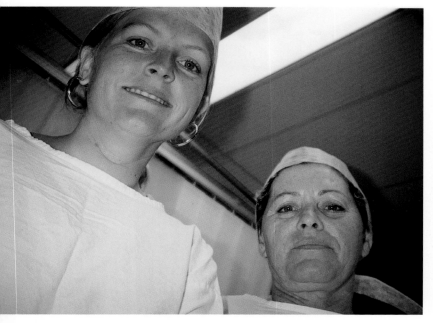

OPPOSITE *Shae and the Rainey family arrived in Italy some 24 hours later. The first thing they did was take a picture of Wayne. And he took a picture of them. Shae and Ila Rainey in the intensive care ward at Cesena Hospital.*
(Rainey Family Collection)

RIGHT *Even to the untutored eye, this X-ray shows the extent of the damage to Rainey's spine, smashed and displaced right across the sixth thoracic vertebra.*
(Rainey Family Collection)

BELOW LEFT *Watched by Rex and cousin Mike Lane, Wayne manoeuvres into position to rise into his standing frame.* (Michael Scott)

BELOW RIGHT *Standing is an important exercise for physical well-being. Climbing is good for four-year-old Rex. Happily, the two things now coincide.* (Michael Scott)

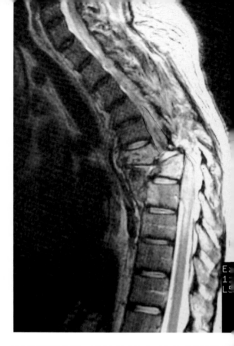

ABOVE *Eddie Lawson built this 150mph hand-controlled go-kart for his old friend and rival. In March 1997, Wayne tested it in California.* (Rainey Family Collection)

BELOW *Wayne's workshop is overseen by a fairing nose cone from his six years as a 500cc Grand Prix rider. The 'Magic Carpet' is bottom left.* (Michael Scott)

ABOVE *Rainey's cycle. 'On a good day, I'll do 15 miles on it.' By early 2010, he had clocked up more than 8,000 miles. The strength in his arms and shoulders is formidable.* (Rainey Family Collection)

BELOW *Wayne, Shae and Rex, at home in 2010, more than 16 years after the crash. The journey continues.* (Rainey Family Collection)

Wayne's crash ended an era in GP racing. The banner at Jarama said it all.
(Malcolm Bryan)

could get two Dunlops with the same number, but they would act completely differently. We were testing different compounds and constructions all the time. It wasn't a lack of effort that did it. Just that Michelin had a better manufacturing process.'

The latest version of the Yamaha had big boxy air-intakes and a large square seat intended to reduce turbulence behind the rider's body. In essential respects it was almost the same as the previous year's machine. The Honda was faster in a straight line, the Suzuki was lighter and more agile. The 1989 Yamaha's strength was in its well-rounded character, which meant that a determined rider could bend it to his will in a wide variety of circumstances.

The 15-round calendar was also little different. The series started once again in Suzuka in Japan, with the cherry blossoms just appearing on the wooded hillsides. Wayne turned up well prepared after two months in a rented house in Modesto for ranch-training, and extensive tests. 'We'd been fastest pretty much everywhere in testing and hadn't fallen off, so we were pretty confident. I wasn't thinking about winning the championship, but I thought I could make the top three.'

The first race combined high excitement with a touch of farce. Revenge for last year's defeat seemed within his grasp as he tussled with Schwantz for the lead, then on the last lap he made a basic error that cost him the race. It is easily explained – and made frequently by riders who should know better. Even Doohan did the same thing in Germany in 1996.

'I couldn't see my pit board so I was watching the circuit's own lap counter over the start line. That clicks down as the leaders go underneath it, but I didn't realise that. I read L2. I was following Kevin and thinking: why's he riding so wild when there's still another lap left? He was being real aggressive, and I was sitting right on him, planning how the next lap I'd draught him on the back straight, then not let him pass me at the chicane. Then we came across the start-finish line and there was the checker. It really pissed me off. Towards the end of 1988 we'd started saying hello to one another. It wasn't just the two of us any more. Now our rivalry started to heat up again.'

To Phillip Island for the first Australian GP. An eye-opener, for an American racer expecting something like the general apathy that had attended the rebirth of the US round recently. Instead, the whole country seemed GP crazy, and the visiting 500 riders were feted by their hosts and pursued by a media displaying a lively and knowledgeable interest. 'We were part of the show from the moment we landed.' And what a race-track. Picturesquely located beside the sea, Phillip Island was fast and open – ideal for close 500-class racing.

'It was such a cool track. The Yamaha could even pass the Honda there because of the downhill straight. You come onto it in fourth, so you're already getting up to high speed. We had the bike geared high, so we could hang in the draught of the Hondas. I was coming on there in a full-lock full-throttle slide. I liked to do it in front of Kevin, and the Honda guys, Gardner, Eddie and Doohan, to show how early I could get on the throttle, and to try and make them get on the gas too early.'

The race was a classic. Lawson was riding hurt after colliding with a broken-down Magee in practice; Schwantz eliminated himself with a hot-headed first-lap crash. Wayne barely had time for a wry smile when he saw that, being rather busy for the next 48-and-a-quarter minutes. Gardner's Honda and the three Yamahas of Rainey, Sarron and Magee were locked throughout in a close slipstreaming battle: they finished in that order, inches apart. 'I duked it out with these guys. Gardner ran into the back of me twice, and didn't even notice. He was one of the sloppiest guys I ever raced – he reminded me of a bulldog on a bike. When he was on a good day, he could ride that thing right out of the saddle. He was a bit like Kevin, but more out of control. Not a thinking racer: he rode by the excitement of the crowd. If nobody was there I think he wouldn't do much.'

Scary? 'No. I felt I was more aggressive than the year before. I knew right away we were in the hunt for the championship. I didn't know who I'd be racing for it, but Schwantz had already made a mistake, Gardner was way back in the first race, and Eddie was way back too. I had a pretty good lead then.'

Wayne won a week later at the jet-lagged US GP at Laguna Seca, starting from pole and defeating Schwantz by some seven seconds. In a fateful weekend, Gardner crashed heavily and broke his leg badly. He was out of the title chase.

Then came Bubba Shobert's accident. A foolish combination of circumstances involving Rainey's own team-mate Magee left Wayne's best man and best goof-off pal in a life-threatening coma with serious head injuries. It happened only minutes after Wayne's win and had him numb with shock. 'That was one of the worst days of my life. Nothing registered about the win. Only Bubba was on everybody's mind. It was just tragic the way it happened. The race was 40 laps, and on the last lap going up the hill my bike was surging, running out of gas. Magee's bike had already been doing that a couple of laps before, and that let Eddie pass him and get third. He was so upset, and about halfway round the track he stopped to do a burnout to let off some steam' (spinning and smoking up the back tyre while holding the front brake). 'He wasn't in the middle of the track, but he wasn't on the side either. Bubba came round shaking Eddie's hand, looking across at him, and never seen Magee. And that was that. Bubba's career was over.'

The finger pointed at Magee, who suffered a broken ankle that wrecked his own season, but Wayne does not condemn him. Everybody knows not to slow down or stop on the track, but at times everybody does it anyway, road-racing having so little to do with commonsense anyway. 'You see people do it today – slow down to pick up a flag. I've done that. There was the time in '84 at Laguna when I slowed down and got hit from behind. And this year, after I beat Eddie at Hockenheim, I stopped to pick up Kevin and give him a ride back, he'd broken down out there. I thought afterwards: that wasn't too smart after what happened to Bubba.'

Shobert was in a coma for 11 days. 'I was in Europe, checking on him every day, and the guy with him told me that he was awake, but he wasn't talking. I said: give him the phone. Then I said: Bubba, this is Wayne. And he goes – Wayne. And that's when he started talking. After the next GP in Spain I flew back to see him. That was the first day he was allowed home, and the day he started to remember who he was. So when I seen he was feeling better, I started feeling better.' After extensive therapy Bubba made a reasonable recovery, but was never to race again.

The Spanish GP was in Jerez. It was won by Lawson with Rainey second: Schwantz had led by miles but fell off. Then to Misano, where changing weather rendered the poor patched surface virtually unridable, and caused the riders to pull in of their own accord after the first start. The works men declined to restart as the rain continued. 'Eddie was the most vocal,' recalls Wayne. 'I think it was a lot worse for the guys on Michelins. My Dunlops weren't so bad. I could have raced, but safety is the strong point, and I went along with the other guys. The problem was the lack of any sort of riders' union, to prevent this kinda thing happening again.' A seed was sown.

Wayne now led Eddie by 10 points. It was half the total allotted to a race win, and still a slender margin. His former Crucible companion expected revenge at the next race. Germany's Hockenheimring comprises a pair of very long warp-speed gallops, each interrupted by a chicane, linked at one end by a very fast U-bend, and at the other by the short, twisty stadium section. Awe-inspiring on a 500cc GP bike, the circuit is 4.22 miles long with the average speed of 123.8mph – fastest of the year. Eddie Lawson, peeved that his new Honda's uncertain roadholding meant he had not so far felt the benefit of its significant power advantage, had a special way of summing it up. The track, he said, had 'Honda-lanes'. He expected his second win of the season here.

Wayne: 'All year long Eddie had been telling me about the Honda-lane. I guess in Germany it started getting pretty bumpy with him, because I was in that Honda-lane. The Yamaha-lane started as we went into the stadium, where I outbraked him on the last lap. It was the only place I could pass him. I hung in his slipstream out of the last chicane and waited until he started to brake. Then I just whipped out and passed him. It's pretty difficult to defend that corner, once you're committed.' There was to be an echo of this two years later, with Rainey as victim to Schwantz.

Eddie was not happy, remembers Rainey: 'I think he was embarrassed, because he'd been badmouthing the Yamaha for being slow, and we'd beat him at the fastest track of the year.' The resentment boiled over a week later at the equally spectacular Salzburgring in Austria, another very fast (and frightening) circuit with a run of flat-out corners clinging to the side of an Alp. 'Schwantz won the race, but my Yamaha couldn't pass that Honda-lane bike up the hill', a breath-taking top-speed surge round the flank of the mountain. 'But on the banked right-hander at the end of that section, Eddie was going really slow, and I could ride round him every time. Then he'd get by me again on power. It was really pissing me off.' When the Dunlops succumbed to the pressure and started shredding, Wayne fell back to a distant third.

'After the race we did a lap on the victory truck. We were laughing and giggling, then when we got to that corner he said to me: I was gonna run your ass right over here. I said: What are you talking about? I'd thought we were just racing. He says: You cut me off right here. You came across the top and tried to take me out. I said: No I didn't, Ed. You were riding so slow, just pole-putting. It was the only place I could pass you.

'Those were the only words spoken, and we didn't talk again for the rest of the year. All us American guys had been lent 944 Porsches, and he ended up putting his in a ditch that night, so only the headlights were showing. I think he was pretty upset.'

As is usual in these circumstances, Eddie remembers the whole thing a little differently. 'It was a pretty awesome move around the outside. It pissed me off more than anything, and he just slammed the door on me. He always rode real, real aggressive, probably more than anyone I've ever raced against. I got him back. I edged him out because the Honda was faster. In the truck after the race, he needled me first. He said: How come you parked it down there in that corner? I said, well it's kinda hard to get that Honda stopped, but I was so close to T-boning you back in the next chicane. And he just went through the ceiling. I can't remember what was said, but I told him if he ever tried that again, be prepared . . .

'I was giggling inside because it was easy to get him wound that tight. I found that kind of amusing. I thought, if he's rattled that easy, just go ahead and stay with it.' Ruthless? Of course. But this is the World Championship. As Eddie adds: 'Wayne is quieter than me when it comes to other people or the press, and always real careful with his words. But he was every bit as strong-minded as I was. When it came to racing, he had exactly the same mentality as I did. If not more.'

It was Schwantz–Rainey–Lawson again at Rijeka, and probably would have been again at Assen, had Kevin's Suzuki not broken a piston on the last lap, giving Wayne his first and last victory at the Dutch track. His points lead when they arrived at Spa the next weekend was 16. After an extraordinary race, restarted twice in deteriorating weather, he thought he'd extended it. After all, he'd won it, when Schwantz crashed out of a secure lead on the final lap. Then, three hours after the race they rewrote the results, as the FIM jury discovered a rule that allowed only one restart. The third leg was discounted, and Lawson awarded victory ahead of Schwantz and Rainey, with only half-points awarded. 'So I won the race, but they gave it to Lawson, because the FIM organisers didn't know their own rules! Schwantz took a big chance and tweaked his neck pretty good, and it wasn't even counted as a race.' After Misano, here was another demonstration that the riders needed to get organised if they were not to find themselves again treated as mere ambulance-fodder.

In France, the tyres failed him again; Lawson claimed a second successive win, then Schwantz, Rainey third. In Britain, the magic of the year before had deserted the Dunlops. 'Tracks change from one year to the next, especially if they get used a lot, like Donington Park. We had a side-grip problem. I rode harder than the year before, but didn't win.' Schwantz narrowly ahead of Lawson, Rainey dropping back in third again.

The crux of the season came one week later, at the scrubby airfield circuit at Anderstorp in Sweden. This comprises a succession of heavily banked U-turns and right-angle bends, then a fast gallop down the runway back towards the finish line. The banking ruled out dirt-track cornering techniques, the long straight suited the Honda. And Eddie's team boss Kanemoto had been working hard at closing the handling gap. Radical strengthening of the chassis had improved the steering, while Eddie's trademark consistency meant he'd never been too far away even before that. Wayne was consistent too, of course. Now the pressure was intensifying. Which would crack first?

'I definitely screwed up there,' admits Wayne. 'I didn't have to beat him there, but I had to beat him at one of the last three races, and I wanted to get it done. I qualified on pole a full second quicker than Eddie. The Dunlops were pretty good on the one-lap fliers. In the race, the tyres were getting less predictable. I was on Eddie, but I couldn't get by, and we were running out of laps. The only place to pass was at the end of the straight, under brakes – but that meant I had to get a good run out of the corner onto the straight to get his draught.

'I was riding more on emotion than brains. Out of that corner, with three laps left, the back wheel stepped out so fast, and it just flicked me off. I was pretty devastated, laying there. I knew I'd lost the championship. I'd let the team down, and everybody down. It had started so well, and in the end it was Eddie's year.'

Lawson recollects: 'What people didn't realise about Sweden – I've never even said anything to Wayne about it – was I had much, much better tyres than his. The Michelins were far superior at that track. We were doing the same times, lap after lap, and my tyres felt like they were getting better and better. That time I grabbed a handful of throttle in the middle, the thing just hooked up and accelerated out. That was my fastest lap of the race; I'd never got on the throttle that early all race. When I cracked it open, Wayne followed me, and there was just no way the Dunlop was going to do that. It wasn't Wayne, it was the tyres.'

Unhurt, but his bike unridable, with a handlebar snapped off, Wayne brushed track officials away and withdrew into the adjacent pine forest to contemplate the meaning of what he'd done. For the first time in 12 races, he no longer led the World Championship. And he knew that was the end of that.

It wasn't quite over yet, of course. At Brno, Wayne barely beat Sarron's Michelin-shod Yamaha for third, while Schwantz won. 'It was the same situation: I just couldn't go where those Michelin guys could go.' The final round was at Goiania. Rainey was third again behind Schwantz and Lawson. And Eddie was World Champion for a fourth and final time.

Wayne had fulfilled his pre-season ambitions of a top-three finish, and typically used his failure to build greater strength. He'd come within an ace of the title, 17.5 points behind Lawson, in spite of the 'wrong' tyres. It is entirely in character that he would blame himself for the failure, and come back even more determined than ever. This was the path to glory. But if this life has a theme, it is that the more successful he became, the more desperate was his ambition, to the point when it drove him to destruction. 'After that year, I promised myself I'd never lose the championship that way again. I was going to be better than ever in my life.

'I was starting to become obsessed with being better than I ever was.'

CHAPTER 11

DOUBLE ACT,
BUT JUST ONE WINNER

'When I crossed the finish line, and I was World Champion, I had this
burst of emotion. I felt really great. For about two tenths of a second.
Then it was gone. It left me feeling really disappointed. It meant so
much more to me emotionally losing the title in Sweden when I crashed
than it did winning it.' Wayne Rainey, on the rewards of victory

Rainey came ferocious to the fray in 1990. Testing, training, as usual, but a bit harder than before. Also as usual. 'From 1988 to 1989 I was a much better racer. But when it came to 1990 I was very very fine-tuned.'

Another factor was a further adjustment to international life. Having done to death the American in Europe number, fed up with motorhome touring and listless sightseeing while inwardly obsessed with the task of racing, Wayne and Kenny together bought a house in Sitges, outside Barcelona. 'I needed somewhere with good weather, where I could train. I felt as I was getting older I needed to train more than before. That was pretty hard in the motorhome. You could lift weights, and I went for a run every night, no matter where we stopped. But we were getting tired of that. Kenny and his wife Pam and Shae and I lived together. It worked out pretty good. Nobody else could get on with Kenny but me, and we were pretty much inseparable. The only arguments we had were at the racetrack, when the bike wasn't good, then we'd yell at each other more like brothers than business partners. He always used to say: Wayne, if you keep winning, how are we going to get them to build us a better bike?'

(The Europeanisation went both ways. Wayne had formed a close friendship with double 250 champion Sito Pons, an old-school Spaniard who gave up a promising career as an architect to race motorbikes. Sito came to stay with Wayne in California. 'He was a really sophisticated European, but I got him Americanised pretty quick. With Sito, you always went to the best restaurant, always booked in advance. I said to him: you wanna try Mexican? So I took him to my favourite Taco Bell, and we ate in the truck. He was amazed at the idea of eating lunch driving down Interstate Five.' Wayne was impressed by Sito's negotiating technique – he was there to buy a motorhome. 'He negotiated the price down and down, until eventually the guy said OK, this is the last price. He went to tell his boss, and Sito crossed out that price and wrote another, $2,000 cheaper.' Sito raced a 500 that year, before retiring after surviving a potentially fatal crash. 'I helped him a lot, on corner lines and gears, and where you have to open the throttle. He didn't want anybody to know about it. He was definitely afraid of the 500. He was really smart, but a bit too smart. He knew what he had to do to ride a 500, but he didn't want to do it that much.'

Then there was the Team-Mate Thing. It was rather special this year. The other guy riding the Roberts Yamahas was none other than his old Crucible companion and victor of 1989. Yes: Eddie Lawson.

The situation was complex. After four years of supporting both Roberts and Agostini's Marlboro-backed team, with the latter the official factory squad, both Yamaha and top sponsors Marlboro felt they'd been let down by the Italian. His bid to salvage the team's position by hiring Spencer in 1989 had backfired when the overweight and under-motivated former 500-class genius had left without completing the year. At the same time, Kenny wanted to expand his team, to add a 250 for up-and-coming boy wonder John Kocinski, and Lucky Strike declined to boost the budget as he required. Meanwhile, Eddie Lawson was about to perform another of his unexpected career moves. Disappointed by Honda's response to his winning the 1989 title for them, and with lots of other offers, he decided to go back to Yamaha, this time with Kenny. The friends/enemies were team-mates again, but with revised status compared with the days at Kawasaki in the USA.

Kenny explains the decision. 'At the time, I thought Wayne was better than Eddie. But both could win races, and I was looking at finishing first and second. That's what I was paid to do. I asked Wayne about it, and he was pleased.' Wayne confirms it. 'That was a perfect scenario for me. I liked having team-mates. I could work off them. When you had me as a team-mate, you had your hands full. Because I would try and beat you at everything. I just wanted to devastate Eddie. I don't think he was ready for a team-mate like me. Maybe he thought he could control me, but at that stage I was past being controlled.

'We didn't do so much pre-season testing with the Michelins as before. I remember he approached testing the same way he did the motocross practice way back – just lap after lap after lap. I'd do five or six laps then come in. That was what I was used to with Dunlop, having all those tyres to test. Wherever we were, I'd always keep an eye on Eddie's pit board. Without letting anybody know. I'd never go and look at his lap chart. But I always wanted to be faster than him.'

Michelins? Certainly. The most important change for the year concerned tyres. Team Roberts made the big switch, from their long-time near-exclusive Dunlops to the class favourite Michelins. Not something done lightly – but new sponsors Marlboro insisted.

'I had a real soft spot for the Dunlop guys. I came up with them, and it was always something like a family atmosphere. Sure, we all blame the tyres, but I'd blame myself a lot too, because I wanted to win for those guys as well as for myself. It was like the little guys up against the might of Michelin. It goes back to my earliest racing days. I would get a bigger rush out of being the underdog trying to win. It would make me even more motivated if I was at some disadvantage.'

Now he'd joined the enemy, using the same tyres as his rivals, and he didn't know what to expect. 'You'd always hear about Michelin that they'd give one or another pet rider a special tyre, without telling the others. I was pretty impressed when I first tested them. I had no more of the sidegrip problem, and I wasn't battling any more the way I had before. And we were devastating the lap records at the test tracks. We went to Jerez for the IRTA tests, with other teams present. I'd always be the fastest guy there, and break the record. With Dunlop we'd always have a mass of tyres to test. Now I'd tested all the Michelins in about two hours – or I thought I'd tested them all. I told Gerard, the Michelin guy, I wanted some more grip from the front tyre. He said OK, let me make a phone call. His boss said OK, give him *this* tyre. And I straight away went another half-a-second quicker. I was amazed. With Dunlop we'd spend days looking for half a second. With Michelin, it was just a phone call away.'

Then there was what Wayne wryly calls 'the Michelin flick.' This was the down-side to the extra side-grip in the corners, and was a major contributing factor to the uncomfortable prominence in those days of the highsider accident, where instead of falling off inside the bike, on the low side as it slid away – the traditional and time-honoured way of crashing – you were instead flicked high in the air to land heavily beyond the bike with the further risk that it might now hit you. The reason was simple enough. The Dunlops would slide earlier, at a lower cornering speed, but in a rider-friendly way, so that you could control the slide with the throttle, with steering input, and your body weight. At this point the Michelins were still hanging on tight, and the rider was enjoying a higher speed mid-corner as well as the chance to get on the throttle earlier and achieve a faster exit. But when they did let go, as inevitably happens now and then when you ride on the limit, it happened suddenly and viciously. And then, with the bike sideways, the tyres would suddenly grip again, flicking it into the air to somersault to destruction, launching the rider even higher as it did so. Highsiders were always painful, often injurious. It is a tribute to Wayne's level of skill with tyres that he made the transition with only one crash during 1990 (in practice in Germany), while experienced Michelin riders like Gardner and Sarron continued to fall off with more or less ruinous regularity.

Wayne led 1990 from the first race until the last. By the time they left Brno after the 12th of 15 rounds, he was unbeatable. It was an indomitable performance.

The season opened again in Japan, with a nasty surprise from the new Michelins. 'My first lap out on the race-track, coming out of the first turn, I almost highsided the thing. Michelin had forgotten to let the air out again after over-inflating the back tyre to pop the bead.' Then followed a curtain-raising battle in qualifying, duelling with Schwantz for pole in the closing minutes of practice. Wayne won it. He recalls how Schwantz had been fastest, at 2:10.4, with time for just one more lap. 'It was the most perfect lap ever anywhere in my racing career. Even then it stepped out a little on the last corner, which cost me a few tenths.' His time of 2:09.589 was Suzuka's first ever inside 2:10. He won the race too, after a start-to-finish run that defied TV commentator Barry Sheene's predictions that he wouldn't be able to keep up his habit of runaway starts now he was on Michelins. 'After that win, I felt so good. We were all on the same tyres now, and there were no more excuses.'

Laguna Seca came next, and again proved highly significant. First came the resolution of the Team-Mate Thing, for a long while at least. A mechanic's error allowed Eddie Lawson's brake pads to fall out on the front straight on the fastest part of the track, leading straight to a looping U-turn taken in third or even second gear. Eddie leapt for safety, and was lucky to escape with only a broken heel. He did not return for several months. (Afterwards, asked if he blamed the mechanic, he gave a typically Lawson response. 'I want him to always do my brakes in future. He won't make that mistake again.')

The second resolution came in the race, when Schwantz crashed after a typical bravura performance reliving their Superbike duels here. It was also the perfect illustration of how well Wayne's push-harder tactics could work. 'We were going really fast that day. He did a 1:25.8, which has never been bettered.' Then as Wayne upped his own pace, Kevin looped it on the corner right by the pits and grandstands. The highsider left him with a fractured wrist; while second-placed Doohan was fully 30 seconds adrift. Laguna was again marked by a tragic accident. This year's victim was, ironically enough, Kevin Magee. The Australian had stayed with Lucky Strike in their switch to Suzuki, and was now Schwantz's team-mate. Left behind with a slow-starting motor, scrabbling to make up time, he'd crashed heavily soon after the start, suffering life-threatening head injuries. He later made a complete recovery. Unlike his racing career.

At Jerez Wayne was second to Gardner, Schwantz third, riding with trademark bravery with his wrist strapped up. Then to Misano, Wayne's fateful favourite, where this time luck was on his side. He was leading, but in serious trouble. 'My brakes were clicking. We were back and forth between carbons and cast-iron brakes at the time, and these were iron. Then before anything else happened it started to rain and they stopped the race. Turned out in the pits one of my two front discs was cracked.' Wayne was able to replace the part, and though he was only fourth in a near dead-heat of the second leg, a half-second advantage from the first leg was enough to give him the win on aggregate. The consequences of the inevitable catastrophic brake failure had the race not been stopped hardly bear thinking about; this very lucky escape was of greater significance than the win. It was almost as if he was being saved for something else. What was it about Misano, and Wayne?

From springtime Italy to the cold and misty Eifel hills of the Nurburgring, and that one crash of the year. That Michelin flick in practice. 'As soon as I went to turn the bike into the left–right, it highsided me. That was the penalty of the sidegrip. The Dunlops always gave you a bit of warning. I was very, very lucky to walk away. I mangled my left little finger pretty good, and broke some bones in my hand. I thought then: I could have really screwed this thing up.' Wayne raced with his hand so numbed up with Novocain he had to keep checking to see it was still on the handlebar. But the field was very depleted. As well as Lawson, Gardner was now out after a heavy practice fall broke his foot. Doohan and Chili performed a remarkable piece of formation crashing in the race, what Wayne calls 'the ballerina backflip.' Thus a distant second to Schwantz was relatively easily achieved. 'I just rode around.'

Austria next, and a whisker-close second to Schwantz, still leading well on points: 111 to 87; then another strong win over Kevin at Yugoslavia to stretch the gap still further. Then Assen, where a fine fairing-banging fight with Schwantz saw the Suzuki rider win by just over a tenth of a second. He was the fastest guy out there, but Wayne led by more than 24 points. With 20 points for a win, it meant he could afford a non-finish and still be in front. A fact that they celebrated – along with the return of Eddie Lawson and Wayne Gardner – late into the night in Wayne's motorhome. So late that Doohan's mother was inspired to shout from her part of the mobile paddock village, 'Knock it off, will ya,' which only inspired Schwantz to hurl more firecrackers. Wayne's 250 team-mate John Kocinski, himself well on the way to securing his debut-season title, was liberally sprayed with fire-extinguisher dust by rival Carlos Cardus. 'I remember telling him not to let it off, then whoosh. It sucked all the oxygen out of the place, and we all came out coughing. John was just covered. He must have been cleaning for a week. It didn't take more than a couple of beers to get us Americans going. It was a pretty stressful time for everyone, living in the motorhomes.'

Belgium, and Wayne's first rain-race win, by miles, on the treacherous and frightening Spa public-roads track. This was bike GP racing's last visit to a magnificent and historic venue that, like the Isle of Man before it, was rendered unacceptably dangerous by the increasing speeds. 'I really liked Spa. It was scary if you made a mistake, and to go fast you had to click it real right. There were those fast lefts' (the notorious widow-making Blanchimont section) 'where if you were too fast you went off the track, but if you slowed up your lap time really suffered.' In the wet it was twice as daunting. 'Coming onto the part where you rejoin the street at the back, that thing would be totally sideways in fifth gear.' Lucky Sandy wasn't there to see that!

France, and third behind Schwantz and Gardner after a hard race. 'I was really trying to protect my points lead by then.' Donington Park in Britain, and another close second to Kevin. Then Sweden, where last time it had all gone wrong.

'The Yamaha was pretty good that year, not fast, but it accelerated hard and handled well. We had it the best it was all year long there – really predictable and easy to ride. Schwantz qualified well, but fell off, and I barely beat Eddie by just over a second, but the bike felt good.'

This time, Wayne left Anderstorp with one hand on the title. With three rounds remaining and a maximum of 60 points for three wins, he led Schwantz by 47 points. All he had to do at Brno was to finish within sight of Schwantz. 'There were all sorts of ways I could win it. There was even a way I could lose it. I thought back to the way Jay Springsteen had won at Ascot, back in the Seventies. He didn't need to win the race, but I really admired that he'd gone out and won the title by coming first.

'I qualified third, then in the race I put my head down. I caught and passed Gardner, and won. I knew I was champion when I saw Schwantz crashed out on the third lap, but I put that out of my mind and concentrated on winning. I didn't think about the championship until the last quarter of a lap.'

'Then, when I crossed the finish line, and I was World Champion, I had this burst of emotion. I felt really great, for about two tenths of a second. Then it was gone, and it was like – wow, what happened to everything? Here I am, with the thing I've devoted everything in me to win, and there wasn't anything there. It left me feeling really disappointed. It meant so much more to me emotionally losing the title in Sweden when I crashed than it did winning it. It felt very strange.'

It was now that Eddie melted down. Nothing to do with handing his Number One plate to Wayne, he insists. His problem was with the team, and the motorcycle. He remains convinced to this day that Wayne was getting better engine and chassis set-up than he was, and better service and support from his crew chief Mike Sinclair than Eddie was from Warren Willing.

Kenny Roberts insists the opposite: that although a rider likes to think his personal crew chief is giving him special attention – 'that's his edge, and I'm happy to let them think that if they like' – in fact the two crew chiefs worked closely together, co-operating to the hilt to give both riders the best possible bike for that race. 'Eddie was struggling towards the end, with bike performance. He thought he wasn't getting the best possible bike set-up. You know, when you're not winning, you need to find a reason why. Eddie wouldn't believe the technicians weren't favouring Wayne, because Wayne was beating him; while Wayne wouldn't believe he was winning because he was on a better bike – it was his riding doing it. So there was no sense in going into it.' He pauses, then adds: 'Life in the team, at its best, is difficult. And it's gonna be difficult whatever you do. That's the business.'

Wayne recalls a third angle: that during the Brno weekend, with his covert permission, they actually swopped one of his motors into Eddie's bike. 'I don't think he knows I knew that.'

Anyway, it ends up that coincidentally with losing his title, Eddie has a serious row after the race with crew chief Willing, and leaves the track directly without bothering to attend the post-race ceremonies (he'd finished third). He insists he did congratulate Wayne before jumping in his rented car and hightailing it out of

175

there; but many observers felt it would have been a more sporting act if he'd done so in public, up there on the rostrum. Eddie completed the year with the team, then left, and now has no kind words to say about them or their motorbike. 'Wayne won the title for the next two years on a motorcycle that shouldn't have been able to do it. It was a piece of crap. Wayne carried that whole team – absolutely. If you listen to them, they made it all happen. But I guarantee you it was Wayne who carried them. They were such a bunch of egomaniacs. And without Wayne, they would be nowhere.'

There were two more races – the year's first non-finish at Hungary after an experiment with a new type of brake master-cylinder went wrong, where future star Doohan won his first GP; then an absolute corker in Australia, won by an inspired Gardner, his fairing flapping loose after a near-crash. Doohan was second, Rainey third, and poor old Kevin underlined the keynote of his season by crashing just after pushing past Wayne in the closing stages. 'That's how I lost the tow of the Hondas. He drafted by me down the front straight, then got into Turn One' (a very fast right-hand kink) 'a bit hot. He always used the back brake a lot. I only used it in left-hand turns, never in right-handers. So at the end of the front straight he downshifted, and used a little too much back brake, and that thing went away on him, and highsided him. I just went: Wow. We were going well over 150mph there.'

The year ended in celebrations. One was in Switzerland, with sponsors Marlboro, who had also won the Formula One car title with Ayrton Senna. 'Kocinski had also won the 250, and Loris Capirossi the 125, another Marlboro guy. They had my bike there, and Senna's McLaren. Ayrton said to me, it scares me to watch you racing those bikes out there. I said, but Ayrton, you know the feeling. He said, I know, but it still scares me.

'I was quite surprised. All he wanted to talk about was the bikes – about some of the tracks he knew, and why the bikes tried to highside you, and how to slide them. He didn't want to talk about the cars at all.'

There was another celebration in America, where they hired the Embassy Suites hotel and golf course for an epic bash with just about everyone Wayne knew. The World Championship made very little impact in the US at large, it being something that happened over there and far away. There were still plenty in the LA Crucible who knew what it meant, and that the kid who'd once dazzled them all, that wisp of a thing, riding round Corona on Shell Thuet's 750 Yamaha dirt-tracker, had just kept on getting better ever since.

Wayne knew too, and he knew he wasn't done yet. And if there was a nagging doubt because of that strange feeling of disappointment after crossing the line at Brno, he knew how to deal with that too. Like a junkie after coming down from a prolonged and consuming hard-drug binge. He had to get another fix.

CHAPTER 12

HEIR APPARENT
TO THE EVIL EMPIRE

'Being faster than John was more important to me than any other team-mate so far. He wanted to do the same thing to me. I knew by the end of this year one of our careers would be ruined. Either him or me.'
Wayne Rainey, on new team-mate John Kocinski

Most of Wayne Rainey's second World Championship happened the same way as the first. Against strong opposition, he was the dominant rider, and the sight of the dayglo-chevroned Marlboro Yamaha bursting straight into the lead from the green light became one of the constants of 1991 GP racing.

Wayne stayed of course with Marlboro Team Roberts-Yamaha. The success of the combination (no matter what Eddie says, and despite how the team foundered after Wayne had gone, it was the combination that made the phenomenon) was such that the whole huge team gained the nickname 'The Evil Empire' after a remark by then-President Reagan about the Soviet Union.

It was an apt title. A them and us thing. As the races and successes clicked on past, Team Roberts achieved increasing stature and self-assurance, and with that a growing isolation. Rainey too was becoming solitary. Racing didn't get easier, however it might look. Quite the reverse. His training and then the injuries took a lot out of him physically. The fearsome focus he could now muster while on the bike drained him mentally. So too did the drive for motivation. He was still seeking that high of satisfaction that he'd thought the 1990 championship would bring, even while his continuing success made it ever more elusive. The smile that he'd once worn habitually now came only sometimes; his more usual expression at the trackside was a frowning concentration. He hadn't changed: he was still courteous and interested, when he had time to be. But he was mostly pretty busy.

Then there was the first venture into running his own team. Encouraged by Kenny to provide an impetus for US racing, and hoping to find some new heroes to follow on behind, Wayne put together a 250 team for the domestic championship. There were two riders, one the teenage Kenny Roberts Junior, the other a would-be GP rider Alan Scott. Sandy was employed to run it: 'The construction industry was pretty slow round about then, so I was pretty pleased when Wayne called me up. It was the first time ever I'd been paid for going racing. Until then, it had always cost me.' Wayne's involvement was necessarily limited. Scott would lead the outlaw WERA championship until Junior crucially knocked him off late in the season.

Meanwhile, in the 1991 GP World Championship things were a little different. A management rebellion led by the teams' association IRTA was brewing, with F1 mogul Bernie Ecclestone involved and the FIM backed up against the wall. Lawyers were working behind closed doors, while paddock rumours dealt more with politics than lap times. The year was to end with open warfare for commercial control. It was business as usual for Rainey and his rivals, however, with the same two themes to consider, team-mates and tyres, each in a new form.

Eddie Lawson had departed in high dudgeon to a pair of lucrative swan-song years with Cagiva, the Italian manufacturer whose machines were consistently the most stylish in appearance, but whose performance and technology was always a step or so behind the Japanese leaders. Eddie did a fine job at Cagiva, not only bringing respectability and his awesome dedication, but also giving them their first GP win in 13 years of trying. But the move put him out on the margins of the World Championships.

In came the next team-mate up to be tested: first-time 250 champion John Kocinski. And here was a real unknown quantity. Only two things were clear. Little John was an odd-ball, a man apart even from the already diverse grouping of professional motorbike racers. He was a loner, with an obsession with cleanliness and a mighty talent for racing. And Little John, far from being over-awed by the prospect of joining the big boys on the 500s, was very, very bullish.

'He wasn't cocky with me,' says Rainey, 'but he was with

everyone around me. He was real secretive, didn't want anybody knowing what he did. And he liked to be different, with suspension and everything. I ran a rear fender on the bike, and so he didn't want to run a rear fender. Didn't make any difference to the bike, but helped him to think he was somebody special. He'd never really had a team-mate like me, so he didn't know what he was in for. He just thought he was going to come in and kick my butt, and kick everybody else's butt. And I was ready for him. Being faster than John was more important to me than any team-mate so far. He wanted to do the same thing to me. I knew by the end of this year that one of our careers would be ruined. Either him or me.

'Our first test together was in Eastern Creek. We were nice with each other – well, not nice, but we would talk. But we were both World Champions, and we severely didn't want the other to be faster. Those tests were pretty intense. I ended up like two-tenths quicker than him, or even less than that.' Wayne noticed that John was doing a bit of window-dressing – altering cornering lines to concentrate on a high top speed through the traps ('whereas trap times didn't concern me whatsoever'), and running extra warmup or slow laps to bump up his overall total to be more than Wayne's. Then came their first press conference together, at the tests.

'Somebody asked John if he thought he was going to win races. And he said: I'm gonna be winning races while I'm learning. And I was looking over, and thinking, wow, you're sure talking a lot. I just didn't know if he could back it up. I just sat and listened.' Wayne was quicker again at the next tests at Laguna Seca. This too was important, this was a favourite track for each of them. In the closing stages, running into Turn Three, Wayne could look right across at the far side of the track to where John was running round what is now Rainey Corner. And every lap Wayne would have grabbed a few more inches on him. 'That was great. That was everything.'

During their joint training earlier at Modesto, Wayne had been far from sure. 'Maybe he could really beat me. No matter how good you are, you need that doubt to keep you sharp. I was pushing really hard to beat him on Kenny's minibikes, and motocross. Every lap – though he never really raced me on the motocrossers because he didn't like to get dirty. He was a really strange guy, you know. Every day after training he'd go home and clean his bike spotless. Next day that thing'd look brand new. His dirt bikes and his truck. He wouldn't drive his truck with his shoes on. To get out, he'd lay this mat down, then stand on that in his socks. It was a show just to watch him get ready. His bike was always immaculate. I remember one time he'd fallen off and Kenny and I went through and did a couple of brweeerarrps to spray him really bad with dirt. He loaded up and went home, and didn't come back for four days.'

And there was a new chapter in the tyre saga. Michelin had, late the previous season, announced that they were to pull out of motorsport completely. The announcement was premature, and in fact they did stay in bike GP racing for 1991, by special arrangement only with the Honda factory team of Gardner and Doohan. Rainey and his team moved back to Dunlops, as did everybody else including Kevin Schwantz and his Suzuki. 'That was fine with me. With Michelin not really being in there, I thought we could win the championship on Dunlop again. Especially with Schwantz riding Dunlop. Having him testing them too would make the job easier than when it was just our team in 1988/89.'

Another minor but possibly significant change was in the World Championship scoring. The FIM reverted to a long-forgotten system where each rider's worst two scores were dropped from the final tally. This rule favoured the inconsistent Schwantz or Gardner more than someone like Wayne.

There were 15 rounds in 1991, starting as usual in Japan. Suzuka is a fine, flowing circuit, where a 500cc motorcycle can run free and there is a chance for riding skill to make up for machine differences. In this golden era of GP racing, that meant a close four-way race of a sort almost forgotten now in the years since Rainey and his cohorts have gone. Kocinski's debut as a 500 rider saw him right up there with the class leaders, and he finished a close fourth behind Rainey, with Schwantz then Doohan up ahead. The first four were covered by just over half-a-second, but Wayne was not too perturbed. 'Practice was wet, and we had it geared all wrong for the dry. I was using one gear higher than usual through a lot of corners. People commented on how John was able to use tight lines, but I had to use those big, swooping lines because I was in a higher gear.'

The next race, at the tight new Eastern Creek circuit in Australia, was more revealing, showing among other things that Schwantz would be consistent in his habit of inconsistency. His Suzuki had a certain over-sensitivity. 'It was either on or it was off: he couldn't make it so it was good all the time like the Yamaha was, and the Honda.' This left Mick Doohan as Wayne's target. 'Gardner could do a fast lap, but Mick was consistent. My plan was to get a lead from the start, as usual. By the time Doohan got to second place, I was about nine seconds ahead.' The first win of the year, and Schwantz already lagging. Kocinski had been beaten twice, Rainey led on points. But Doohan was just one behind. Clearly the intense Queensland rider was a matured talent in his third year.

There was some John business to get out of the way at Laguna. Who would win the American arch-rivals' home GP? 'I remembered reading in the paper on the way to the track John saying: I guess we're gonna find out who is King of Laguna Seca. I thought: I guess you're right. I outqualified him by about a tenth for pole. That really screwed him up. But I still didn't know I could win. I always wanted to be fastest qualifier in 1991. Being on pole would give me a couple of hours of calm and happiness. Then you'd start thinking about the race. After that year, I was happy with anywhere on the front row.' Wayne took six poles in 1991, and only one more from 1992 onwards.

'The race, it was the same old thing. Get a good start, and race the second lap like it was the last, just as fast as I could go. When John got to second, I'd taken three seconds in four laps. I just had to maintain that lead. I didn't look behind. I rarely did. I knew what was going on from my pit board. I had John screwed, because he knew how hard it would be to chip away at me the whole race long. He knew how fit I was from training with me. I think he got frustrated after a couple of laps, lost concentration, and crashed. That night, he ended up in jail. John was never really a problem after that. I think he felt so deflated.' (The distressed Kocinski had driven wildly away from the circuit, then refused to stop when challenged by a police officer. He was arrested later as a result; his eventual penance was a short stint of community service.)

Once again, the early rounds had narrowed the focus. Rainey led Doohan by four points, then Mick moved ahead by one point with a win at Jerez. Kocinski was second, Rainey third. The blight of the Dunlops was responsible. Rainey had fallen in practice, on the first lap, caught out for once by his fast-from-the-start tyre testing techniques. 'That's when I knew the tyre was too hard,' he comments wrily. Then in the race, right after he set a new record on the second lap, going away again, the front tyre showed a construction fault – a blister formed in the tread, the size of a silver dollar. It was on the right-hand side, so on right-handers the bike would understeer horribly. From then on, he was nursing it: 'slow into the turns, then early on the gas to take the weight off the front wheel.'

By the finish, a flap of tread was peeling right off the tyre. Wayne remains amused by Kocinski's reaction to beating him. 'It was like he'd won the race.' (This was, in a way, John's other 'local' GP, since he'd adopted Spain as a second home; the feeling was mutual, the Spanish fans rather liking John's unexpected character traits.) 'Doohan and I were waiting and waiting for him on the rostrum. Now John thought he was a Spanish guy, and he's stopping in the track and waving. He picked up what he thought was a Catalonian flag to carry round. Turned out it was the oil warning flag' (same colours, stripes running the other way). 'I thought then: this guy's really screwed up. In the pit afterwards, I made a point of calling him over to see how bad my tyre was, with the flap hanging off it. His happiness turned right there.'

Misano was weird, once again. Rainey took his fourth pole in a row, and got fastest lap again, while overtaking winner Doohan. He was unlapping himself at the time, after another Dunlop constructional failure, and a stop to change the rear tyre. Unlike car racing, this simply does not happen in the short 45-minute bike GPs and the bikes are not configured with quick changes in mind, so not surprisingly he lost a lot of time in the pits – 80 seconds, compared with 10 for a specially-prepared endurance-racing bike, or less than seven for all four wheels of a GP car. He finished ninth; Schwantz, who also had a rear tyre break up, soldiered home seventh, ignoring the vibration. Rainey did not approve of the risks of such a strategy. 'My life's more important to me than seventh on a tyre that could break up at any moment.' Doohan now had 14 points in hand.

By now, there were serious concerns about the Dunlops, especially since the next race was at superfast Hockenheim. The carcase failures continued as practice began. Then came an overnight delivery from Fort Dunlop of an emergency batch of rear tyres. But by the end of the weekend, it was Michelin who had tread patterns all over their faces, after Doohan's rear tyre shed a chunk of tread – ripping off his rear fender and sending Wayne, just behind, swerving to avoid the possible impending top-speed disaster – just as he was moving away to win in the closing stages.

The race was even more memorable for the finish. It was a TV spectacular that has been played over and over again. Rainey leads the last lap, and into the corner that begins the tight bends of the stadium section. But as he sits up to brake, the Suzuki bursts into view alongside, tying itself into knots as the rear tries to come past the front in what looks like a masterful outbraking move. Riding the thinnest of lines, Schwantz may have been sideways, but he was in front, and held Wayne off to cross the line just 16 thousandths of a second in front.

Schwantz insists his move was not the master-stroke that it looked – just accident avoidance. 'Everyone remembers that race, but to me it's not that important. It wasn't like I outrode him. I still think he made a mistake. He braked much earlier than I expected – my first move is evasive. If I'd have been expecting it, I'd have been more focused. I had to swerve to avoid running up the back of him.'

Rainey reads it differently. 'I braked deep, but Schwantz was concentrating so much on me he'd forgotten where he was. I think what surprised him was that we were already in the corner. We were both in there deep, at probably about 180mph. That corner has only one line on the way in, so I had to save him some room. If I would have leaned on him we both would have been off the track. That was Schwantz's way of racing. He didn't always think about it a lot. If the positions had been reversed I think he'd have leaned on me, and we'd have both gone down. It was a good race. And I thought I was pretty lucky that we beat Doohan there when he had a problem. That's who I was racing for the championship.'

An epic at the Salzburgring the next weekend saw Doohan win again, his lead growing again to 15 points. The Honda was built for these fast tracks: Wayne puts the top speed advantage at about 10mph. Running free, the Honda produced so much horsepower that even at the top of the Salzburgring's punishing climb, in sixth gear, Mick had to sit the bike up a bit to stop it wheelspinning through the kink. Even so Rainey's Yamaha was less than two-tenths behind after shadowing him all the way.

Rainey beat Doohan by a comforting margin in the blazing heat at Jarama. It was in gruelling conditions that he relished because he'd trained for them. Then came another of those landmarks at Assen – a negative landmark. Wayne (who never really liked being called Mr Perfect) made what he described later as 'a rookie's mistake', in full view of the grandstand and within sight of the chequered flag, spoiling what had until then been a faultless race. Schwantz, who had an 0.44 second advantage in a race split into two legs by bad weather, had already accepted second. Wayne, however, was riding too ferociously to accept first. He hadn't done that since Sweden in 1989.

'People all remember me going off the track, but they don't know why. I'd had to start the race on a new tyre, changed on the grid after trouble on the warm-up lap. At the end, I was leading, and Schwantz started chipping away at that. We were running a second faster than we'd qualified, and at the start of the last lap I had point zero. I put together such a lap, because I not only had to beat Schwantz to the line, but also by half-a-second. (Kenny Roberts) Junior timed it recently from the video, three corners from the end on the previous lap to the same place on this lap, and it was 2:01.9, half-a-second faster than the lap that gave Schwantz the record. Then I just went a little bit too much into the last chicane. The front pushed' (slid away) 'on the brakes and I went off the track.' He recovered, fighting for control across the grass, and while he did so Schwantz flashed past. For once, the tables had been turned, and Kevin was jumping for joy. 'On the slow-down lap, I patted him on the helmet, and he kinda shoves me away. Afterwards, I said: I think I induced that mistake from when I passed him in Germany. I just said it as a joke – he gave me a look.' But it was not a total loss. Doohan had crashed out, and Wayne's impressive accident avoidance meant he took the points lead again. He was not to lose it even though he didn't finish the year.

The next race was in France, at the revised and shortened Paul Ricard circuit on the Côte d'Azur. Special tests were laid on first for familiarisation with the new layout, and Wayne was disgusted, as he was freewheeling back to the pits at the close of them, to feel Kocinski give him a helping push as he came alongside. 'I knew right away he'd been faster than me. I was real mad. And John was telling all the journalists about how the bike was finally right for him, and he was going to win the race. The car just wouldn't go fast enough on the drive home to Barcelona that night.' The balance was redressed in practice, however, with Wayne on pole and John third. Then Kocinski muffed the start, and crashed out on the first lap, to be stretchered away mortified. Wayne was racing Doohan instead, gaining a clear win by the finish, using the experimental Ohlins electronic rear suspension for the first time.

Mr Buzzy came out to play that night, betting Kenny Roberts $50 he wouldn't be able to climb the ramparts opposite the restaurant. He lost. The day before, a friendly pilot had taken Wayne for a flip in his stunt plane. 'We did one inverted loop, and afterwards I said to him: I seen black up there. He said: So did I.'

Wayne beat Doohan again in England, although narrowly behind Schwantz after an overtaking move round the outside at the penultimate hairpin that Kevin remembers with real pride. Wayne had half-an-eye on Doohan and the title, but was still pretty flabbergasted by the audacity of it.

The next win came at Mugello, at the circuit rebuilt (by Ferrari) in the Tuscan Apennine foothills. It was an idyllic spot, and a sweeping racetrack in the grand old manner. 'The Honda was faster, but the Yamaha could go from corner to corner better.' Doohan was third again, Rainey leading Schwantz by almost three seconds. And thence to Brno, and Doohan second. This surge put Wayne in a commanding position, with two races to go.

Partly this was because they'd left the fast tracks behind. It was only in fifth and sixth gears that the Honda would start to run away. But partly it was the accord that rider and team had struck with the Yamaha, able to get it settled to a wide variety of tracks relatively easily. And it was because of Wayne, and his determination. Wayne had found a technique that worked with

Doohan. 'I'd just sit on his back wheel in the middle part of the race, and I'd make sure he could feel me, so he'd work his front tyre harder, braking later and going deeper into the bends. As the tyre got used up, his bike'd start to push and run out wide. Then I'd pass him and up the pace, and he couldn't stay with me.'

The climax to the title coincided, appropriately enough, with another set piece with Kocinski. After Brno Wayne had tested a different chassis made by Yamaha engineer Nakajima-San. 'We called it Naka's dream.' This was 'cut-and-shut', the steering head angle radically steepened to give it lightning-quick steering at the expense of straight-line stability. Wayne teased the anxious designer by making it wobble viciously as he went past the pits. Naka immediately called him in. 'He was so worried. He was really dark, but he was white when I came in. I told him I'd done it on purpose, but he didn't believe me.' The chassis was fast, a full second quicker at Brno, with its quirky off-camber corners, where you are obliged to ride the front wheel more. But at Le Mans, the next track, the corners were different, and Wayne would be able to use his power-on rear-wheel technique, so he stuck with the chassis he already knew. Kocinski hadn't been at the test, but in France he found the new chassis worked well with his different riding style. Quickest in every practice session, he was soon talking again about victory with the right bike at last. 'It didn't bother me, because all I had to do was finish behind Doohan. I was only thinking of the championship. Kenny asked me before the race if I wanted John to help me. I said no, he hasn't helped me all year, and I don't want him to help me now. And I told him: the best thing you can do for me is win the race. That'll make it easier for me to out-point Doohan.'

Schwantz won, Doohan was second, Rainey passed Kocinski for third. Point proven, championship won. And this time, if it was an anticlimax – well, he was used to that.

Kocinski did win the last race. His maiden 500 victory came on the first-ever GP visit to Malaysia, at the Shah Alam circuit outside Kuala Lumpur. Kocinski's lap record still stood five years later, but the fact remains that his first 500cc GP win was in the absence of Schwantz and Rainey. Both had crashed at special pre-race familiarisation tests. Kevin needed five pins in his shattered hand.

Wayne had only broken one bone – but it was the biggest in the body. The smashed right femur was his worst injury yet, in terms of sheer damage, and the ordeal began as he hit the ground, after running off-line in sixth gear onto a slippery piece of track to avoid Niall Mackenzie, travelling slower on the racing line.

'There was a kind of a raised kerb by the track, and I hit my knee on it. I remember trying to get up, but I couldn't. That was the first time I hadn't been able to stand up. At San Jose as a Rookie Expert, I'd knocked myself out, so I didn't know nothing. This time I was dingy, but conscious. The next thing I remember is laying in the track hospital. I was in my leathers, I could hear 500s going round, but I couldn't figure out where I was. It was really a strange feeling. I didn't like it at all. Then a corner popped into my brain, and I followed it round, and I realised I was in Malaysia. I'd broken my femur at the knee joint. It was a pretty bad break.'

Wayne was in hospital for 24 hours, then elected to go home for the surgical rebuild. He barely remembers the visit from Rajah Muda, the local prince and patron of Shah Alam, a bike racing enthusiast and Harley-Davidson rider. His royal interest in the case was to prove crucial the next day, when China Airlines refused to let the injured rider, his leg in a straight cast and his condition poor, aboard their aircraft. 'Unbeknown to me, Rajah Muda had come down to see me off. And now the plane was getting ready to leave without me. So he disappears, and next thing I know, the Rajah comes back out, and three guys take me to the aeroplane. I asked Trevor Tilbury from my team, who was looking after me: what's going on? So he says Muda went in there, and said if Wayne's not on board, this aircraft doesn't leave Malaysia.'

After 20 hours of flying, he arrived in San Francisco dehydrated and exhausted, his blood count very low. Then followed three hours of somewhat radical surgery, necessary to avoid the risk of serious damage to the knee. Surgeon Arthur Ting (nowadays a well-known osteopath to the racing world) had to saw off part of the tibia below the kneecap to detach the tendons, then flip the kneecap back so he could then put three screws into the badly damaged base of the femur, then re-attach the tibial tuberosity with two more screws.

Rehabilitation was an ordeal, especially the way Wayne forced the pace. 'After two weeks I had to start moving it. This was kinda good for me, because it was another motivation. To come back and win from this accident, to show everyone I could do it again, and to show myself.

'The problem was when they took the knee out of the straight-leg cast, everything's fused straight. You have to get it bending gradually. I had Dean Miller staying in my house, in Downey. He had a machine to bend it. You could adjust how far it would bend, and I'd just lie there. Bit by bit every day we tried to bend it more. The knee was full of adhesions – bending it made it snap, crackle and pop, like dried-out spaghetti.' Progress was slow, then they got the advice: drug him up, then while he's really relaxed, bend it all the way, bust through the adhesions. 'So Dean gets me home. I'm lying on my stomach, and he's icing and rubbing my knee. I was really relaxed. Then all of a sudden he takes the knee and tries to bend it. I just went through the roof. When I came down, I said: Are you on drugs? What is wrong with you? Dean couldn't believe how I was freaking out.' Arthur Ting eventually did the job, with Wayne under anaesthetic. 'He had to use all his weight, he told me, and it sounded like a machine-gun going off.'

The result was so much pain and inflammation that the problem recurred and the treatment had to be repeated. By December the knee at least had a few degrees of movement. Wayne was desperate to get back on a bike, but when he tried – joining Marlboro-backed 125/250 riders Ralf Waldmann and Doriano Romboni on minibike practice at Kenny's ranch – his leg wouldn't bend enough. Determination? Get this. Dean Miller: 'We went to the pain centre of the Sequoia Hospital, where they inserted an intravenous tube right into his spine. It was left in place, looped around the body. This meant I could give him epidural anaesthetics right there when he was done riding, to numb him so we could work on getting the range of motion back.' Rainey gritted his teeth and carried on. 'I needed to kill the pain. At night when I was done riding Dean could screw on this big old shot to numb me from my waist down. I couldn't even walk then. Again, it just wasn't enough. I ended up getting another general anaesthetic to bend it up again.'

Wayne still wonders what the European riders thought of this American guy, who'd already won two World Championships, and was now so badly injured that he couldn't walk. And here he was, out sliding the tail of his oval-track minibike, just impossible to beat.

CHAPTER 13

RACING
AGAINST A GHOST

'I got a bad start because I wasn't there physically or mentally.
I had injections in my back, my hand and my knee. Just to numb it.
I was saying to myself: Wayne you should really start thinking
about your life now, instead of trying to be the one who carries
the whole thing. I really felt I was gonna hurt myself bad,
because the bike wasn't good and I wasn't good.'
Wayne Rainey, on the struggle to win his third and last title

Those who thought Wayne's 1990 and 1991 world titles were achieved in typically determined and thoroughly professional style were right, but only halfway there. The changing circumstances of the third put the new double champion under different pressures and made a number of new demands. Hitherto, it had been enough to aim at self-betterment. Now he had a huge injury to overcome, and he did so by trying to ignore it. This led directly to the loss of consistency and further physical and mental damage. As seems to happen in racing, once you start getting hurt, you go on getting hurt.

Then there was a technical weakness. For all sorts of reasons, Wayne's Yamaha was outclassed this year far more thoroughly than when his only problem had been the quirky Dunlops. Looking back, 1992 was the year when things began to become unhinged – his obsessive need to win hardened into self-destruction. Yet it was also his greatest triumph over adversity, and the finest of his three successive crowns.

The common ingredient with previous years was his determination. The circumstances of 1992 culminated in a triumphant fight-back. Battered and apparently beaten mid-season, he showed a steel focus, creating opportunities by sheer willpower. You make your own luck in racing: at least that's what riders tend to say when it's running their way. He realises now that the other side of the coin is just as valid.

Wayne's return from his leg injury was nothing more than normal practice for dedicated road-racers. The impressive part was that he could muster the dedication, aged 32, having already achieved such greatness. But his motivation was still acute. The goal of equalling Kenny's three titles in a row, the need to stop Schwantz from taking over, and the same racing drive that had sustained him from childhood helped overcome the pain as well as the creeping complacency of financial success and the growing home comforts of his adult life.

Away from the track, life was definitely good. Marriage was good. Shae was good. And then, after season's end, his son was good too, born in October 1992. They called him Rex, meaning King, and his birth affected Wayne deeply, following all the trauma of his nightmare triumph. Wayne was present as a difficult labour got worse over 32 gruelling hours, and as they screened Shae's body from his view to perform C-section (Caesarian) surgery.

During this ordeal the unborn child had swallowed his meconium (pre-birth waste matter), which can lead to pneumonia, among other things. When Rex did emerge, he was pale and apparently lifeless. Wayne watched, helplessly holding Shae's hand. 'They never said anything about C-sections in pre-natal classes. When I saw them beating on Rex's chest with a tube down his throat I thought they were trying to start his heart beating, rather than removing the meconium. Shae asked me how he was. He didn't look alive, but I said: he looks great. They were working at emergency speed on her, and at that time I thought I was going to lose them both. Then Rex came to life and started peeing all over them. From then on everything was OK – though the doctors told me that 10 years before they might both have died.'

Wayne and Shae had also settled down – in the sense of moving out of suburban LA where they had both grown up. Rainey was now, quite literally, rich beyond his dreams. The scale of his earnings was huge. Back in 1989 he had turned down $2 million to switch from Team Roberts to Team Agostini, when the Italian former multi-champion was desperate for a big-name rider to save his team. It wasn't enough to tempt him. During 1992 Rainey had a major flirtation with Cagiva. He visited the Italian factory in secret during June with Claudio Castiglioni, one of two brothers who owned the firm. He was impressed by their passionate commitment to racing – 'Claudio had tears in his eyes when he was trying to persuade me to sign' – but resisted their blandishments. This was mainly because the pull of the World Championship was too strong, and their motorcycles were not as reliably competitive as the Japanese machines.

Cagiva came back at the British GP a couple of weeks later with an offer said to be around $10 million for two years. It ended up with a bitter argument in my motorhome in the paddock, with sponsorship overseer Leo de Graffenried flatly saying: 'If Wayne goes to Cagiva, Marlboro will pull out of racing.' Gary Howard, representing Wayne, was livid. 'He went ballistic, saying: you can't put that sort of pressure on Wayne. You can't blackmail him like that.

'I had my leathers on and I went out to practice, leaving them all shouting. In the end I stayed, after a big effort by Kenny, Yamaha and Marlboro. Looking back, it may have been good if I'd gone. Cagiva's love of racing was higher than where I was at, but I stayed because I wanted to continue to race for the World Championship.'

In any case, the money was still pouring in at the rate of several million dollars each year. 'It wasn't the motivating factor, but I did want to be the highest paid rider, and I believe that I was.'

Wayne could have joined the movie set, in Beverly Hills or the fashionable canyons; bought himself a chunk of the High Desert perhaps, where once he'd chased rabbits on home-made dirt bikes; or got himself a ranch somewhere in the Central Valley, like Kenny. Instead he chose a hilltop property on an exclusive estate outside Monterey. It has that section of the Laguna Seca racetrack bearing his name almost visible in the Salinas valley below, the ocean away on the other side, and the soft heights of the grassy coastal range rising out of the sea-mist that floods the valleys in the mornings. This is a beautiful spot. Gnarled oaks and tall pines are festooned with Spanish Moss, quail scurry by the roadside, and deer gaze mournfully into your headlights at night. Sometimes you can see a bobcat make his evening rounds. A short drive takes you to the compact city, with its jazz festivals and historic Cannery Row. The millionaires' Pebble Beach golf course lies adjacent, and then there's Carmel, where the mayor was local restaurant owner Clint Eastwood. But more compelling than all of these – Bubba lived at Carmel Valley. That's how Wayne knew just how cool it was out there. He commissioned a fine timber multi-level house, with a large sun-deck, a pool, and an annexe gymnasium. It was ready by the end of 1992, but he only had a few weeks there before returning to Europe. And then they had to call in the architects and builders again – to instal wheelchair ramps between the split levels and an elevator from the garage. Wayne can, however, still use the swimming pool and gymnasium.

The knee injury cast a long shadow in 1992. It messed up Wayne's training, because he was unable to run. He punished himself in the gymnasium instead. It was another 12 months before Wayne was able to get back to road work – mainly because of the way the screws projected from the bone, and snagged the ligaments as he bent his knee, whether running or riding the bike. This pain remained until they were removed at the end of the season.

Residual weakness led directly to another injury. Testing at Barcelona, Kenny observed that 'Wayne just didn't have the strength in his leg to apply pressure to the footpegs to control the bike the way he needed to.' As a direct result he was unable to prevent the Yamaha – Michelin-shod again, and prone therefore to the Michelin flick – from hurling him over the highside. The crash ground away most of the little finger on his left hand. 'I made the mistake of forgetting about my condition. When the doctors said they had to amputate, that just devastated me.' (The mutilation did have its lighter side. Later in the year, on the road across Europe, he ordered four sodas from a roadhouse. He was served three. I ordered four, he said. No, you ordered three. 'I held up my hand, fingers outstretched, and said: Does this look like three?' Oh. Yes. I suppose it does.)

More crashes were to follow, as Wayne tried too hard against manifold disadvantages; and another looping highsider in Germany left him so badly battered, with back and hand injuries, that for the first time ever he actually pulled out of a race because he was not strong enough to continue. Things might have been quite different for the rest of this year, and for the next, if similar unkind fortune had not stricken Doohan mid-way through the season at Assen. Until then Doohan was seemingly set for a runaway victory – but his crash gave Wayne a glimmer of hope. It was just what he didn't need for his own well-being.

The switch back to Michelins had come, says Kenny, at the request of both riders – Kocinski was again his second man. Kenny had misgivings. 'I didn't rate Wayne's chances much against the Honda on the same tyres.'

Then the world's biggest motorcycle company upped the stakes still further. At the first race of the season, Doohan, Gardner and new team-mate Shinichi Itoh astonished everybody by appearing on Hondas that looked much the same as last year's, but sounded quite different. In place of their previous tortured treble warble, the new bikes had a sort of a flat drone. And instead of their hysterical wheelspinning response to a touch too much throttle, the new droners simply dug in and accelerated out of the corners. Even in the wet. Wayne recalls watching them exit the pit lane at the first round at Suzuka. 'They'd slot it into gear, and do a wheelie right there. The Yamaha would never do that. You had to get it above 5,000rpm into the power range. I knew then that the Honda must be really good.'

This was the new 'Big Bang' concept: firing all four cylinders at almost the same time. The engine delivered the same amount of power as before, but it came in a series of pulses instead of a smooth push. This inconstancy helped the rear tyre to maintain traction in much the same way (though at a lot higher frequency) as some car anti-lock brake systems prevent skids by repeatedly applying and releasing the brakes. Big Bang was a big breakthrough. In retrospect, it was rather overdue. Many years before, Harley-Davidson had employed the same thinking to help their 750 V-twin dirt-trackers to hook up under power. Their version was dubbed 'the Twingle'. It seems GP racing happily adopted former dirt-track riders, but did not pay the same attention to their engineers. Anyway, Yamaha and the other companies scrabbled to catch up, determining the Honda's unorthodox firing pattern by analysing tape-recordings of its exhaust then hastily converting their own V4 engines to match. All were remarkably successful given that they were rush jobs. However Honda not only had half-a-season advantage by then, but also the luxury of having done their testing and development in private in the winter, rather than in action on the racetracks.

For once, the Team-Mate Thing was unimportant. Kocinski was buoyed up by his 1991 last-race win, but Wayne dismantled his confidence easily, as Roberts watched, carried along by events. 'The trouble is, me and Wayne were like brothers, and John wasn't. Probably didn't want to be. In '91, it had been kind of a fun thing. Wayne laughed about a lot of the stuff John had trouble with. He thought it was a pretty good kick, though it wasn't for John. In '92, I think Wayne just got tired of hearing John say how bad the bike was. We all did.

'Like in Barcelona for the GP of Europe, the mechanics worked so hard, doing everything he wanted. And John wanted soup to nuts every weekend. Soup to nuts, soup to nuts, soup to nuts. And back to soup. Put it back the way it was when we got here. Then in the race he got fifth, came in, and said: this is the worst piece of crap I ever rode. You can't steer it. Nobody could ride that bike any faster than me, because they'd kill themselves.

'It was difficult to listen to that when Wayne had just won the race. When John's good, he's very good, and easy to work with. But the minute somebody goes faster, he turns into John Kocinski. And that's when we'd have a problem.

'Wayne would do it on purpose. Every time John went fast in testing or practice, Wayne would go right out and beat it. It drove John crazy – to the point that he just *knew* that Wayne's bike was better than his bike. It wasn't true, though there was no way I could prove it. And John was very good at saying something, then believing it. By the end of the year, it was getting ugly.' Kenny dropped Kocinski, and kept Wayne. As Wayne had predicted, one of their careers would be ruined.

There was no questioning Wayne's status within the team, or in the paddock. In an era of greatness, he was the 500-class king. He was the target for all the other riders: beat Wayne and you'd truly beaten the world. Schwantz, Lawson, Gardner and Doohan commanded respect, but when Wayne walked in the room went quiet. It didn't make him happier. Old friends from the laughing days like Mike Minnig and Itchy Armstrong worried at the magazine photographs of his grim and hawkish face – but he shouldered the responsibilities of a double World Champion with conscientious resolve. On the one side this meant playing the sponsors' game: Marlboro were heavy hitters and big payers, and they expected a lot of their men, in terms of meeting dignitaries and the press. On the other hand, they also knew how to treat a guy, mostly, and when not to distract him too much, and it wasn't all bad. One laugh in a year of not too much humour came at a Marlboro pre-race press conference. Wayne's sombre presence could easily fluster his interlocutors, like the one who asked: 'Do you have any secret plans or tactics for the race Wayne? Er, that you're obviously not going to tell us about . . .' Wayne waited just the right amount of time before saying, firmly: 'No.'

But there were more serious issues at stake. Racing had been through a huge political upheaval. There was discontent among the entrants. Kenny Roberts was a prime mover in the increasingly powerful International Racing Teams Association which was in league with the stirrings of a powerful commercialism and the new explosion of cable and satellite TV markets. A complex power struggle had taken participants through several blind alleys and sudden U-turns. The uneasy resolution for the 1992 season put Dorna and F1 mogul Bernie Ecclestone in commercial control, with the Geneva federation – the FIM – having leased off all commercial rights and most of the others as well in return for a tidy and inflation-proofed $10 million-plus per annum. IRTA had a major management role in the new regime. The sands were still shifting (and are five years later), and Ecclestone's involvement was to be both short-lived and financially costly to erstwhile partners Dorna.

Something had been forgotten in all this high-powered melee. It was rider safety. Ironically enough this was the political raft upon which Mike Trimby had floated to an influential position as a high-level IRTA functionary. The new regime paid lip-service to the riders' interests, but the team-led structure subjugated riders to their team managers in various ways, and showed that hard-won rider power within IRTA had melted away. At least that was how Rainey took it when the new calendar revived two Ecclestone circuits with highly dubious safety provisions – Hungary and Brazil.

'All through my rehabilitation I'd been thinking about how I broke my leg in Malaysia because of the kerb. Not because I crashed, but because I hit the kerb with my leg, and it was too steep. I thought: how are we going to get the kerbs changed? And I realised I was the guy to do it. The riders were the only people in the paddock who weren't organised.' Wayne called a meeting at the first round, in Japan. Some 20 riders (out of about 100) showed up. 'It was easy for them to say yeah, we're behind you, then just forget about it. But I didn't forget, because of my own experience, and because I wanted to do something for racing. The riders had tried to get organised before, but when it really came to crunch time it would always break up. This time I wanted all the riders involved, from privateers to the World Champion. I thought if we put in $1,000 per rider we would get a lawyer, an office and all the supplies and so on. And we did it. Some riders couldn't afford it, so we let them pay half or pay the next year. Some guys never came to a meeting, never paid. I don't respect guys who don't give a damn about their fellow riders.'

Loris Reggiani represented the 250 class, Jorge Martinez the 125s, and the organisation was dubbed IMRA – International Motorcycle Racers' Association. They'd meet at every race. Wayne took to showing up a day or so early, canvassing support. 'I was racing the championship and I didn't want to be doing this, but I knew if I didn't it would just fall apart. Every time more and more riders would show up, and it was starting to come around, though the meetings were pretty disorganised, because everybody had a different problem.' One was with the new method of prize money. In the past this had always gone to the riders, who would have their own arrangements over how much they would keep, and how much would go to the team or the mechanics. Now the money went to the teams instead, and arrangements had to be made the other way round. There were complaints also about the new restrictions to free passes, which meant riders couldn't invite their own guests. And stringent new rules requiring team uniforms at all times, and spick and span vehicles and equipment (and no washing hung out in the paddock to dry). To Wayne, these were side issues. 'I said hey: this is a safety organisation. There's a lot of things wrong, but they're a done deal, and we missed our chance to negotiate because we weren't organised. Now we've got to go for things we can control. Which is safety.'

He wanted IMRA to have a seat on IRTA's committee, which would give them the right of approval over safety provisions at all tracks. 'But IRTA wouldn't even talk to us. Because they knew from the past that riders would go out and ride and just worry about themselves.' Matters came to a head at the Hungarian GP, round nine out of 13. 'These guys were all set to strike for the last two races. I said: guys, you're wanting too much. You've got to go a little at a time.' But feelings were running high, and now IMRA put together a petition signed by almost every rider, threatening to boycott the Hungarian race if they didn't get a sympathetic hearing at once. Rainey and six or seven others formed the IMRA deputation, among them not only Schwantz but also Eddie Lawson, who had paid his dues but otherwise remained aloof. 'I told Eddie we needed him to show he was with us. And he wanted to go in there and tell Trimby and Paul Butler (now president of IRTA) what he thought of them.'

Eddie turned out to be a loose cannon – highly impressive as he launched into the IRTA mob. 'Although it wasn't really what the meeting was about, he just flew off the handle and started telling Trimby what he thought about him: you used to work for the riders and now you don't give a damn about us. You're just a bunch of fat dickheads who sit around eating steak.

'We sat back and let him have his say, then I said: what we really want is a seat on the committee, so we can figure out what racetracks we're going to, how we can make them safer, and approve the racetracks before you guys say they're OK. They still didn't think we could stick together, but when I showed them the signatures we had, we got more or less what we wanted.' But the situation didn't really ease until some behind-the-scenes work. Wayne found unexpected help and co-operation from Dorna, who wielded the real power. As a result they got more of the same from IRTA as well.

The role of riders' representative went to ex-racer Didier de Radigues, a Belgian with extensive experience, who set about inspecting the remaining tracks on the calendar. (From 1993 this role with IRTA was taken by former 500 champion Franco Uncini, while – without Wayne's drive – IMRA quietly fell dormant because of the predicted lack of unity.) But the whole safety business was to backfire on Wayne. This caused a serious rift with

Lawson and allowed others to question his principles, when the exercising of them happened to coincide with his own desire to claim a third successive World Championship.

It happened in Brazil, for the penultimate round of 1992. For the previous two years the GP there had been cancelled, on the grounds of bad track safety. The local organisers at Sao Paulo did some work on the circuit, and promised some more, and here it was back on the calendar. Just the job for IMRA's new representative. Didier duly visited the track in the company of FIM and IRTA representatives, noted the alterations and the promises of more work, then returned to the riders with a fistful of photographs. They decided on his advice that yes, this time they would go to Brazil.

Trouble started soon after arrival at the Interlagos venue. What may have seemed safe out of the window of a rentacar or in a wide-angle photograph looked very different from the saddle of a speeding 500. Retaining walls were simply too close to the trackside, and a bout of dreadful weather only added to the obvious dangers. The riders met en masse once again, to hear two very opposed arguments. Eddie Lawson felt very strongly that they should all pack up and go straight home at once. Rainey propounded a rather different viewpoint. Yes, maybe they'd screwed up. Maybe Didier had got it all wrong. But they had already had their chance to judge the issue. They'd sent their representative, and they'd voted to come and race. To pull out now would be grossly unprofessional. In the end, torn also by their own needs, the riders made a woolly decision: to race, but reserving the right to withdraw if it rained.

Wayne remains adamant. 'This race-track was very, very dangerous. There were parts where it was just walls. If you made a mistake there, it'd wipe you out. But I'd started this rider thing and we'd sent our guy down to check it out. There was no way we could back out now. I was thinking about the championship, but believe it or not I was thinking more about the state of the championship series. The promoter had hocked his house to run the race, all the teams were down there. If we'd pulled out now we'd have looked like idiots.' He adds, convincingly: 'I know what Eddie would have done in my situation. He'd have raced.'

But Lawson has not shifted his opposing view either. 'I was in a similar situation in 1988, when there was a dispute among the riders whether we should race in Argentina, and I was going for the title. I just kept out of it, and Wayne should have done the same. He said to me: you don't have to race if you don't want to. After he'd asked me to get behind him for IMRA, I couldn't believe he said that.' Lawson stormed out of the meeting, vowing: 'Whatever you guys decide, I'll do the opposite.' And he did. The next day, when practice was wet, only one bike went out as the others huddled in the pits to await developments. It was Eddie's defiant Cagiva.

That was a turning point for the two old friends and rivals. They'd started the year off well together, taking a break at Hamilton Island off the Australian coast, where Mr Buzzy had dared Eddie to go sky-diving, and in the sober light of day, neither was quite able to back out. 'Eddie went first, then me,' remembers Wayne. 'I'm afraid of heights: stepping out onto the undercarriage then jumping out of the aircraft was the scariest thing I've ever done.' But now Lawson was burning mad, and he didn't mind who knew it. He'd already decided this would be his last 500 season. He left few friends behind, and that was the way he wanted it. 'After that, I was done with other riders.' Yet in the future, while pursuing his own not-quite-successful Indy Lights car-racing campaign, he would again be a good friend to Wayne.

But all this was yet to come.

The 1992 season was 13 races long, a shorter calendar with a revised points-scoring system, for the top ten instead of the top 15. The bias was skewed to give greater advantage to race winners at the expense of the other rostrum finishers.

Wayne had worked his way gradually into testing – or tried to. His goal for the opening round of tests in Malaysia had been to drag his knee on the ground. 'I did that on my first lap.' He'd ride 20 laps or so, then change out of his leathers to go and watch Kocinski. The gradual approach didn't last. In the second round of tests at the new Montmelo circuit outside Barcelona came the crash and the hand injury. He was still in pain for the first race in Japan.

Suzuka was wet, and Wayne struggled to qualify ninth, hampered by his injuries. 'Then I made a really stupid mistake on the second lap of the race. I was looking up ahead to see where everybody else was, starting to panic a bit.' He was, after all, accustomed to leading the early laps, not brawling with the underdogs. 'Then in Dunlop Corner' (a medium-speed left-hander over a crest) 'it stepped out on me and I was down. Later I was watching the race on TV, and I could see Doohan was wheelying out of some corners. I was just amazed that they had so much grip in the rain. He and Gardner were lifting the wheel while everybody else was just struggling to stay on.' Kocinski also fell in the race, leading to Team Roberts's first ever double non-finish.

Wayne was unhappy about the feel of the chassis. Final development had perforce been done by John, whose high-corner-speed style required completely different characteristics. The team got going with Yamaha to knock together a revised-geometry chassis for Wayne in time for the next round, in Australia two weeks later. It was still not ideal. 'We'd gone to bigger front forks this year for greater stiffness, and we had this real stiction problem' (static friction, which stiffens up the initial suspension movement). 'The forks would bind up when you braked, so you had to release them then take a second handful.'

His hand and knee were both troublesome, and for the race he took a course of painkilling injections from Dr Costa, to help him support his weight on the handlebars under braking at the tight and technical Eastern Creek Raceway outside Sydney. Doohan was on pole, but Wayne was happy to be second-fastest, while Kocinski fell heavily in practice, suffering his own hand injury and was out for two races. Wayne managed to lead from the line, and made himself very difficult to pass. When Doohan did get by he couldn't lose the persistent American until they ran into some backmarkers. He won by seven seconds.

'I was really happy with that result, my first finish of the year. Doohan had won two races already. But I wasn't too concerned because I knew he might make a mistake. I knew he was really talented as a rider, but I didn't think he had the tactics or experience to put everything together. He was always riding hurt. Doohan was quick, but I never thought he had that good racing intelligence. He thought only about winning everything, and not at the big picture.'

Malaysia came next. This was another runaway win for Doohan, though Wayne set fastest lap and finished second – Schwantz had crashed out in practice. Wayne was happy again. 'It was hot, and I wasn't trying to win the race, just do the best I could while I was gaining fitness.'

Now the European season began, at Jerez. Doohan won again, this time 18 seconds clear. 'Mick was just stretching this thing out, and my knee was getting worse because of all the bending. I was constantly having to adjust my leg in right-handers, which was dangerous; and I could see on TV my foot was hanging out. And I was getting this sharp pain from the screws on the ligaments while I was racing. Doohan just smoked us, but again I was happy with second, with the condition I was in. At that point, I still wasn't desperate about the championship.'

Most European racetracks run clockwise and have predominantly right-hand turns. Including Mugello, where they arrived to race two weeks later. 'By now it's May, eight months after the accident, and I'm still battling with this knee something fierce. This really started working on me. I was more than a second slower than Doohan in practice, but I raced him and Schwantz on the Sunday, and actually got ahead of them both. I could have won the race. I was starting to pull away – I opened up about a one-second lead. At last things were seeming to go my way. But as I went faster there was this vague feeling from the front forks. I was so used to blaming everything on my leg and my condition that I decided not to think about it. I went into one of the ess-bends on the top of the hill – pushed the front, and crashed. My feeling had been right, but I tried it anyway because I was so desperate to win.

'I was devastated. I was very very upset with myself, sitting up on this hill crying. I was losing the World Championship, and I was starting not to be able to deal with it. I'd hurt myself, and I was willing to hurt myself more to win. I'd never crashed before much. Now I'd crashed twice, so early in the year. We were so far behind physically and technically and I was trying to make up for everything, and it was too much. But I hadn't realised it at that point.'

Less adventurous souls might think that Wayne was coming to his senses. If so, the reversal came one week later in Barcelona, with the long-awaited first win of the year, defeating the mighty Honda and its rider in a straight fight. 'John was back now, and he outqualified me, and he was obviously feeling pretty cool. I just said: Hey John, d'you think you're going to do those times in the race? He kind of winced. I knew he was junk after that. He was real easy for me by then.'

The crucial change to the bike came on race morning, when Wayne asked crew chief Mike Sinclair to move the footpeg down and forward by about 20mm. 'It made all the difference. I could brake and go off into the corner without my leg being in a bind. My foot was dragging on the ground more, but my leg was in a more comfortable position and I could exert some leverage on the footpeg.' Now Doohan, pole qualifier, had his hands full. Rainey: 'I was with him the whole race and I was trying to pass him anywhere I could. About three or four laps to go, I got a good drive onto the straight and outbraked him at the end of the straight. Then I just kept the hammer down, and he ran out of laps to get back at me. I think if the race had been one lap longer he'd have beat me.'

The respite from pressure was only temporary. The next track took them back to the old Honda-lanes of the Hockenheimring, where Doohan was again vastly superior in practice. Wayne's desperation returned, stronger than ever. 'Michelin had brought out this new rear tyre, and I remember telling John Hogan' (Marlboro's top man) 'before that practice session how it had such unbelievable grip, but that I couldn't feel what it was going to do. If it did let go, it felt like it would throw me into the grandstands. I got hooked up with Mick in the last session. I'd actually caught up with him a bit on his fastest lap, because I really didn't want him to be on pole again. But I was way above the level of the bike, and myself. Then coming out of the first-gear Sachs corner, it just went brrrrrp and stepped out. Next thing I know I was hitting the ground really hard. I broke some ribs, broke my hand again, tweaked my knee again.

'I was in a lot of pain after that. Mentally I was really down, probably the worst I had ever been in my GP career. I'd screwed myself up trying to race with Doohan. And I didn't feel I was getting the support from Yamaha. I was still on the same bike, it was still slow. And I was still having problems tyrewise, though

Michelin had made some more tyres around me. We'd actually fixed the front tyre problem they'd had. What they developed round my bike is what they're using now.

'I got a bad start because I wasn't there physically or mentally. I had injections in my back, my hand and my knee. Just to numb it. I was running down the straightaways, lying about eleventh, and my mind wasn't on the race. I was saying to myself: Wayne you should really start thinking about your life now, instead of trying to be the one who carries the whole thing. I really felt I was gonna hurt myself bad, because the bike wasn't good and I wasn't good. I wasn't even up to speed. Doohan was gone. He was all I was concerned about. I wasn't racing for second place. I ended up pulling in, for the first time in my career, because I was just too hurt to continue. I didn't feel I needed to abuse myself any more than I had already. I was comfortable after making the decision. It went against everything I stood for, but in the end it was right for me.

'I hadn't given up on the championship. Doohan won the race – he had 130 points, I had 65. I knew anything could happen, but the only thing for me would be if Mick made a huge mistake. That was possible, because I knew he only thought about being the fastest guy, winning every race and devastating everybody.

'There was one weekend off, and I went home to Spain and just did nothing. When I got to Holland for the Dutch TT at Assen I decided to start training. I went cycling, but I couldn't even hold on to the handlebar. I thought maybe the suspension of a 500 would make it easier, but I did eight laps on the first morning and I could only think of the pain. So I pulled out of the race. To listen to my body again. Shae and I went home to the US that day, and I was really happy with the decision. There was this fax waiting for me. Doohan was out, and Schwantz had crashed. Then I knew I'd done the right thing. Later, I got to thinking if I'd stayed I could have got some easy points. But at the same time I knew I couldn't have because my brain just wasn't into the racing. I also thought, if I was there maybe Mick would have been focused more, and wouldn't have crashed. I'm sure he thought: oh man this is going to be easy. And he made that mistake.' So too, in the depleted race, did Schwantz and Lawson, knocking each other down while disputing the lead, handing a first victory to new Spanish rider Alex Criville.

Doohan's injury was disproportionately grave. He'd broken his right leg below the knee, and complications set in during what he insists was sub-standard care in the local hospital. As a result, he came close to losing his leg. He was out for months, spending several weeks with his legs joined below the knee, sharing blood vessels. His leg is permanently withered now, his ankle locked in position, and he has a limp.

Nobody at the Hungarian GP knew how serious it was. The race was at the mercy of the weather, stopped and restarted in falling rain. Conservatively, Wayne and the rest all chose wet-weather tyres. Cagiva-mounted Lawson alone felt able to take the risk of fitting intermediates, in case the track dried. His gamble was richly rewarded, and the ex-Crucible Kid and great grand prix hero gave the Italian firm their first win in 12 years of trying. Wayne, riding cautiously, finished fifth. 'Before the race, I'd called Mick, and said: I hope you're feeling better, but I'm trying to catch you. We thought he'd be back at the next race or so.'

Wayne knew an opportunity when he saw one, and would finish the remainder of the season gaining strength rapidly. Now he wanted to get some testing time: Yamaha's own Big Bang had finally arrived for the Hungarian GP, and they needed to find out how to make it work best. The team went to Jerez, where Rainey was his old intense self, trying all the combinations including slotting the older pre-Big Bang engine (known as 'the 180' for its even crankshaft spacing) into his latest chassis, against the wishes of the whole team. 'The new motor vibrated real bad – it was breaking gearbox bolts and the primary drive gears, and the 180 felt unbelievably smooth. It seemed easier on the chassis and the tyres, but it would spin the rear wheel and step out a lot quicker out of the corners because it had less torque down low, and the power came in harder. We decided to stay with the new engine for the rest of the year.'

Wayne won the French GP from Gardner and Kocinski at the new circuit of Magny-Cours, only his second victory in ten rounds. The next race was the British GP at Donington Park. 'When Mick didn't show up people started to realise how bad his leg was. I was racing against a ghost. By then I was talking to him probably once a week. Giving him support, and letting him know I was chipping away. I always found it easy to talk to Mick. If it had been Schwantz, I probably wouldn't have.' Gardner won an extraordinary race, in which two of the new Big Bang Yamahas blew up dramatically, Niall Mackenzie's out on the back straight, and Kocinski's right in front of the pits, where it laid an invisible slick on the entry to the first corner that brought down both works Suzukis and another rider. Wayne's bike survived for a close second place.

Then came Brazil and the uproar over safety. Wayne was 22 points down, 20 were available for a win. But now Mick was back, albeit as a pale shadow of himself. Wayne, like everybody, was shocked. 'Skinny, white, could barely walk. I felt sorry for him. I'd put him in the situation where he had to come back to try to save his World Championship, but he was far from ready.'

At the big riders' meeting 'Mick and Eddie were the only guys who agreed that we shouldn't race.' I reminded Wayne that Mick says he sat on the fence. 'No way. At that point he was saying we shouldn't race. Which would make him automatically World Champion.' As we have seen, the race went ahead. All were cautious, and as a result (mercifully) there were the least number of crashes of the whole year. Wayne's race was perfect. He led from the start and pulled away to win over Kocinski and Suzuki-mounted Doug Chandler. 'I got to the hole shot, and the first 10 laps I just had my head down. I was running a full second quicker than in qualifying. My pit board was right at the end of the front straight. I was doing about 185mph, braking for the first turn, and I could just glance across, and all I had time to read was Point Zero. I very seldom looked behind me when I raced, so I had no idea who was second. Finally I decided to brake early to have a good look at the board. I saw it was Gardner, and I had a 10-second lead. I just thought: Wow.' Mick struggled home 12th, for zero points. 'So now I'm two points behind going into the last race. Wild, huh.'

The task was straightforward. Wayne had simply to finish in front of Doohan, and higher than sixth, should the Australian be right behind. The only difficulty would be finding the right focus. There was one weekend off: Rainey worked on acclimatising to the 6,000-foot altitude of Kyalami, where bikes – and people – would lose power quite noticeably. He trained at Lake Tahoe, so when he arrived in Johannesburg he was already adjusted to the thinner air.

'Mick looked a lot better, and the Honda was going good again. At that time I was really imagining myself riding a Honda, because it did the stuff right. Kocinski was on pole, and Mick outqualified me. Again Kenny asked me if I wanted John's help, again I said no. We had another problem – we were out of parts. We even thought about putting the 180 engine back in. Garriga had fallen off there, when his Big Bang motor broke a transmission bolt again. Then I said, let's just go with what got us here. Just give me the best bike you can, and if the transmission breaks, I wasn't meant to be in this position anyways.

'I led the race, then Kocinski went by. The only thing I had on my pit board was Doohan. I could see he was sixth, and falling back. Gardner passed me. He would much rather me win the championship than Mick, so for once he gave me a whole lot of room when he went by.

'I got third, and I wasn't even sure if I was champion until I came in. They told me I was. It was all pretty unbelievable, but I said: We'll take it.'

And he knew he had deserved it, too. 'That year I'd suffered a great deal, by abusing my body, and I'd abused my team, and Yamaha, and everybody around me. Just to be World Champion. Mick made a mistake. That's racing. That's the risk you take. And I'd been making them before him.

'Some people think I lucked into it, but I've never felt like that. It's a cruel sport. I believe that year I beat Doohan because I took advantage of the situation he put me in, but he didn't take advantage of the situation I put him in.'

A third successive title put Wayne with the greats. The last to achieve this in the 500 class had been Kenny Roberts; before him Giacomo Agostini, Mike Hailwood, John Surtees and Geoff Duke. He was on a high, a great achiever. Just one thing was missing. The satisfaction. 'You'd think it would be satisfying, but it just made me more determined. Because something was missing, and I had to find out what it was.

'Winning the championship screwed me up. After that it was more important to keep the championship than win it the first time. People say when you're on top there's only one place to go. I always said no, it's not down. It's staying there. And my life was built around winning the World Championship. I just wasn't focused on anything else. I was way too intense. I was willing to try anything to race. I knew I might die, but I was willing to risk that to avoid getting beat. I was afraid to wake up, when I did retire, and look in the mirror and say: did you do the best you could?

'In 1992 I pushed myself so hard that I was a pretty miserable guy to be around. I remember going to racetracks and sitting at the red lights just hating it. Because the intensity was so much greater than ever before.

'By the time '93 rolled round I was going to be World Champion, and I was prepared to do whatever it would take.'

CHAPTER 14

COUNTDOWN
TO CATASTROPHE

*'This was the year Kevin finally started to think about the World
Championship. That was much more dangerous. This was the most
concern I'd ever had about winning the championship, because it was
going to have to be against Schwantz. And when he raced me,
it was fierce.'* Wayne Rainey, before his final season

If 1992 had been a bad year for self-destruction, it was only a dress rehearsal. For 1993, Wayne was fully fit, training hard. But more than ever, he was tortured and perplexed by his corrosive dissatisfaction. It was now even more important to hold on to something which gave him no pleasure.

'I'd won the championship three years in a row, and now I was possessed in a way that nobody understood. I was trying to talk to Kenny about it, but he had never been in that situation. He got hurt early the year he was going for his fourth. I think if I'd have gotten hurt early in 1993, I'd probably still be racing now.'

The challenge was spiced by another tyre switch – back to Dunlops. This was entirely Wayne's decision and Kenny forged an exclusive deal with the otherwise disfavoured company, who also backed a non-racing test team, Randy Mamola riding. 'They really made a big commitment. I wasn't happy with the feel of the Michelin, and I really liked the guys at Dunlop. They were more like family. I'd always liked trying to win on something different, and I really needed something to make it more interesting for me.'

The winter was marked by a rare month of doing nothing, with Shae and Rex. They moved into their new house the day after Christmas. 'I was there for about two weeks before we went to Australia to go testing.'

A serious shock was waiting. Not new Marlboro-Yamaha team-mate Luca Cadalora. 'He was the least challenge of any team-mate.

But he did surprise me with his speed at some tracks.' The new bike was the problem. Yamaha's latest version of the V4 YZR theme was their biggest change for years. The engine was basically the same, but the rest was all new after a major redesign – in entirely the wrong direction. Last year's bigger front forks led to problems with tyre chatter and suspension stiction. They'd sought a solution in increasing stiffness elsewhere in the machine. The all-new chassis used Honda-style deep-section aluminium extrusions and, as well as being more compact than the old welded-up pressed aluminium 'Deltabox', it was very much stiffer. From this were hung even larger-diameter forks, and bigger wheel, steering and suspension spindles. In this way, they hoped to eliminate the wobbles and weaves and (as the dirt-trackers would say) 'squirrelly' handling of the grossly overpowered 500s. In providing a more rigid platform for the suspension, they were following normal racing car practice.

That the experiment was a failure did not reflect badly on Yamaha or on the team, whose idea it had been in the first place. They had to find out, after all, and motorcycles – half man, half-machine – respond to far more complex and obtuse physics than mere motor cars. The fault came in not learning the lessons quickly enough. It is typically Japanese to stick with a problem until it is solved, rather than stepping back and starting again. Wayne made his own unwilling contribution to this process. While complaining continuously about the bike's serious faults, he happened to win two out of the first three races. No wonder Yamaha didn't take him too seriously: there couldn't be that much wrong with their new wonderbike. 'I felt I'd won because of my own effort, and Luca agreed. So then we proceeded to lose the next four races.'

Wayne and Luca first rode the new bike, in poor weather, at Phillip Island in Australia. Wayne wasted no time in finding its limits. 'After the first five laps I came in and said: this bike feels really good. Except for this chatter-bounce going into the turns.' The juddering was to prove impossible to eliminate over the coming months. 'I knew we couldn't win on this thing. The bike was stiff in the wrong places, so that when it was leant over, the tyre sidewalls had to provide all the suspension. As soon as you put pressure on it, it'd start to bounce.'

There were other problems. The compact chassis was so narrow that it trapped engine heat, and running hot cost horsepower. There was also a redesigned clutch that was not to Wayne's liking. In the launch off the line, it tended to grab, almost stalling the motor, so he'd have to declutch and get the revs up again, losing ground and positions. But the chatter, making it impossible for Wayne to flick the bike into the corners, was the biggest drawback, and it quickly became clear that the new chassis was impervious to any of the usual improvements by adjustment. Wayne used an old bike to run through the new Dunlops, while Kevin Magee (now contracted to Yamaha to race in Japan) joined in the tests to try and pin down the problems.

'The bike was junk' at Laguna Seca, likewise in more tests in Malaysia. 'This was for sure the worst bike I'd ever ridden.' There remained just the IRTA tests (open to all teams) at Jerez. And, in spite of the best efforts of factory and team, 'after 15 days of testing, the bike was the same. From here and for the whole year, almost, we went slower than two or three years before. Everybody was concerned why: I kept saying it was because the feeling had gone away from the bike. On Dunlops on the wobbly, slow old bike, I could ride the crap out of it. I could make it corner the way I wanted it to. Now that feeling was gone.' Wayne left the Jerez test early, face of thunder, and his problems became public knowledge.

Eastern Creek, Australia, 28 March – Eleven races to go

'Gardner and Lawson had retired, Kocinski was on a 250, Doohan was hurt from a pre-season crash. Doug was on the Cagiva now: I knew he was fast by himself, but felt if I could put some pressure on him, I could beat him. Kevin and I battled for pole. He won it.'

It was a good race, early leader Daryl Beattie (Mick's new Honda team-mate) was pegged down by the Americans, who laid on a three-way battle to finish Schwantz, Rainey, Chandler. It had been close enough at times for Doug's front wheel to have scuffed the leg of Wayne's leathers.

Wayne already knew Schwantz would be the greatest threat. After all those years of 'racing on emotion' the Texan had finally gotten smart, while Wayne had been growing more obsessed with winning the title no matter what. A role reversal. 'This was the year Kevin finally started to think about racing, while I was kind of going into the mode he'd been in.

'I'd been reading what he said during testing and I realised that he'd changed. He wasn't just looking at the lap time, but the overall package and the balance of the bike. He wasn't talking like Kevin Schwantz, he was talking like a guy that's thinking. That was much more dangerous. I knew he could go fast, but he'd never known how to go slow when he needed to. Right away I thought he would be the challenge. When he raced against me, it was fierce. This was the most concern I'd ever had about winning the championship, because it was going to have to be against Schwantz.'

This was only proper. Wayne and Kevin had been racing's great double act for years. From 1990 onwards, as mature 500 riders, they had been locked in inch-close combat at almost every race. They were what the GPs were all about. When in 1995 both riders had gone, the last survivor of those days, Michael Doohan, would be moved, while winning everything, to complain about how boring it had all become.

Wayne and Kevin were the double act not because there was nobody else, but because they made it so. They'd left the no-speaks behind on the US Superbike tracks, but everything else was the same. They were racing only each other. Each could be crushed with frustration when the other stole a mere couple of hundredths of a second off his best practice lap. It might not be for pole position (though it usually was); it might make no discernible difference to the starting position – anywhere on the front row being good enough. But that unimaginably small time margin would be the major driving force.

In this way, they brought out greatness each in the other, and gave greatness to racing, and to those few rivals who were able to join in.

Shah Alam, Malaysia, 4 April – Ten races to go.
'Schwantz was pole, I was third, Cadalora was again one-and-a-half seconds off. It was 104 degrees, and I was really happy that it was super super hot, because the bike was no good when the tyres gripped, but in that heat they'd start to slide after about five laps. Then I'd be

212

able to ride the bike like I wanted without it getting this chatter-
bounce. They shortened the race by two laps because of the heat, and
that really pissed me off. Most riders were getting IV drips' (to combat
the loss of body fluid in the saturating humidity). 'When I saw that,
I went outside and got changed into my leathers in the sun.

'In the race, I pulled away a couple of tenths a lap, and ended up
winning by six seconds. Beattie was second, Schwantz third, but I
was still concerned about him. He was the danger, because I knew
the first three were just bonus races.'

Wayne was ahead on points now, but he felt the difference in
the ebb and flow of their long-standing rivalry. Measuring out the
honours is revealing. During almost six years of direct GP
confrontation, Kevin showed a marginally greater aptitude for
sheer speed, reflecting his reliance on pure talent; while Rainey's
ability to win when he could, and also to finish well when he
couldn't win, reflected his more considered approach. Not that
there was a great deal in it.

Schwantz took 28 pole positions to Wayne's 15. Schwantz took
one more best race lap than Rainey, 23 to 22. The balance tipped
the other way with the more important race wins. Out of a possible
85, Wayne won 24 and Kevin 23. Their nearest rivals, Lawson and
Doohan, each won ten in the same period. And more telling still
were the number of top-three rostrum finishes, the ones that back
up the wins with valuable points. Wayne was second or third 40
times from 1988 to 1993; Schwantz only 21 times.

Schwantz was obliged by circumstances to reach an
accommodation with himself about his talent to win races and lose
championships. '1990 kinda set the pattern. For some reason, it didn't
burn me up. Winning titles was what I wanted, but at the same time
I was still proving the point that I could be the fastest guy out there. I
could win, win, win. Ah shit, so I made a mistake and it cost me the
championship.' To Rainey, the title was everything. Winning it was
what he did better than Kevin, on a ratio of three to one. He was
leading on points again for a historic fourth in a row when he met his
fate at Misano. The way was finally open for Kevin to claim what
Wayne had denied him for so long. Afterwards Wayne was insistent
that his career-long sparring partner deserved the crown. Yet the

ironical taint remains: to become World Champion, Schwantz had to wait until Rainey was crippled.

He deserved it, says Wayne, because of how he'd changed. 'Before this he never had a game plan. He just raced with whoever he had to race with. He raced on emotion, rather than his brain. He was a lovely rider, to watch. He'd go way past what the bike should be doing. He'd do anything to beat me. I'd think: he's just not riding it right, yet he could pull it off sometimes. I believe we raced each other differently from how we'd race anybody else.'

Wayne's tactics reached a pitch of refinement in 1990, and remained effective for three seasons. 'In training I'd work on my heart rate, so when I got tired I could push again. I'd start every race as fast as I could, then if I got a good lead that was usually it. He knew if he tried to catch me then I'd speed up again. But if we were still close at the end, I could up the pace a bit more. Then if he went with me, that was that. Sometimes he'd beat me, though usually only by a little. But what would usually happen is he'd make a mistake. He fell off a lot in 1990 that way. He won five races that year, and five in '91. But he just wasn't ready for the championship then. It wasn't until 1993 that he put together a good season. He rode like I rode. It took all those years, all those crashes, all those wins to put 1993 together – and he did it better than I did. He forced me into the mistake, whereas before I'd always done it to him.'

The next race was to be their last close finish. Inches apart, after 76.5 miles of racing. Rainey won, in a vintage performance that both he and Kenny Roberts regard as the best of his life. The victory, on a third revision of the flawed new bike, set back his campaign for a replacement by several races. It was, furthermore, magnificent.

Japanese GP, Suzuka, 18 April – Nine races to go

'Schwantz was on pole, I was third, with (Shinichi) Itoh between us. His Honda was a real screamer. Honda's pride is not to win the race, but the straightaway. The Suzukis were also fast this year, while my bike was running hot and slow.

'I got a bad start. First lap I was 12th, Schwantz was leading, and I thought: he's gonna be gone. But it was like he was waiting for me. Luca pulled in, said the Yamaha was unraceable. But I was getting

inspired because I was catching up, chipping away, passing people in the Esses, then they'd just blow by me again on the straight.

'About half way through the race I could start to slide the bike like none of the Michelin riders. I was enjoying myself so much – it was now I had an out-of-body experience, looking down on myself riding. I finally caught and passed Schwantz – that really screwed him up – and was fighting it out with Itoh.

'I could pass him in the corners, but when it came to the straight he came by so fast it would blow my bike over by two feet. I wanted to lead him into Turn One, so I could pull out enough lead he wouldn't pass me again on the straight, but I couldn't do it.

'The tyre was going off, and sliding nicely. Now I thought maybe I could use that to antagonise the other riders – win the race by intimidating them. On the last five laps I made my run.'

Itoh succumbed to a demonstration of radical rear-wheel steering through Dunlop Corner. Wayne could see he was getting fatigued. Now for Schwantz and Beattie.

'In the last few laps I had that thing really pegged and it was sliding everywhere. I knew that frustrated Schwantz, because that's what he wanted to do but his tyres wouldn't let him. I had about a 1.5 second lead to start the last lap, but then I had a huge slide in fifth gear on the right-hander after the hairpin, where I'd been passing everybody. It should have been a highsider, but I was riding so far ahead of the bike I was able to save it. But I lost about a full second, and they were all on my ass as we ran onto the back straight.

'Beattie's Honda drafted by me, but he went into the last corner too hot and ran wide, and I went back under him. Then I had to make myself unpassable at the chicane.' He finished ahead of Schwantz by less than a tenth of a second, Beattie two more tenths back, Itoh close behind.

Best-ever? 'For sure.' The victory was achieved on a slower bike, by a devastating combination of tactics and aggression on the limit, measured out in breathtaking angles of slide. It was vintage Rainey. Wayne admits he was helped by the slow pace. 'I could slide it where I wanted to. I was having so much fun. But I couldn't have gone any faster.' Wayne remains puzzled that Schwantz set best lap in the last lap. 'I was wondering: what was he doing the whole race? If he'd done that earlier on, I'd never have got near him.'

Victory at Suzuka is always special to the Japanese factories. There is an added dynamic here: the circuit belongs indirectly to Honda, so that winning is extra sweet to their rivals. Yamaha were jubilant, and Wayne's continuing complaints were ignored. Indeed, they seemed barely plausible to outsiders. Kenny: 'I told Wayne, how am I ever going to get them to make the bike better if you keep winning on it?' That situation was soon to be corrected with the start of the European season.

Spanish GP, Jerez, 2 May – Eight races to go

'Kevin and I were racing it out, then Barros caught us. And again Kevin was clever, because he didn't let that mess him up. Barros had us both beat, then he lost the front and crashed. In fact Schwantz pushed him into it. He took off from me to chase him down. I thought: OK. I knew I couldn't win that day. I thought he might make a mistake, but he used his head.'

Wayne still led the World Championship, 90 points to Schwantz's 86. Each had two wins, but Wayne had two seconds and Schwantz one second and one third. And he was riding clever. 'I was still on the same bike, and Yamaha's just depending on me to ride the thing.' The next track, the speed-bowl Salzburgring, would show up its shortcomings in speed, and lead to a rare public row with Roberts. Kenny remembers saying: What do you want me to do about it? Go and eat some aluminium chips and crap you a new crankshaft? Wayne: If you could, I sure would appreciate that right now.

'I was feeling the pressure much earlier in the year than ever before – because it was Schwantz.' The chatter-bounce was still there too, but Wayne found a stop-gap solution that at least reduced the problem at the crucial Fahrerlager corner, a looping banked U-turn near the end of the lap, where a lot of overtaking takes place. 'On race morning I watched the 250s from the top of my motorhome, and I noticed the Dunlop riders were all having the same chatter there. The Michelin riders weren't. Because of all my experience tyre testing, I felt we might improve the Dunlop with more pressure, so I got my tyre technician Jim Murphy to go from two bar to 2.1 – about three psi more. We didn't even have a chance to test it, but it did cut the chatter at that corner. As a result I could ride round people there, and when I passed Barros there on the last lap I was so happy.' Barros had played joker again, to Wayne's benefit. The Brazil nut had defeated the American and was safe in third when he wrong-footed while trying to lap a slower rider. The backmarker – Spaniard Juan Lopez-Mella – hadn't done much wrong, but Barros blew a fuse, closing the throttle at the start of the climb up the flat-out hill to aim a few wild blows at the flabbergasted privateer. Rainey was by now so close behind that he was lucky not to cop a flying fist or two himself.

Austrian GP, Salzburgring, 16 May – Seven races to go

'A great race. I was more happy to get third than Schwantz was to win. I was seventh on the grid, 1.3 seconds down on Schwantz. In the race, him and Doohan took off. I'm just struggling, racing with Criville, Barros, Cadalora, Itoh. With the clutch problem, I'd lost touch with the leaders at the start. On the last lap I was fourth, two seconds behind Barros. He messed up trying to outbrake Lopez-Mella at the chicane, which made him slow into the next corner. I still wasn't close enough to draft, but I aimed to pass him at the Fahrerlager. So we're going up the gears, in fifth round this bumpy left, when all of a sudden Barros shuts off, reaches over, and puts his finger in front of this guy's helmet. We're going about 180mph there, and I just thought – wow. I shut off and swerved to the right. Luckily there's an ambulance road outside the corner, and I ran right across it. Barros saw this streak on the grass, and he gassed it again. When I got back on the track I was behind him. But I passed him on the Fahrerlager. I thought this was so good.

'When Kevin saw me walking up to the rostrum, his face looked like – what are you doing here? I was so jazzed I stayed in my leathers for a long time after the race, carrying Rex around . . .'

His elation was appropriate. He shouldn't have been able to get on the rostrum. Not with that bike. And a more natural order would soon be restored too, at the horsepower-hungry Honda-lanes of the Hockenheimring. As well as the over-stiff chassis, Yamaha were also lagging in another important area – the development of ram intake systems that used the machine's speed to pressurise a sealed carburettor airbox. Honda had been first, Suzuki now had their own version up and running. Now at last Wayne had one too. 'It worked great. I passed Schwantz and the Cagivas down the straight, but it was eating holes in the pistons, so I couldn't use it. Without it, the bike instantly lost five mph.

German GP, Hockenheimring, 13 June – Six races to go
'I was just never in the race. The bike would pull 12,500rpm, but when Itoh caught up it would lose 1,000rpm pulling him along in my draft. Then when he passed me it would blow me right over the track. I could feel him from behind when he'd move to pass, because he'd suck me over the same way. I'd already started turning left when he'd pass me on the right. I ended up fifth, and Schwantz was getting a good lead on me – 131 to 117.

Wayne had another lucky escape in Germany from the unexpected antics of a different young up-and-coming rider. Honda-mounted Alex Criville, behind him, had braked too late for one of the chicanes, and run straight on through it, dodging the barriers. This is a legitimate accident avoidance, but he should then have stopped until signalled back onto a clear track by the marshals. Instead he came straight out, at low speed, right in front of Wayne. 'He just about took me out, and it lost me a place.' His protest was over-ruled, rather surprisingly. But this was the sort of thing he was having to get used to, racing against people like Criville and Barros, whom he really didn't believe had any right to be anywhere near him. 'I just didn't want to race against them guys. I didn't feel they were at the same level. The only guys I liked racing with were Chandler, Doohan, Kocinski, Schwantz, Lawson and Gardner. I had in my mind that when I was back with those other guys I was in the bad stuff. Don't try and race it out with them.'

Getting fifth was especially uncomfortable. Worse in a way than getting sixth, or seventh, or breaking down. Because it was one of Kenny's jokes. In previous years, some time or another after the race, and often as not at the victory dinner, someone in the team would ask: 'Who got fifth?' And the cry would be taken up. Who got fifth? Who got fifth? It was one of those things that mattered so little that it was always funny. No-one was laughing now. 'Before; when I was winning, the Marlboro guys always celebrated with me. When I didn't, then I didn't see them. And for the guys in the team, when we got second or third it was as though we'd finished tenth. A few years before we'd have all been happy with third. It seemed we were so used to winning we didn't know how to lose.' This was a real reason for dissatisfaction. Wayne typically looked inside himself for the solution. 'I felt I wanted more of a challenge. I was talking to Kenny about 1994, and trying to do more. I wanted to ride in 500 and 250 classes.'

Dutch TT, Assen, 26 June – Five races to go

'Oh, man. Again we were really slow. I tried an ROC chassis, but I raced the usual bike, and it was terrible – bouncing everywhere on the brakes, and you couldn't turn it in to the corners. For the first time ever Kevin was getting the better end of it. He won it, Chandler and Criville both passed me, and I ended up fifth. Cadalora was more than thirty seconds behind. Two races in a row, I'd gotten fifth.

Back to the future. The ROC chassis had been introduced in 1992, along with the British-built Harris. Both were closely supervised copies of Yamaha's own 'Deltabox' chassis from Wayne's winning 1991 model: ROCs were built in France, Harrises in England. The Yamaha factory also supplied 'works-replica' engines to make a package for privateers, to add numbers to alarmingly small grids. In retrospect, it is rather surprising that they didn't try it sooner – bolting a '93 works engine, suspension and brakes into an ROC. It was only in the seventh round at Assen, when Wayne was bouncing and faltering round a track which demands fluency and smoothness, that 'I got so disgusted with the bike I got them to go buy an ROC. I tried it in morning warm-up' (a brief 20-minute gallop some three hours before the race). 'And I loved it. But everyone said: Wayne, we have no experience with this bike. We don't know what it's going to do to the tyres. I said: we're losing this championship. We've got to do something drastic. I wanted to race it, but they wouldn't let me.' But by the time they got to Barcelona for the next round, there was no doubt. Wayne was on an ROC, and the Yamaha chassis was in the back of the truck.

European GP, Catalunya, 4 July – Four races to go

'The reason I won was because of the wind. The tailwind down the straight helped the Yamaha's speed, but coming the other way I was able to use the wind to help get the bike to turn in. It was solving problems for me. On the ROC we were still having problems with the chattering. The track got hotter on the day, and the Dunlops seemed to work better when they were sliding than when they were new. So they threw me another harder tyre. Doohan got second, Schwantz was third. He was doing it Rainey's way. He was a distant third, but he knew the bike wasn't good, and he was preserving his position.'

This was a turnaround, and that night Mr Buzzy came out in a big way. Upper-crust diners in a restaurant stuffed with antiques and quiet decorum watched in growing horror as Kenny's team and Yamaha's staff started noisy and ended up riotous in a full-scale food fight. 'That cost me some money,' recalls Kenny with a mixture of pride and regret. Mr Buzzy, for his part, made a short but memorable speech. 'I'd like to thank Yamaha,' he said, standing in the centre of the long table. 'For nothing.' Wayne insists today that he doesn't remember that at all.

'I was very very happy. Finally I'd gotten on a bike that felt good, after battling with the other chassis. The next day we stayed on testing, and I remember Oguma' (Yoichi Oguma, head of the factory Honda team) 'had all his HRC guys standing in a big circle around him, and as I walked past he stopped talking and just pointed at me. The next year I asked him what was going on. And he says: I never had children, and the NSR Honda was like my only son to me. And you beat it three years in a row. Then when you did it on an aftermarket standard chassis, I was talking severely to my engineers. I wanted to know how that could happen.'

The ROC allowed Wayne to ride the way he did best – nice and loose, pitching the bike into the corners smoothly then getting right on the gas, to throw all the work into the back tyre. But the problems were not solved, mainly because things had changed since 1992, and the rival bikes were that much better again. The biggest change was the Big Bang engine, which must bear most of the blame for a curious and still not fully explained fact – that the lap times now were by and large slower than in the early 1990s.

This went against all notions of progress. But in one regard things were a lot better: the number of highsider crashes had fallen significantly, as tyres, suspensions and chassis technology improved. This puzzlement was another contributing factor to Wayne's own darkening mood. At IRTA tests at Misano he'd even had a row with Mike Sinclair, the studious and soft-spoken New Zealander with whom he'd hardly ever disagreed in five years together. 'I had three bikes – we were testing the Yamaha again, and we were getting blown away by Schwantz. That really upset me. At that time everything was different. I was really intense, and if something on the bike didn't work I was all over everybody. I was real . . . unhappy in '93, and I was taking it out on people round me. Mike just reamed me.'

San Marino GP, Mugello, 18 July – Three races to go

'I qualified fifth. Cadalora was almost three seconds slower. Doohan and Schwantz just took off. That's when Kevin's tyre threw a chunk and he got second. I was a distant third, after being with Criville for a while. I didn't like that.'

There were five rounds remaining, and Schwantz led by 23 points – almost a one-race margin. Doohan wasn't a factor, nearly 50 points adrift. Wayne's title hopes were beginning to depend on the 'Anything Can Happen' rule. And things, several of them, were about to happen, one after the other.

The first concerned the motorcycle. The team stayed on at Mugello for three days of intensive testing. The first two were tiring and fruitless. Wayne was testing alone on the third day: 'Luca hadn't shown up. By about 11am they phoned around. He's in bed at home, and he says: I'm sore and I'm tired. That pissed me off.' Wayne dug in and did another 100 laps, and was so fatigued at the end of what was now six days in succession that he kept running into the sand trap at the end of the front straight. 'The sand trap was raked into furrows, sort of whoop-de-doos, and it was really hard to get the bike stopped over them. They were the same when I crashed later at Misano, and if it had been raked smooth I might not have been hurt. I should have said something at the time, but I didn't.'

They had something else to think about. This time they'd made a discovery that neither Wayne nor Kenny is even now prepared to discuss in any detail. 'That's when we came up on this spring centre thing – how we could really change the bike by just moving the spring centre around. I don't want to get too detailed, because it's something the other teams could find out. It's a click on the clickers on the front or on the preload on the spring, not a geometry change. And we found out about it on the last day.'

The next 'anything' event was cataclysmic – for Schwantz. It happened at Donington Park, a favourite track for the Suzuki rider, and it came in two parts. First came a heavy tumble in practice, causing wrist fractures that meant he was unable to ride to full capacity again that year, though typically it didn't stop him trying. Then came a first-lap spectacular – a multiple pile-up among the leaders at the end of the back straight. It was triggered by Doohan, who ran out of room to stop. His fallen Honda struck Schwantz's rear wheel, sending the Texan cartwheeling out of the saddle, and also knocked the other Suzuki rider Barros flying. Mercifully, nobody was hurt. For Wayne it was a gift. Particularly since he was involved in a drama of his own.

In practice, Luca had enthusiastically taken to the new chassis balance. Wayne was still angry with him, and didn't like the time-sheets at all. 'I was having trouble because the track had gotten bumpy. I called the last corner' (the final hairpin onto pit straight) 'the Staircase. I decided to put in one good lap to try and get onto the leaderboard, but I got onto the Staircase a little wide, to get a fast run onto the straight, and when I got on the gas, that thing spat me off and threw me on the ground.'

As is often the case with low-speed accidents, the landing was hard. Wayne tore two fingernails off his left hand, and sustained a compression fracture in his back. The sixth thoracic vertebra, to be precise – T6. But of more immediate concern was that he had also banged his head.

'As soon as I hit the ground I got up and walked away like I always did. My hand was bleeding pretty bad, so I thought what I'd do is get the other bike and go back out. I ran across the track, and I was still not really thinking clear. Shae was looking at me, really concerned. I did three laps and pulled in. I had no depth perception.

'I told the medical guys my back was really sore, but I didn't say anything about my head. Back at the motorhome that night I found my vision was lagging. I knew I was concussed, but the doctors hadn't checked, and I wanted nobody to know. Next morning I woke up and swung my head, and again my vision was behind the movement. I decided to do the morning warm-up to see how it would feel. I was two seconds off the pace, but I could choose my line. What concerned me more was I couldn't judge distance, so I couldn't pass anybody.

'After practice everyone was saying, is your back OK? I finally told Sinclair: it's my head, not my back. I said, I'm blurry. I don't know if I'm going to race or not. I'll let you know in a few hours. I still didn't tell nobody else. I didn't tell Kenny, or Shae.'

Back in the motorhome, he debated the situation. Should he pull out, and just give the title to Schwantz? There was also the possibility of another crash, perhaps involving other riders. The obsession won the day. 'I ended up getting dressed. Being World Champion was more important than anything. I couldn't live with myself giving it away. It was terribly dangerous. There was no way I should have been racing. And I knew it. Before the race, I said to Sinclair: I can't pass anybody, so I'm gonna try to lead this race on the first lap. Then when somebody comes by I'll just try and stay with them.

'I started in second gear, to save one shift before the first corner. I knew I couldn't win, but I was trying to make something happen. And I got the lead from the second row, so maybe I did force the incident.'

British GP, Donington Park, 1 August – Two races to go

'I got into first like I planned, so I didn't even know what happened behind me. Past the pits I saw my sign out, saying SCHWANTZ OUT. I couldn't believe it until I saw it again next time round. And I was still leading. I thought: this is great. I put that thing on cruise control and rode two seconds off qualifying pace.'

Cadalora dutifully followed behind, for 28 of the 30 laps, dogging his team-mate's rear wheel, baffled as to why he didn't go faster. Then the temptation to take his first 500-class GP win became irresistible. 'He could see I was going slow, and I just thought, if he was going to pass me, he would have passed me by now. We had

*something like 10 seconds on the next guys, Mackenzie and Fogarty. I
just assumed Luca was going to let me win. But he was in a hard
position, and nobody told him what to do. Being the way he is, he
won the race. I was mad, but I couldn't blame him. Anyways, I'd
never had any help before from my team-mates.'*

Now things had changed. Without knowing how badly
Schwantz was injured, Rainey again had the chance to turn
everything upside down. There were four rounds remaining, and
he was suddenly only three points behind Kevin. And three of the
upcoming tracks – Brno, Misano and Laguna Seca – had the mark
of Rainey stamped on them very clearly. 'The championship had
turned in my favour. I knew at Czecho Schwantz would struggle.
He'd been riding brilliantly all year. I'd been riding good but the
bike had been terrible. But at Brno the Yamaha was easy to ride
fast. I had acupuncture for my hand and my back. We had the
spring-centre deal right, and the bike just clicked. I was on pole.

'I could see that Schwantz was feeling the pressure. On Sunday
morning I followed him. He didn't know I was behind him, so I
knew where he was having trouble, and that was where I was going
to get him. The TV cameras were on us. And I stuffed the crap out
of him. After the end of the session, he came by me so close he
almost hit me. And I thought yeah. I've got him where I want him.'

Czech Republic GP, Brno, 22 August – One race to go
*This was one of the easiest races of my career. The easiest race I ever
won. And the last race I ever won. I was pulling away at about a
second a lap, but I wasn't concentrating on the race. I was thinking
about Shae, about Rex. Thinking: do you really enjoy racing? Because
I wasn't having any fun. Afterwards, I'd won the race, taken over the
championship lead by 11 points, and it was probably the most upset
and unhappy I'd been all year. It was different from the anticlimax
of winning the championship, because this was too easy. I like it to be
difficult, I guess.*

Shae and Rex went home after that. Wayne was to follow soon
after. There was just the Italian GP to go, then one week later the
US GP, backed this year by Kenny Roberts (an expensive attempt

at playing impresario and US racing benefactor), and featuring Wayne heavily in the pre-event advertising. It was at Laguna Seca, just a couple of miles from their new house: they expected a houseful for the weekend.

Wayne always had a cocky way of walking. A strut, almost – although lacking pomposity – certainly a business-like quick stride. Back very straight, shoulders emphasised by the protective padding in his leathers, his red-white-and-black helmet instantly recognisable, he walked out to his Yamaha, in second position on the starting grid for the Italian GP. Luca was on pole by less than a tenth, but Wayne wasn't even watching him. Only Kevin. 'I was fit now from the Donington crash, ready to race, with an 11-point lead, going to my favourite race-track. The three lefts onto the back straight were still by far my favourite corners. This year I was going through the last one in sixth gear, where I'd only ever used fifth before.'

Talking about this final race is clearly difficult. His telling of it wanders as he puts off journey's end, as if it could be undone. He recalls the visitors – skier Alberto Tomba was Luca's guest; all Marlboro's top brass were there too. He recalls listening to loud music to get himself going. Madonna, Jon Anderson, maybe some Van Halen. He recalls trading times in wet morning warm-up with Schwantz. 'We were half-a-lap apart, but every time I'd see the pit board with his time, my own on-board timer would click my time, and it'd be faster.

'Somehow I was over-amping myself for this race. I knew I could win the championship here. Not finally, mathematically, but if I beat Kevin it would be the last nail in the coffin. I didn't know how bad his wrist was, but I'd seen him race hurt when it should have slowed him down, and it didn't. Howard Gregory, my mechanic, was always the last guy to push me off. He wished me luck as usual, and I said: Yeah, it's going to be a long race. Then I thought, I've never ever said that before. Why did I say that?'

Italian GP, Misano, 5 September – Last Race
'At the start I was following Luca for two laps, then I passed him on the fast lefts. Schwantz was 1.5-seconds behind. On lap seven, I upped the pace a little. Luca was with me, but the only guy on my board was Schwantz, and I was taking like two tenths from him every lap.

'I was riding so hard. What had been so easy for me in Czecho was the complete opposite. I was out of breath, like my tongue was dragging. It was way harder than I wanted to ride. But I was riding at that edge to keep pulling away from Schwantz. I was starting gradually to draw away from Luca. It was a 30-lap race, and I was a third of the way into it, and I was exhausted already.

'That lap, when I went into the first turn,' (a right-hander) 'I got in a little bit too hot. So when I flicked it, I had more lean angle than I wanted. I really had to lay it off in there hard to keep it on the right line. When I went to accelerate my lean angle was still too great. As I cracked the throttle, it stepped out real quick. and then came back. So it didn't highside me. It threw me off on the inside.

'The first thought was: F***! I've lost the World Championship. Right when I was going down.

'Then I'm on the ground, and sliding. Then all of a sudden I start flipping. And I thought: wow, I am going fast. It's a third-gear corner, so I was probably going about 130 mph. I was thinking: I hope I don't hit nothing here.

'When you're flipping you don't know which way is up and which way is down. I can remember hitting the ground, and not knowing if anything was hitting me. The ground or the bike or the guardrail feels the same.

'It seemed like I was flipping for quite a while. I was thinking, please – I gotta be coming to a stop here any time.

'Then right before I stopped I felt this huge pop in my back. And I had no idea what it was from.'

In those first few seconds, Wayne's life was changed in oh so many ways.

'I laid there in the sandtrap. The pain I was feeling was . . . unbelievable. I'd never felt pain like that. It felt like there was a hole in the middle of my chest.

'My first thought was, get up. Because I'd always gotten up before. I thought if I could get up, it didn't matter how bad the pain was, I would live.

'But I couldn't get up. I was moving my hands, trying to sit. I could see my hands were moving.

'Nobody had gotten to me yet. I thought then, something's not

226

right here. I felt my legs, but I couldn't feel anything. And I thought, OK. I've hurt myself bad this time.

'I was thinking, don't these people know I'm hurt? Another fear I had was somebody crashing into the sandtrap and hitting me.

'At that stage, my left eye went completely black. And then my right eye, I could see my vision going away. So then I thought I was dying. Because the pain was still way too much.

'I remember a real peace came over me. A real easy feeling. Everything was real calm.

'I was never a religious man before, though I did believe in God, and I knew that to go to heaven you had to ask forgiveness of your sins. I knew all this stuff, but I'd never . . .

'I spoke out loud. I said: God, if I'm dying, I'm sorry for all the sins, and the bad things I have done. But I'm not ready to leave yet. I want to see Shae and I want to see Rex.

'As soon as I did that, all of a sudden my eyesight came back.

'I felt as if God told me: OK Wayne. Your life's going to be very difficult. But you're going to have to work.

'I thought what He said was I've got to work for Him. I've got to do something that will bring people closer to God.

'I wasn't worried any more about anything to do with racing. It was completely gone from my mind.'

A far greater battle had already begun.

CHAPTER 15

GOING
HOME BROKEN

'I'd always known that one day I would wake up, and everybody would be talking about who was racing that day, and I wouldn't be one of them. I didn't know how I'd be able to deal with that. Now it was done.'
Wayne Rainey, reflecting on life after the crash

Wayne's fight to survive consumed the first 24 hours after the crash. His condition was critical: tubes drained blood and fluid from each lung, other internal injuries contributed. 'I knew it was up to me. I could live or I could die. Living was harder.' He was determined to hang on though, at least until Shae arrived, on Monday afternoon. 'When I saw her, and my mom and dad, then everything got easier.'

Wayne spent five nights at Cesena Hospital, each one a little better than the last as he gained strength. The days were desperate. Yet for the family there was also a sense of relief. Ila's view was simple: 'As long as he's alive, I'll take him any way I can get him.' For Sandy this clearcut end meant an end also to waiting for those early-morning phone calls. No more dread, now this dreadful thing had happened.

Wayne felt the same. 'It was tough at that time, but I was pretty happy it was all over. I didn't have to race no more. To put myself through all that. I'd always known that one day I would wake up, and everybody would be talking about who was racing that day, and I wouldn't be one of them. I didn't know how I'd be able to deal with that. Now it was done.'

The cards, calls and faxes flowed in from all over the world. Shae started a collection that would grow and grow. This was a small distraction.

Wayne wanted to get home, just as soon as possible. There was no more doubt now as to the extent of the injury. The sixth

228

thoracic vertebra – about in the middle of the chest – had snapped, and the spine was displaced by almost an inch at that point. The broken bones could be repaired, the severed spinal cord could not. For the meantime, Wayne had to lie still on his back, while he recovered from his other injuries. The risk of death would remain acute until after orthopaedic surgery had realigned his spine. Until then, too heavy a jolt could displace everything again.

The journey home was, of course, awful. They put him in an inflatable body cast, then found it could barely fit into Marlboro's light aircraft, commissioned for the first leg of the journey. They took a scheduled flight to LA from Geneva. Wayne's stretcher was curtained off, and he had a male nurse with him. 'His job was to see that I got to America pain-free. He had me so tanked up. He sat at my feet and watched my face, and if I had a little pain he would just give me more morphine. I can see how people can get addicted to it: it just took me away from everything. Later, after the operation, I started getting these headaches, and they told me it was withdrawal symptoms.'

The escort party included Shae, Sandy and Ila, Shae's nephew Scott Copeland, team physio Dean Miller, and IRTA neurosurgeon Peter Richards. Shae: 'We had to take turns to be with you. It was so cold in there.' And all the way Wayne sucked on the oxygen, finishing all three cylinders supplied. It was a relief to arrive in LA, and make the final transfer to the Centinella Hospital.

Medically, his condition needed to stabilise before surgery could take place. He waited for three more days. Kenny was with him, and Rodney and Renee as well, someone always there. It was now that the calls started to come in. 'I'm sure I'd talked to Bubba and other people, but Jeff Ward the motocrosser is the first I remember. Ayrton Senna sent a fax, and Mario Andretti. I started to realise that the world outside was affected. It wasn't just me going through this thing. It was everybody.'

The shock and grief in racing was palpable. Numbed, the circus went through the motions, with the chief lion-tamer conspicuous by his absence. The calendar took the bikes, riders, mechanics and camp followers directly from Misano to the West Coast, to Laguna Seca, just down the road from Wayne's home. (Kenny was personally promoting this event, in a vain and expensive attempt to save the US riders' home GP.)

Kenny's reactions were those of everybody, to the power of ten. He was devastated. Had been ever since stepping into the trackside hospital on Sunday afternoon. 'I knew at that point it was more serious than Wayne knew it was serious, and though I didn't want to believe it, Wayne saw it in my face.' Wayne had wanted Kenny to go with him in the helicopter ambulance from the track, but there wasn't the room. He drove up by car, with GP medic Dr Claudio Costa, for years now the racer's first and sometimes last resort in the case of injury. 'Costa was great. He never got emotional. He said to me right away: You have to be strong for Wayne now. Wayne has another world ahead of him. Another career, that he's going to be good at.

'I just couldn't gather my thoughts quick enough. Wayne was like my son. I just couldn't piece it together – how did all this happen? I knew Shae needed to know, but in some kind of strange way she already did. She was very prepared for this moment. I think she was proceeding along a path she'd already considered. Being a sensible and very level-headed person, she'd had to think about that stuff. I kept going through in my mind how I could have prevented it. I knew Wayne wanted to win that race too much, but I didn't know how to stop that.'

Kenny had to leave on Tuesday. He had plenty to do before the US GP, much of which involved making public appearances. He looked like a ghost, his skin pale and pulled tight with the effort of fighting back the tears. 'It got worse as the days went on. I couldn't control my emotions. It's like a glass of water. Your emotions fill up then start to overflow, then when the water goes out you're OK again. And I just went through this stuff until the water didn't fill up so fast or so often. At first I couldn't go more than an hour without crying, unless I was with Wayne. I was better when I was with him.' He was by no means the only person to find himself drawing strength from the victim.

Wayne arrived back in the USA the day official practice began. Kenny flew down to LA to be with him, and then back the next morning. Sandy was with him. And he was a tower of strength, receiving messages of sympathy from still-shocked paddock people, and dispensing down-home optimism. 'I had to be like that,' he said later. 'It was what Wayne wanted. He didn't want to take nobody down with him.'

Then came the fax. Written in Wayne's handwriting, addressed to Chuck Aksland at Team Roberts, it read: 'Just because I'm not there doesn't mean you can quit working. Where are today's times?' It was a forgery. In fact, Shae had written it to his dictation, imitating Wayne's distinctive block-capitals style. 'He knew when practice was done, and if that fax machine in the nurses' office wasn't going he wanted to know why,' she recalls. Why on earth, when it couldn't possibly affect him one way or the other? 'Because – that was me. My life. Racing. I had nothing else to think about. I just wanted to know what was going on. It was the easiest thing for me to think about.' There was more to it. He understood how it would make his team feel, and everyone else in the racing paddock (photocopies were eagerly distributed). This was his way of relieving the shock.

He also made sure to speak with his principal former rivals. 'Mick called me. I never did have any problem speaking with him anyway. Kevin called. I said to him: You deserve it. And hey, I made the mistake. It doesn't take anything away from what you did to win your championship. I also told people: I always knew this could happen. I'm just glad it didn't happen on the way to or from the racetrack. If it was going to happen, there wasn't any better way.'

He kept up the front in public from then onwards. It has never slipped. Now, looking back, he admits it was just an act. 'When I look back at some interviews I gave after the operation, I think: Hmmm, you sounded pretty good.'

The surgery took about six hours, and was performed by Dr Robert G. Watkins, a specialist in this type of injury (and later the author of a book on the subject, using Wayne as a case history). He observed what the other doctors had already seen: 'That there was bone touching bone, where the spinal cord should be. It was completely cut, though the dural sac surrounding the column was intact, which saved some other complications.' Inasmuch as these injuries are classifiable, it conformed to a particular model – of a miner on his hands and knees, struck from above by a falling coal face. Watkins's first view was that it had been caused by a twisting jack-knife movement; but he accepts also the possibility of Wayne's later conclusion, after examining his leathers, that he had been hit by the bike.

The surgery was simple in principle, delicate in execution. The aim was to realign the spine, then hold it in that position until the bones fused together. This is done by fitting hooks to the two vertebrae above and below, which are then clamped to a pair of rods either side of the spine. A bone graft (from the pelvis) encourages the spine to fuse in that area, and then the rods can be removed. In Wayne's case, this was done at the end of 1996, more than three years later, and to his considerable relief.

Part Two of Rainey's life began after that – and getting used to his new situation was to be as vast a challenge as any he had imposed on himself in the past. Even absorbing the full implications was not easy, and took several years.

When your spinal cord is cut in this way, you lose all muscular control from the point of the injury downwards. In Wayne's case, this is from about the level of the nipples. The list of what you can do is short. You have to use the muscles above there for everything. In addition to the usual manipulative skills, your arms and shoulders have to take on the duties of moving your body around. The strain is considerable.

The list of what you cannot do is formidable. You cannot stand or walk. You can't even sit upright, without at first acquiring the trick of balancing. Wayne found it was in banalities that it hurt the most at first. 'You can't reach up to grab something from the top of a cupboard. I couldn't pick things up from the floor. I couldn't pick up my kid when he was crying.' And when you get yourself a cup of coffee, balance it in your lap, and roll back across the room, you're liable to find upon arrival that it has spilt and scalded you. All this you must learn. You can't even lie down, without taking special precautions. Although there are no feelings, the legs are still prone to cramps. Pressure sores are a serious threat; these can develop within two hours.

Then there are the bodily functions. These continue of their own accord, stealthily. And they have the capacity not only to take you by surprise on a daily basis, sometimes in the most humiliating of ways, but also to lay long-term health traps.

It took Wayne more than two years just to avoid wetting himself repeatedly. The bladder operates normally, filling up at a steady rate from the kidneys. Mainly because of Wayne's posture, the capacity is reduced by about half, to 250cc. When full, the kidneys send a signal to the brain via the spinal cord. In the normal course of events, you go to the lavatory. But when the cord is cut, the message bounces straight back downwards and the flood gates open unbidden. And there you are, covered with pee again.

One way of dealing with it is to wear a sort of a condom fitted with a tube, running to a bag worn on the lower leg. This is especially useful on long flights, for example, or when you sleep. Trouble is, it keeps falling off; or the bag gets a knock, or overflows. The other way is to monitor your fluid intake, and anticipate the event.

What, you might wonder, about solid wastes? Bowel movements? Or, as Wayne bitterly puts it, 'shit accidents'. What indeed. The bowels give trouble less frequently, but even more treacherously. Let's get this over with. The trick is to establish a daily routine. As every well brought up Victorian child knew, strictly timed daily visits to the lavatory train the bowels; your body sooner or later falls in with this arrangement. Paraplegics can exploit this tendency. Wayne's difficulty is that he works in racing. He flies constantly around the world, from one time zone to another: Malaysia, for example, entails a 16-hour displacement, and he goes there two or three times each year. The stress of grand prix travel is hard on an able-bodied person; it is much more than doubly difficult if you are paralysed. But his techniques have improved, and at the end of 1996 he was happy to say: 'I haven't had a shit accident for months.'

There is more. In spite of being disconnected from the conscious mind, the reproductive system continues on its merry way, producing hormones at the usual rate for a man in his thirties. The thoughts don't go away; simply the capacity to do something about them. This involved another area of highly personal difficulties for Wayne; again by the end of 1996 he had found some sort of improved resolution.

All this was to come in the bleak time after the operation, the gathering of the nightmare. 'Other than that I wasn't going to walk again, I had no idea. After a couple of days I started asking questions: am I going to get any feeling back? Will I be able to have kids? The doctors told me: no, you'll never be able to do any of that stuff again. That's not exactly true, but I was really devastated then. It was just getting worse all the time. I was finding out it was going to be a lot tougher than I thought. If I'd just lost the use of my legs, this would be an easy injury.'

They put Wayne in a special $35,000 bed that moved his position constantly to avoid pressure sores. Even so, he developed a pair on his heels. One time, they had to put the bed in the elevator, and the wheels got jammed in the gap at the doors on the way in. 'I was stuck there for 45 minutes. The bed was so heavy that they had to get jacks to lift it up. I was pretty scared, wondering what would happen if the elevator decided to go up or down. It was real claustrophobic.'

Another treatment involved a tilt-bed, that would move him upright, good for the inner organs and general condition (he has a standing-frame at home, and tries to use it daily). 'The first time, they hadn't got me upright when I started to pass out. Turned out they'd forgotten to drain my bladder. The doctors were real mad at the nurses: that could have caused serious kidney damage.'

Wayne had company most of the time. Sandy, Ila, Rodney or Renee, Shae, Bubba, Kenny. He was in the Centinella Hospital on his back for six weeks, then – rather earlier than the doctors would have preferred – he talked them into releasing him for rehabilitation. Now he went to the Long Beach Memorial Hospital, where he was scheduled to stay for 12 weeks. He left after five.

Dean Miller was in constant touch and, from his experiences with the leg injury, could have told the doctors what to expect: 'incredible, incredible, incredible determination.' Dr Watkins was astonished. 'With this sort of injury, you have to learn to do everything: how to roll over, sit up . . . You lie on a mat like a baby, helpless, with a physiotherapist teaching you the techniques. We try and get patients to do three sessions daily, though most can't manage that. Wayne always wanted four. All the way he was just pushing and pushing. He didn't want a training wheelchair; he wanted the Grand Prix model right away.'

The first time on wheels was not so propitious. 'Kenny and Junior were with me when I got in a wheelchair for the first time. And I started bawling, and they were crying. I was thinking: this is my life now.' Even the half-hour ambulance journey to Long Beach saw a poignant moment. From the window Wayne spotted a freeway billboard for the US GP. It was a picture of him, racing.

After the complete but impersonal care in hospital, with the rigid 6am starts, the new hospital improved the quality of life right away. 'I got there on Sunday, and there was nobody there except my nurse, Debbie. She was young, enthusiastic, very good-looking. I felt like she was someone who was willing to make my life good. I had no idea if my life was ever going to be good again. The first thing she did was show me a dinner menu – you could choose different things. I thought this was pretty cool.

'I said: what I'd really like is a shower. For six weeks they'd washed my hair with dry shampoo. I felt like I had two or three inches of it caked in my hair, and my head itched so bad. So she takes me out of bed, whips me straight in the shower chair, and wheels me in to the shower and – it was great. My first shower in six weeks. The best shower I'd ever had in my life.'

Wayne was there with 10 other patients. Their injuries helped to put some perspective on his own. 'One Mexican guy had been swimming in the ocean. He dived and hit a sandbar, and was paralysed from the neck down. Nothing. Another guy was riding a bicycle in Long Beach. He swerved to avoid a trash truck, and hit a tree. He had minimal use of his hands. He was a poet – a really funny guy. There was a roadie from a carnival. He'd been working on the Ferris wheel when the wind took him and he fell 80 feet. He was paralysed at a lower level. And there were gang members. One of the biggest causes of spinal injury in the US now is bullet wounds. They'd be checked in under John Doe names, because they didn't want any assassinations there.

'There was a psychologist there, and they always tried to get me to go to these group meetings. The other guys swore by it, because they could talk about their experiences. I said: it's my body that's screwed up, not my brain. There was a young guy who'd lost his leg in a motorcycle accident. He came to see me, looking for support, but I was the wrong guy to talk to. I told him: you're going to get an artificial leg and walk out of here. You don't have a problem. You still have control over your bowels and your bladder. I didn't see him again after that.

'They liked me at Long Beach because I was really gung-ho.' Wayne was soon treating the wheelchair in the same way as every other vehicle: going full tilt, and laughing when it all went wrong. Like the time he fell forward in the chair while speeding along. Unable to sit up again, he crashed head first into some metal filing cabinets. 'It was such a heavy crash that the nurses thought a truck had run into the building or something. It was just me, out of control.' The hospital had a wheelchair course, and a time record for it. A red rag to a bull. 'By the time I left, I'd set a new record.'

Upbeat Wayne was an inspiration. Downbeat Wayne he kept to himself as much as possible. And he was living a nightmare. 'Getting worse all the time' hadn't stopped yet, by a long chalk; there was a long way to go with adjustment to his new life. As he discovered with a jolt on his first 'home leave' outing, to Shae's parents' house in Lakewood, for the trick-or-treating on Hallowe'en Night, 31 October, just over six weeks after the crash. Wayne was dressed in a Kydex jacket, a sort of straitjacket/body cast which held his torso stiff – he had to wear that every time he got out of bed.

'My hair was really long, I was pale and skinny. I looked bad.' Sitting there, 'all of a sudden it feels like there's this chrome bowling ball, a little bit smaller than a real bowling ball, and it's trying to get pushed out of my butt. It feels like chrome – hard and shiny. But I've got no sensation down there, so what is this?' It was a first encounter with phantom pain; the first of many. 'I was lifting myself off the chair, because it felt as though I was being turned inside out. Then my heart started racing. I was white and sweating. I said: Shae, I've got to get back to hospital. Something's not right.' It was dysreflexia, caused by impacted constipation.

The phantom pains got worse. 'I started feeling pins and needles all over my legs. Then my feet felt like they weighed 3,000lbs. They were on fire, and someone was hanging off them.' Morphine was no relief; the reasons were complex. Even a healthy nervous system can produce referred pain, where the wrong part of the body hurts. When there is radical damage, the effects are unpredictable.

'This was a new problem for me. I still have it. From my injury up, everything's normal. Downwards, my body was just going nuts. I didn't understand it; I couldn't control it. I was totally, totally miserable. I thought there's no way I can live like this. If it has to be like this every day I'd much rather be dead. It was just so uncomfortable. That's when they started giving me medication to control that part.'

The drug regime brought only partial control. Two years later Wayne still had the bowling ball, the pins-and-needles, and the heat; while sometimes he'd wake up and find his legs were in spasm. 'You get them straight, and they vibrate and kick. It's as though your body's being just tore up, and I can't do nothing about it.' Another 12 months on they had subsided a little more. The medication had its own difficulties. 'I take Baclofen, which controls the spasms and the chromer. It relaxes your whole body. It even relaxes your mind. I take it daily, because without it I am just miserable.

'But it also relaxes your bladder, so for a long time I had to wear the leg bag all the time. The way to deal with that is with another drug, Ditropan. That controls the bladder, but it also really dries you out. My hands are always cracked. The two drugs are constantly cutting in on each other. It made me real tired, and I didn't think too clear. I'm completely used to it now, but at first my head was so heavy I couldn't get out of bed.'

By far the biggest hurdle was learning to move around with more than half his body a cumbersome deadweight. 'Transfers', in the parlance of the afflicted – whether it be from bed to wheelchair, from 'chair to lavatory or shower stool, or (the hardest of all) back up into the wheelchair if you should fall out of it. You have to climb up the side of the chair, and it requires not only physical strength but also mastery of technique. 'You have to kind of flick your legs, and use your balance,' explains Wayne. All this, of course, has to come one stage at a time, starting off from being unable to roll over while lying down.

'I looked on everything as a challenge. In the hospital they said there's no way you can get in the chair from the ground by yourself, but I was determined to do it. But it's still a real struggle if I fall. I've only done it twice with no help.'

It is still hard to think about this man who only weeks before had toyed with the awesomely difficult task of riding a 500cc grand prix bike to its limits now reduced to expending similar efforts on just moving a couple of feet. At least the task was absorbing. 'A lot of times I'd be trying to drag myself back into the chair, and I'd look down and my pants would be down around my ankles, and my butt'd be hanging out. Everyone would be staring at me, and I'd wonder why. But they thought I was great because I was really trying. A lot of guys are so devastated they don't even think of getting better. I was fortunate because I'd done all this to myself. I knew it was either this or death; and I'd always known this could happen.'

Not surprisingly, Wayne soon grew impatient with the measured pace of rehabilitation. 'After three weeks I already wanted to get out.' At first it was weekending, at a hotel with Shae. 'Then I was going out for a few nights during the week. I still had to go back every day; Debbie had to show up at the hotel at 5am every day to clear my bowels. I still had the Kydex jacket on, so I couldn't bend over.' In among this were constant mood swings. Hard work engendered optimism, a shit accident would plunge him back into despair.

He tried to cut a deal with his medical insurance: that instead of them paying $1,500 a day, he could check into a hotel for $30 a night and just go in as an outpatient. 'They said no way. You leave that hospital, and we've done with you. They'd rather pay the $1,500, but they knew I wanted to leave so bad they were putting pressure on me. So finally I was the one who said – damn it. I'm going home. I checked out of there after five weeks: I should have been there three months.

'At that stage I could not transfer, I had no control of my bladder or bowels, and all of a sudden I go home to Monterey. All the doctors, the nurses, the rehab people, everybody else tried to talk me out of it, but I just wanted out.'

Scott Copeland came with them as they moved the whole family up north again, to help Wayne with all the transfers. 'I had Shae doing my bowel programme, but I wasn't happy with that. It wasn't her problem, so after three days I said no, I'll do it myself. There were no elevators or ramps in the house, which made it a big struggle moving around. I was sleeping down in the back room, because I couldn't get up to our bedroom.

'On the first night home, I had to get out of bed, and I didn't want any help. I fell out of bed so hard I bent one of the rods in my

238

back and broke my foot. So I was in a lot of pain again, at home. I began to wonder then whether I'd made a really big mistake.'

It was support from outside that made a big difference. All the cards and visits and phone calls even in hospital. 'I was taking them all, and seeing everybody because it took my mind off my problems.

'I got hooked up with some good guys in chairs. Specially Jim Knaub, who won the Boston paraplegics marathon five times. Here's a guy who was 18, going to the Olympics with the US pole-vaulting team, sitting on his motorcycle at a red light. He saw this accident happening, and he was thinking how he would tell the guys about it when the car swerved and ran over him. He'd been in a chair for 17 years. I had a lot of questions for him. He was probably the one who helped me most.'

It was Knaub who stopped Wayne from installing chair lifts throughout his multi-level house. 'He told me: you may want that now, but in a year or so you won't. So I held off a couple of months, then I had ramps put in. Now I can get to the bedroom quicker than Shae can.'

Far away in Spain, Wayne won the Athlete of the Year award by a landslide, defeating basketball star Michael Jordan, cyclist Miguel Induran and the usual gang of footballers. In the USA, coverage outside the specialist press was limited to a carelessly misinformed caption to a crash picture in the *National Enquirer*, four months after the event. 'This 24-year-old World Champion sadly will never race again.'

Wayne had also kept his spirits up by setting goals of such vaulting ambition that in retrospect they seem laughable. They evoked very different emotions at the time. 'When I was lying in hospital, I was determined to put my leathers back on and ride the 500 at the first race of 1994. It was the biggest challenge I could imagine, and I was thinking about all these ways I could do it without using my legs. I was going to have to have someone to hold me up to start, then take off and do a victory lap for the fans. Then I'd come back in and that would be it.' He did actually ride a bike at home, with Scott on pillion to hold him in place. They ran for about a mile on the roads round his house, but never got out of first gear, and the experience was so fraught that he has not repeated it. 'As the time came closer, I decided I'd already done everything I wanted to do on bikes.' But during that year he started thinking about going for the motorcycle Land Speed Record, which stood at a temptingly low figure of less than 400mph. Hell, why just beat that? Why not go for the sound barrier? He researched the project enough to discover that to go that fast he'd need rocket power – a single driving wheel would run out of traction long before he got there. Again, with some relief he shelved the notion.

Instead, encouraged by Formula 1 team owner Frank Williams, himself almost completely paralysed after a road accident, he decided to throw himself back into work. 'At first I missed the thought of not racing most of all. Then I started missing having physical control of my body. Then the simple things, like reaching up and grabbing things. Then I started thinking about what to do with the rest of my life. I didn't need the money, but I needed something to get me going, and racing seemed to be it. Kenny had put together a 250 team with Marlboro, with his son Kenny Junior as the rider, as something I could look at. I didn't know if that was what I wanted to do. They called it Team Rainey, but it was really Kenny's team.'

The doctors didn't approve, but in this respect at least Wayne was already off on his own. Thus when the 1994 Grand Prix season opened in Australia on 27 March, almost six months after his crash, Wayne Rainey was back in the paddock.

It would be nice to say the ordeal was over. In many ways, it was just beginning, and the darkest days were yet to come. For throughout this period the family had been living through another nightmare. Shae's mother Shirley was dying of lung cancer. Her last ordeal was frightful. Her condition had been deteriorating over 18 months or more. The crisis coincided with Wayne's own catastrophe. As he lay in hospital in Cesena, she was starting a course of high-dosage chemo-therapy. When Shae came back from Italy, after just a few days away, her mother was bald. Shirley finally lost her battle for life while Wayne was in Australia in his wheelchair. It was almost enough to crush the woman, wife and mother from whom everybody else was accustomed to drawing strength.

After he came back, Wayne saw a new perspective. 'Shae had been struggling much more than I knew. She'd lost me and her mother also. She was trying to be strong for two people. She managed for a while, then in 1995 she tanked it. She went real, real deep into a really bad depression. That's when I figured I'd better start getting better, because I could see she needed some help.'

Wayne's own resources had been heavily depleted. But something else had happened to him on that awful afternoon in Italy. Lying in the dirt, he'd spoken directly to God. That was what he believed. And he'd taken on an obligation, though he wasn't quite sure how this should be discharged. First he had to find the way. Together he and Shae read the Bible, and they found it of great comfort. It was a second personal encounter that really strengthened the faith. 'We were in Spain in the middle of the '94 season, and at about 2am I woke up and Shae was crying. She said: I want to know if my mom's OK. Because at the end she suffered unbelievable pain, and that is what Shae remembers most. So I said: let's pray about it. And I said: God, can you do something right now to let us know that Shae's mom is OK? As soon as I said that, our bedroom window blew open and a breeze came through. It was so weird. To me, that was proof that she was all right.'

As time passed by, they started to attend the Calvary Chapel, where ceremonies of simple singing, shared experiences and inspirational addresses by a pastor of notable eloquence encompass a community of love and faith and comfort. With Shae by his side and Rex downstairs at the Sunday school, this natural gentleman, this former master of one of the world's most difficult sporting disciplines, this broken victim of his own courage and determination and self-reliance – they fitted right in. And it is clear to see also, over the years of sometimes bitter hardship since the accident, how serenity and grace have come to both of them as a reward for their faith.

CHAPTER 16

CHAIR-BORNE
WARRIOR

'I thought I could pass on my race thinking to other riders.
But I found out you can't explain it. Not in a few months, anyway.
And unless the rider's willing to go out and be the World Champion,
it's not going to happen.' Wayne Rainey, 1996

The loss of Wayne Rainey as a rider hit two teams very hard over the next three years. One was Kenny Roberts's empire, which at a stroke went from the glorious 'Evil' days to become an overstaffed and aimless giant, achieving success only haphazardly. The other was the new Team Rainey. It was one thing for Wayne to bring with him the determination that had made his own career, but quite another to find a rider of the same calibre, capable of learning from Wayne's own experience and knowledge.

At his old squad, team morale (and Kenny's own) was very seriously damaged for well over a year, and the deterioration in results played a big part in events that followed. By 1997, Kenny Roberts and Yamaha had split after 25 years, with Kenny reviving his interest in racing by taking a new role, as a manufacturer in his own right.

The Yamaha factory now relied on a new team owner: Wayne Rainey. But racing's biggest sponsor, Marlboro, went along with Roberts.

Two major episodes were crucial.

The first was the creation of the Team Marlboro Rainey 250 squad by Kenny for 1994. This was a magnanimous act – though the benefits did not flow only one way. But it quickly led to friction, with Wayne's desire to exercise authority throwing the two into conflict.

The other was the Michael Doohan affair. This complex tale rewrote the rules of engagement between Kenny and Wayne, and

242

showed the power of Marlboro, playing Devil's advocate in a drama that ran behind the scenes for most of 1995. As it transpired, it all came to nothing. The Dream Team that Wayne had all but finalised turned out to be just that: a dream. However the ramifications were long-lasting. In the end, while Wayne may have ended up with Yamaha for 1997, it was Kenny who retained the coveted Marlboro millions.

It all started, Wayne now believes, rather too precipitately, when he returned headlong to Australia for the first GP of 1994. 'Six months after the accident, I wasn't really thinking clearly, with the drastic changes I was going through. I just didn't know if it was right to go, or stay at home. Shae's mom was real sick, but there was a big push from people around me to go to the first race. I was listening to everybody's advice, and nobody said to stay home. Except the doctors. The promoter paid me, the TV people wanted me to do some commentary. I'd been thinking about racing and what I wanted to do about it, so this was a way for me to try and find out how I really felt. Probably it was too soon to make a public appearance – I looked terrible.'

Wayne was still struggling to adapt to the difficult and time-consuming disciplines imposed by his paralysis. Nonetheless he embarked on the 14-hour flight to Australia with Scott Copeland to help out ('he literally had to carry me to the bathroom'). He arrived at the Eastern Creek circuit two days before practice, and was immediately overcome with tears. He had the same problem on race day, watching from the commentary box as the 500 race got under way. For the first third of the race, his comments came terse and seldom as he fought to control himself. 'It was an emotional time for me.'

Hardly less so for the world of racing. Thin and weak, his complexion chalky and his eyes haunted, Wayne looked like the ghost he had come to lay.

He remembered how, when able-bodied, if he saw anybody in a wheelchair at the racetrack he would walk around them, closing his mind to the spectre of his own fragility. Now cast in the opposite role he observed how a few people treated him the same way. One was Kevin Schwantz. 'I didn't realise until later how my injury had screwed him up.'

He did make one victory lap on race day, to wave to the fans; but instead of the 500cc GP bike he had earlier hoped to find a way to ride, it was in the back seat of a garish pink Cadillac convertible, Elvis Presley style. His other public appearance was at a Press conference to announce his new team.

In fact, Team Rainey belonged to Kenny, lock, stock and barrel. He'd put it together to give his elder son Kenny Junior a berth in the GPs, to short-cut the tedious business of working his way up through the ranks toward his eventual 2000 World Championship. At the same time, Kenny Senior had in mind that if Wayne wanted it, here also was a job for him. Wayne did want it, but the misunderstandings started right away. Rainey believes his presence was a pre-condition of Marlboro backing, and certainly an important part of the package; Kenny says the team would have happened anyway.

Circumstances took the pressure off. Junior was already out injured – he'd broken his arm in pre-season testing. This injury would prove slow to heal, delaying the likeable youngster's debut until the 11th out of 14 rounds, at Brno in Czech Republic. It took the heat off the team as they missed the first race altogether, then soldiered through the early part of the year with a series of non-finishes and other lowly performances from substitute riders Jimmy Filice and Yamaha's nominee Toshihiko Honma.

Neither was helped much by the motorcycle. Yamaha had won the 250 championship the year before, after a season of sustained brilliance by GP newcomer Tetsuya Harada. But when the Japanese rider (riding another works YZR V-twin for the French importers) crashed in practice for the first round of 1994, Yamaha lost interest in the 250s and threw their efforts and resources into the 500 class, where Doohan's Honda was already marching off to a clear overall victory.

Wayne was soon proceeding as he thought appropriate for a team boss. At the Japanese GP, the third round, a new star burst onto the scene. Long-haired teenager Norifumi Abe, riding a works Honda in the domestic championship, made his mark with an extraordinarily spirited ride, contesting the lead for most of the race with Schwantz and Doohan, before crashing nobly. While others were still laughing in admiration at this precocious talent,

Rainey was talking turkey. The negotiations over the next two months were conducted strictly in private. One problem was Abe's existing contract with Honda. Yamaha were reluctant to poach a fellow-factory's recruit.

'I was looking to the future. I wanted to go to the 500 class, and I thought the best way to find a sponsor would be to find my own rider. I thought Asia was the place I could find money. I tied Abe up on a three-year contract, on condition that he would have a 500 from 1995 onwards.' By mid-season, the news had leaked out. Honda had released the youngster, and Wayne wanted to get him going in international racing right away. What's more, with Junior still absent, he had a bike for him. Abe's planned foreign debut was for the Czech Republic GP, riding the Rainey Yamaha 250.

That's when the trouble started. For one thing, the bike was Kenny's, and earmarked for Junior, at last showing signs of recovery. 'Kenny just said: You can't do that. This isn't your team. And that bike's for Junior. So I went: Well, I thought you said it was my team.

'That was the first time we'd ever had any friction, and the first time Kenny was looking at me as a competitor.'

Events conspired to provide a solution. With Cadalora taking over Rainey's top position in Team Roberts, Daryl Beattie had moved over from Honda. Now the Australian was out after a grisly crash in practice for the French GP had removed all the toes from one foot. Wayne lent Abe to Kenny to make way for Junior at Brno, so that the Japanese rider could get some 500cc experience. The loan would become almost permanent.

Wayne's ambitions to join the 500 class were thwarted in 1995, but he did achieve independence as a team owner in his own right. 'Yamaha had offered me a bike for Abe. I had everything except a sponsor. Marlboro were already tied up with Kenny in the 500 class, but they told me there was the budget again for a 250 team, if I ran Harada. So I stayed another year in the 250 class, with Harada and Junior. And it was OK, because I built the foundation of my own team. I negotiated the budget. Tim (O'Sullivan, US-based Briton formerly in partnership with sponsor Bob MacLean) came on board to help me manage it and help me travel.'

The year was not particularly distinguished, although there were some moments to be savoured. Particularly when Wayne was hoisted onto the rostrum at Jerez after Harada's only race win. But the Yamaha rider wilted under the onslaught of Max Biaggi's Aprilia, to finish second overall. Junior had some fun, however, with a best of fourth, and a generally encouraging showing that suggested his short-cut to a works team had not been altogether inappropriate.

The significant events of the season took place off the race-track.

The first concerned Kevin Schwantz. The Texan's title defence in 1994 had been scuppered by wrist injury mid-season that required drastic surgery at the end of the year. He came back for 1995 physically weakened to fulfil the last year of his contract with Lucky Strike Suzuki. The mental toll was probably more significant, and it all crystallized after a strangely below-par performance in a wet third race of the season at Suzuka.

Kevin had avoided contact with Rainey throughout the previous year. Now the two talked for the first time, and it became clear why. Schwantz had been shattered by the consequences of the Misano crash to his long-term adversary. To continue racing he had to close his mind to it. This was not a state of affairs that could last.

They spoke in the pits at Suzuka, and Wayne could see the turmoil the Texan was suffering. Then they flew home together, and each poured out his heart to the other. From the sitting position, Wayne's advice had special impact. 'It was obvious Kevin was having a huge struggle with his commitment. He was obliged to race, but he didn't want to. He told me that ever since my crash it had been getting worse. It was shock at my injury, fear that he might get hurt, and also not caring so much about beating the new guys.' Wayne told him to stop and think again. To hold your head up in the 500cc class you need total commitment. Anything less than that is just – well, too risky.

Schwantz never raced again. 'Talking to Wayne crystallized everything in my own mind. Racing had been everything to me, but now I felt I was only doing it because other people wanted me to. Wayne said he'd felt the same way.'

A conversation with another ex-rival, Mick Doohan, also started off casual, then became very serious.

Rainey still wanted to go 500 racing, and was looking to 1996.

'I had Abe under contract, and that opened up some doors, but they weren't the right doors. Nobody wanted to come up with a 500 team.

'In Malaysia I'd started talking to Doohan – not going after him at that stage, just chatting about things I'd been going through at the end of my career. He was starting to have similar problems, the way the sponsors' guys would always be with you if you won, but if you got second they wouldn't. I felt I often worked harder losing than when I won. It really hacked me off, and he was feeling the same thing. Then in the Japanese GP he had a big near highsider, and lost first place. And it happened again. Nobody was there for him. That really established a good line of communication.

'I was thinking I needed a big-name guy. And maybe Mick really needed a change. So I put it to him: How'd you like to ride for my team? And he thought it was kinda cool.

'We talked back and forth during the year. I talked to Yamaha, and they gave me the OK after two months. And I ran it by Marlboro.'

Marlboro's first response was disbelief. Capturing the dominant 500 rider would be more than just a major coup. It was also a chance for them to regain the pre-eminent position they'd held when Wayne was riding. This seemed too good to be true. Even Mick's verbal assurance wasn't enough to convince them of his intentions. They wanted something in writing.

'We'd negotiated a price, but he wouldn't sign a letter of intent. Mick and I both felt that if Kenny knew there was something in writing, he would tell Honda, and Mick was afraid Honda might somehow sabotage his championship. They had other riders who they could push forward at his expense.

'Mick wanted a bit more money to sign the letter, then he did sign for one-year plus an option, and I faxed a copy to Marlboro.'

Now, with the deal apparently done, things got rocky. And the reason was Marlboro, who told Wayne that his dream team would be entirely at the expense of Kenny Roberts. 'We had all the money agreed upon, Marlboro had agreed upon everything. Then they told me: now Kenny doesn't have a deal. I said: that was never a part of the programme. You guys have a contract with Kenny. They said: yeah, but he doesn't have a rider. He has to have a top rider to fulfil that contract.

'Leo de Graffenried was Marlboro's front man at the tracks, reporting to Graham Bogle in Lausanne. Now, already knowing about the letter of intent at the British GP in late July, he was telling Kenny: you have to have Doohan to keep the contract. He didn't tell Kenny about my deal with Mick, and Kenny must have been desperate to keep his team. He ended up offering Mick an unbelievable amount – $2-million more than I had.

'Mick came straight to me. He liked the new numbers, and though he said he didn't want to ride for Kenny, he wanted me at least to get closer moneywise. To him, it showed how much Marlboro were prepared to pay. I said: Mick, obviously Kenny hasn't talked to Marlboro. There's no way they're going to agree to that. Marlboro doesn't know about this, and it isn't part of our deal. And when Marlboro did find out, they didn't want to pay the money.

'That's when it got cloudy.'

They all moved on to the next race, at Brno. With everyone still at loggerheads, Wayne threw up his hands and withdrew. 'If it hadn't been Kenny, I'd have gone for the jugular. Mick and I had a deal, and it had all been pretty straightforward until Kenny threw in that extra $2-million. I didn't like Marlboro telling me that Kenny would lose his team. I told them: something's not right here. You deal with Mick.'

It was only a matter of time before it all collapsed. Straightforward Mick found himself befuddled by the conflicting messages, while Honda had got wind of the affair and came up with an attractive counter-offer. He decided to stay.

'So everybody ended up with nothing. Marlboro floundered for another year. So did Yamaha. So did Kenny. And Mick won. He ended up with the better deal because he probably doubled the money he was getting from Honda.'

Was it as a consolation that Marlboro then found Wayne a rider on their own account? Or was it, as Wayne thinks, that they saw how his own ties with Yamaha were getting stronger, while Kenny's were badly on the skids? Either way, or even both, for 1996 Wayne retained Harada in the 250 class, but did at last move up to 500s. Abe stayed with Kenny's Marlboro-Yamaha team, while Wayne got the chirpy young Italian Loris Capirossi, who at 17 had been the youngest-ever World Champion when he took the first of two 125cc titles.

'Loris was a Marlboro guy, and he brought some Marlboro Italy money with him. As a team manager, I said yeah. It was good business, and Loris's attitude when he started was real good. He came and stayed at my house, trained hard, said all the right things.'

The good omens didn't last the season, as Wayne learned finally that his expectations of how he could pass on his racing knowledge were not to come to pass.

The tyre question played a crucial role. It was a decision by Marlboro and Yamaha, and this time it was away from Dunlops to Michelins. The reason was the French tyres' superiority in the 500 class. The exact opposite was true in the 250 class. Dunlops ruled, and the handful of top contracted Michelin runners struggled to achieve more than sporadic success. But Michelin promised to put greater efforts into the smaller class for 1996, and on balance, the decision made sense. In the details, however, it was to founder, because Harada's whole career had been on Dunlops, and one single incident on Michelins at only the third race of the year was enough to turn his mind and ruin his challenge.

Harada had always seemed perfect for Rainey. Their racing had much in common. The Japanese rider had always been with Yamaha, which meant that he was used to riding something slower than the rival Hondas and Aprilias. But the machine had sweet handling, and Harada rode the wheels off it round the corners, making good the deficit with his own resources. Very Rainey. His first year with Wayne had been promising, until his plucky fight against the dominant Max Biaggi was spoiled by a heavy practice crash at Assen.

The 1996 season started the same way. Harada was second to Biaggi in Malaysia. Then in Indonesia he out-thought and out-rode the Italian to claim a victory that was resounding in spite of the small time margin. It was vintage tactical racing by the 1993 World Champion, and he arrived in Japan with an important psychological advantage, at a track where he flies like a bird. He qualified on pole, but started poorly. Determined not to let Biaggi get away, and perhaps forgetting that the Michelins (among other quirks) need more time than the Dunlops to develop maximum grip, he gave it a touch too much throttle coming out of the last of Suzuka's Esses, slid and flipped in a punishing highsider that broke bones in his hand, and damaged his spirit for the rest of the season.

From then on, nothing was right. If it wasn't the tyres it was the lack of top speed, or poor throttle response. Valid complaints – but a rider who aspires to the Rainey mould does not succumb to problems like these. He is inspired by them to even greater efforts. So signally did this fail to happen in Harada's case that he did not even finish the season. His efforts tailed off, and by the 12th of 15 races he had split with Yamaha, and his place was taken for the last rounds by rising Spaniard Sete Gibernau.

Rainey believed he could pass on his own race thinking to other riders. 'But in '96 I found out you can't explain it. Not in a few months, anyway. And unless the rider's willing to go out and be the World Champion, it's not going to happen. Harada won it in 1993, and he rode like he was nobody, trying to make a name. In 1994 he was hurt, but when he came back he tried hard. In '95, with me, sure he rode well. But when the bike wasn't that good, he wasn't going to hang it out. Then in '96, we got Michelins. It wasn't his choice, but he should have tried to find a way to make it an advantage. Then he fell off at Suzuka, and he was never the same after that.'

Capirossi's season, conversely, ended on a high note with a maiden 500-class win in the final round in Australia, after new triple-champion Doohan and Honda team-mate Criville had knocked each other off in a last-lap fracas. But the road had not been smooth. On the one side, the language barrier had become increasingly difficult (this was not the first time Loris had tried to improve his English, with only limited success), while the youngster was not immune from the odd silly mistake. But the team also made one embarrassing glitch, leaving him short of fuel at Assen, costing him a safe fifth place.

Loris finished tenth overall. Wayne was prepared to continue with him for 1997, alongside his newly returned rider Abe. They'd even been discussing the winter programme in preparation for the season to come. Then, out of the blue, early in November, a fax arrived from Italy. Loris was repudiating the contract and switching back to the 250 class, to ride a factory Aprilia. Wayne was not heartbroken at losing a rider who had not quite come up to his expectations. But the timing was unfortunate. It arrived while Wayne was in hospital again, having the rods removed from his back.

Looking back now, Wayne contrasts Capirossi's approach with his own as a rider, and blames the young Italian's early 125 success for the lack of dedication he demonstrated when trying to progress to the big-boys' 500 class. 'He came up – like most people in the world – without a lot of money. He had to work for everything. Then suddenly at 17 he was World Champion. That gave him star status in Italy. He'd jumped about 20 steps. He won the title again the next year, so it all came quickly and easily for him. That's what hurt him on a 500. He didn't want to work at it too hard.'

This unexpected development complicated the position, at a late stage.

Wayne had a contract with Yamaha to provide bikes for two riders, as the official factory team. In proof of Wayne's original vision three years before, 'Norick' Abe had become Japan's (and Yamaha's) darling after a cavalier first 500-class victory at Suzuka in 1996. More importantly, he'd followed up by a campaign that gained strength in the closing stages. And the emotional youngster had never been short of willingness and spirit, in the two years he had taken to polish his craft.

Now Wayne needed another rider. And the way it was panning out, in discussions with Marlboro, it would have to be their nominee. Wayne had put together a proposal with Max Biaggi, but Marlboro were pushing him towards a 250 Honda deal at the same time. Then Marlboro told him to speak to Frenchman Jean-Michel Bayle. 'I said: hey – no. He's Kenny's rider. I never did speak to him, but Marlboro told me: he'll go wherever we tell him to go. It seems that's the way it is with riders now.'

Then came the next bombshell. 'All through the winter, Gary Howard, Tim and I had been in constant contact with Marlboro in Switzerland. There was never any question but we were going ahead. It was just a question of getting the second rider.' But in the second week of January 1997, less than three months before the start of the new season, and with the test programme getting under way in just one week, he called Leo de Graffenried. 'You'd better have a stiff whisky, Wayne. We have no sponsorship for you this year.' Instead, in a decision whose timing had whimsical overtones surprising in a multi-million-dollar organisation, Marlboro were putting all their backing into Kenny Roberts's new project, the British-built Malaysian-backed Modenas KR3 500 grand prix bike.

Accustomed to fighting back, Wayne embarked directly on a globe-trotting rescue mission. First stop Yamaha in Hamamatsu, fellow victims of this shock decision. Marlboro had come into team sponsorship in 1982 backing factory Yamahas, and had been with them ever since. Fully committed to a two-rider team, the factory also had no inkling of this abrupt abandonment.

A plan of action was quickly decided. Yamaha would underwrite the team themselves. From there, Wayne went directly to Australia for the first IRTA tests. Abe was ready to go, of course. More high-speed negotiations saw Gibernau drafted in as number two rider: very much a trainee, but still an honourable choice.

Wayne did his best to play the nice guy, in spite of his anger at the way he'd been left in the lurch. 'Marlboro supported me for years, and they were good sponsors. Then they decided not to support me. I can respect that decision. But it was pretty unprofessional the way it happened – with no warning, and much too late for me to find a replacement sponsor.'

Looking back from the perspective of 2010 shows the continuation of a downward path for Yamaha that would last several more years. Wayne won the factory's last championship in 1992; it would not be until 2004 and the arrival of Valentino Rossi that they would prevail once more. Certainly the difficulties of 1997 and 1998 finally wore out Wayne's desire to run his own team.

'We kind of all lost our way there. After my accident in 1993 no Yamaha team was at the same level. Never challenged for race wins or championships. We were all trying to do the best we could but I think mentally and spiritually we were lost. At that time we didn't really know it. Now in 2010 you can see it.'

Abe had come a long way since Wayne signed him up as a rookie, and was the factory's darling. 'Inside the Yamaha camp he was like a protected little boy. Nobody liked to try and put a pressure on him to try to change his riding habits. He was really hard on the back brake. Sometimes he would wear out the pads before the end of the race. I thought in testing maybe we could saw the pads in half, try and break the habit. But he just absolutely refused to ride the bike like that. It's very difficult to go out there and change.

'Also he was so fragile mentally that I didn't want anything to happen to him on the circuit, because he was such a beautiful kid. So that was one side of the garage.'

Sete's presence in 1997 was at Wayne's behest: the factory wanted a one-rider team, but Rainey had mechanics on strength, and the equipment for two riders. 'I thought we could keep going on a reduced budget and do just as well, and try to build from that.

'Sete was not at the level he reached on the Honda four-stroke when he raced against Rossi. He struggled mightily on the 500 two-stroke ... as most people do. I remember he would chuck it down the road, and be just devastated. Not very strong mentally, and that concerned me, because I wasn't used to seeing these things. But I wasn't surprised. I was kind of past the shock of it all, because of my other riders, how each and every guy was completely different. At that stage I learned to limit the damage by trying to encourage them, and trying to help them ride better. And don't put the pressure to where he feels he needs a super result to keep his ride.'

The bigger problem was inside Yamaha. The bikes were using up a crankshaft every practice session – hard on the mechanics, and on Yamaha's dismayed engineers. But there was no impetus from above to improve. 'At that stage Yamaha was just kind of idling along. There was no big commitment. And that kind of frustrated me also, because they put up the budget for the team, and they were calling the shots. And from my side I was already seeing the end in terms of my commitment.

'To do this thing absolutely right I would have to move my family to Europe, and chase sponsorship. And figure out a way to change the culture within Yamaha to try to win championships again. I wasn't ready for that big battle. My spirit was broken as far as wanting to carry on in GPs as a team owner/manager. I knew if I wanted to do a good job I would need the same level of commitment as when I raced, and I was not prepared to do that.

'It was a very frustrating year, 1997. I was still giving it my all, trying to do the best I could. But with the results we were getting it was really hard to get a sponsor interested.' Abe made the rostrum only once on the factory machine.

'Sete was very inexpensive, and I could see something in his riding. His weakest point was mental ... he didn't believe in himself enough.' At the end of the year, his contract was not renewed. 'He was devastated, and I felt bad ... but Yamaha put pressure on me. They wanted to bring in Bayle. They felt they could get some sponsorship with him. I didn't battle hard enough to keep Sete, but I didn't think Bayle was a rider who would bring different results.'

Bayle was a motocross superstar, and new Yamaha racing chief Mr Iio had been Yamaha motocross team manager. Bayle was his choice, and the Frenchman had already made a better-than-average 250 debut.

'I think Bayle did a decent job, to come from motocross and supercross to riding 500 GP bikes. But he banged his head at the very first test in Malaysia, and he never recovered from that. He was very fragile. He did get one pole position in Imola, beating Mick for that one lap. And I thought that was pretty cool. Didn't do nothing in the race though.' (He was fifth, best result of the year.)

When Bayle was away, his place was taken by Yamaha's nominee Kyoji Nanba, with a best of fifth in Japan, and more notably former team-mate Cadalora for a couple of races. 'Luca was interesting for me. He'd challenged me in a way no other team-mate did. He has devastating speed, but he could only find it once or twice a year. When he was on, I loved that I could be challenged like that.

'At Jarama, we paid him a little bit of money to ride it, but with a big bonus for a win. He came within one or two laps of winning ... and the crank broke. We were all devastated – we thought we had it won. When he came in he said: Are you still going to pay my bonus? You know I would have won. But I never heard of anybody who got a first place bonus who didn't win the race. He did a good job but we didn't have the budget to bring him in on a full-time basis.'

The year went somewhat better: Abe was on the rostrum three times, with one second and two thirds – but for Rainey the die was cast. He had had enough. He chose Assen mid-year to make the announcement, by when he had arranged with Yamaha's new racing manager, Englishman Lin Jarvis, that the factory would take over the whole team for 1999, including his mechanics.

It was small comfort that over the following years, with Max Biaggi and Carlos Checa on the factory machines, the team would continue to fail against Honda. But not much, because Wayne remained, and remains to this day, a Yamaha man.

Now, more than 15 years later, Rainey follows bike racing 'from afar'. He has watched with pleasure as Yamaha's commitment was revived when they signed up Valentino Rossi in 2004, and the factory once again started to win races and championships.

Rainey acknowledges Rossi's importance, as the dominant premier class rider for the past decade. 'He has phenomenal focus, concentration and desire. But he's got a spirit in him that he really loves to ride the motorcycle, and he likes to race hard. He's been able to maintain that desire. That's amazing to me. I think it is much easier if you are getting it back from the factories that you race for. Yamaha is doing everything they can to keep him happy.'

But Wayne has his own perspective on the Italian phenomenon. 'When he first got on a 500 he struggled mightily. And by that time those 500s were pretty good, not like what they'd been ten years before. He was handed a bike that Mick Doohan had developed, and by then the tyres were also very good. But he tossed it a lot, and I think even he was glad with the move to four-strokes. He only had a couple of years on 500s and that was probably enough. And then with the four-strokes, he just took off, that's for sure.

'He gets the effort from Yamaha. Every year they provide him with a machine that is better than the year before. And that is incredible. It shows a massive change of culture within the factory.

'When I raced with Yamaha I think they just wanted to be part of the show. I know for a fact they were okay with us not beating Honda. But that all changed after Honda had beaten them for 12 years.'

Rainey is still in 2010 a consultant for Yamaha. The revived US GP, at Laguna, where Rainey Curve now bears his name, is one regular appearance, and 'a chance to see my racing family'. Along with Eddie and Kenny, Wayne is regular guest of honour at Yamaha's annual GP party in Monterey.

'I think Yamaha's loyalty to me has been more than I could have imagined.'

EPILOGUE

*'For 33 years I was an independent guy, and now I am not. Difficult as it
is, I have to accept that I need to ask for help from time to time.'*
Wayne Rainey – Monterey, 2010

Wayne's story runs from rags to riches to despair to renewal.
Exceptionally gifted on a motorcycle, he also had a fearsome
determination that took him to the very top. Along the way it
became an obsession, an inner rage that drove him painfully beyond
satisfaction towards his destiny.

'Why was I that way? I think it was dealing with the unknown.
I could train a certain way, and set the bike up a certain way. I
could choose tyres and suspension, decide how I wanted to run
the race. The only thing I didn't know was the outcome.

'The way I trained and prepared for racing was very unforgiving.
I didn't want to leave any room for error. That's why it took over
my whole life. My satisfaction was to do that, then go out and
push it right to edge, to the limit, and see what would happen.
And you never knew. I never thought about how good I was. I had
to keep proving it to myself. I never ever started a race with the
feeling that I knew I would win. That's what kept the excitement.
Never knowing.

'I had a lot of success in racing. There were some disasters
along the way, but we kept on going. In my life, Misano was a
disaster along the way. I fell down, and now I can't walk any more.
But that was just a setback. I'm still going, and I'm still looking
for that part of life where I'm not quite sure of the outcome. I'd
felt really disappointed the two races before the crash because they
were too easy. There was no challenge. Well, God gave me my
challenge back at Misano.'

Rainey's new life started at the precise moment of spinal
fracture, but it was the same person living it, and the same
determination that forced him to attack the many difficulties in

his own inimitable way. It's now been 17 years, of unrevealed anguish alongside consistent determination to do more than merely exist. With conspicuous success.

Go-kart racing was a way of assuaging the racing bug. Eddie was already active, and built Wayne a hand-controlled kart. Wayne went in with some enthusiasm, along with Sandy - tuning and preparing the karts, fiddling and developing on the dyno just as he always had. But for Wayne it was a quite different way of racing. 'I got a little bit serious - testing a bit, tried a few different chassis. I would travel to Las Vegas and southern California, and I was able to bring a few karting races to some Laguna Seca events, with drivers from all over the world.

'I was able to challenge myself to compete, but it was very strange. I was never going to be within a couple of seconds of the fastest guys. I needed my feet, and needed feeling in my butt to do that.'

But now he started having serious carpal tunnel problems in his left wrist every time he raced - something that had never happened on motorcycles. The doctors explained that the stress of wheeling his chair was crucial, and that either his wrist or his shoulder would eventually wear out. For a while, cortisone injections helped prevent the numbness, but it was a short-term fix with likely long-term complications. 'The doctor told me I needed surgery, or I would eventually lose the use of my hand.'

The six or eight weeks of recuperation would leave him helpless - unable to make the transfers in and out of bed or his car, unable to dress himself. 'It's okay if you're walking around and you can hold your hand up. In my case it would be like somebody cutting your foot wide open then having to walk on it the same day. I didn't want to go through that.'

For two years he continued with the cortisone, then in 2008 'I had to make a huge decision. Then I found a doctor in Monterey, right across the street from my home. One of two or three doctors in the US doing a new procedure.' This was keyhole micro-surgery, within the fascia lining the carpal tunnel, and in spite of conventional advice not to risk such a new procedure, Wayne went ahead. 'The doctor told me he'd done 1,300 procedures, with not a single failure.' The surgery was accomplished with a tiny cut and only a local anaesthetic. 'It's been two years now with never a problem. It's perfect. I look at the racers with cuts all over them to relieve the pressure, and I think: wow.'

At the same time, the racing bug was finally letting go. 'I started thinking about things I never thought about when I raced ... and that was getting injured. I thought if I injure my hands racing this kart, then it would have a huge impact on my quality of life - my hands are also my legs. And then I knew I couldn't race any more. I couldn't commit to corners as I once did. And the kart is so fast it's not a toy to have fun with. It's a weapon, with lap times like a MotoGP bike. I go out and play with Eddie every once in a while, but I have not raced in over three years. I miss going to the races with Eddie and my dad, but I don't miss the racing.'

Wayne is still physically very fit, and with immense strength in his arms. 'If I can reach something, I can lift myself up on it.' Apart from regular swimming, one major factor is the cycling.

Cycling? Certainly. Wayne started at the end of his racing team days, after he was introduced to a three-wheeler hand cycle that he can ride on an asphalt trail. Wayne liked the idea. 'I had to work out how to get into it, and how to carry it to the track in my Suburban. Now I can load it up by myself, and on a good day I'll do 15 miles. I have 8,000 miles on it now.'

In 2010, after 17 years and on the verge of turning 50, it's no easier. 'For 33 years I was an independent guy, and now I am not. Difficult as it is, I have to accept that I need to ask for help from time to time.

'I've forgotten to be self-conscious. At first, I had difficulty being around people while I was in the wheelchair. I was trying to hide. I felt so exposed. At the race-track, I'd just wheel between the pitbox and my motorhome. Now half the time I don't even think about it. I'm used to being me, in a chair.

'It's still a battle, and each day brings its own situations to get through. When I stopped the race team it made my life much easier, to be in one time zone, and without all the pressure and stress - I was beating myself up quite a lot. When I got home it helped my body settle down, and I got to know it a lot better.'

One big change was acceptance that he'd have to leave the fine hilltop house he'd built just before the crash. It hadn't been designed with a wheelchair in mind. 'I moved in six months after the accident - had to put ramps and elevators in, and I dealt with it. After four years I told Shae we needed to move somewhere easier for me.'

It took another four years or so to find a suitable lot that could be levelled for a single-level house with a pool, workshop and all the amenities. It was across the road from the church they attend. And it took another five years to design and build. 'For that time, the house was my major project.' Living is much easier now.

Throughout, he has been supported by his family. Most especially Shae and Rex. 'I have been very blessed. Shae has been just tremendous, and so patient. There is no stronger person I know than my wife.' Rex, now 17, is soon to finish high school. Currently it seems his interests after university will take him into sports marketing or management. He was never bitten by the racing bug, preferring stick and ball games, and he is a member of the school baseball team. He has never really known his father except in a wheelchair. 'I've had to use Rex for all sorts of chores, much more than a boy that age would normally be used. He just does it as normal. Never complains and never asks why. So I've been blessed with a wife and a son who deal with it, and we continue the journey.'

Meanwhile Sandy and Rodney work as carpenters in LA, with Sandy still running his own private race workshop, with a dyno, for Eddie's karts. Ila bowls and plays bingo, Renee brings up two children. 'We're still a tight-knit family. We talk all the time, spend holidays together, get together on the boat in the summertime ... '

Wayne keeps a close eye on his investments and has some small-scale property interests in Monterey. And a full life.

'Today Rex is playing for the school baseball team. We'll pick him up from there and drive 350 miles down to LA to spend the night. Tomorrow we have tickets for an LA Lakers professional basketball game. After that, we'll drive home again ready for school on Monday. That's what we do now, instead of going to racetracks.

'We're just like a normal family, trying to get through every day, just like anybody else.

'After the first 24 hours, when I figured out that I was going to survive, I felt a calm inside myself. All that inner rage was done. I've had a lot of comments about how my face softened from that time. I knew that deciding to live was a tough option, but I know the decision was right. And I have no regrets about racing, and about what happened.

'My journey continues.'

GRAND PRIX AND US CHAMPIONSHIP ROAD-RACING RESULTS, 1982–1993

Key – DNS – Did Not Start; DNF – Did Not Finish; * – Fastest Lap of the Race

1982 USA NATIONAL CHAMPIONSHIP

Kawasaki Superbike

5/3	Daytona, Florida	Fifth
14/3	Talladega, Alabama	Third
18/4	Riverside, California	Third
22/5	Elkhart Lake, Wisconsin	Third
19/6	Loudon, New Hampshire	First
10/7	Laguna Seca, California	Tenth
8/8	Pocono, Pennsylvania	Second
21/8	Sears Point, California	DNF – crash
12/9	Seattle, Washington	Third
3/10	Daytona, Florida	Fourth
11/10	Palm Beach, Florida	DNF

Championship Position – Third

Other Results – Formula One – Fifth overall

1983 USA NATIONAL CHAMPIONSHIP

Kawasaki Superbike

11/3	Daytona, Florida	Fourth
21/3	Talladega, Alabama	Second
17/4	Riverside, California	Second
21/5	Mid-Ohio	DNF – crash
4/6	Elkhart Lake, Wisconsin	Second
18/6	Loudon, New Hampshire	Third
26/6	Pocono, Pennsylvania	First
16/7	Laguna Seca, California	First
24/7	Portland, Oregon	13th
20/8	Sears Point, California	First
3/9	Brainerd, Minnesota	First
11/9	Seattle, Washington	First
18/9	Willow Springs, California	First
2/10	Daytona, Florida	Second

Championship Position – First

1984 GRAND PRIX

		Circuit	Qualifying	Race Position
24/3	South African GP	Kyalami	Fifth	DNF – gearchange
15/4	Italian GP	Misano	19th	Third *
6/5	Spanish GP	Jarama	Seventh	Tenth
20/5	Austrian GP	Salzburgring	Third	DNF – Crash
27/5	West German GP	Nurburgring	Fourth	Sixth
10/6	French GP	Paul Ricard	Sixth	Sixth
17/6	Yugoslavian GP	Rijeka	First	Fourth
30/6	Dutch TT	Assen	Fourth	12th
8/7	Belgian GP	Spa-Francorchamps	20th	DNF – overheating
5/8	British GP	Silverstone	19th	14th
12/8	Swedish TT	Anderstorp	17th	13th
2/9	San Marino GP	Mugello	11th	DNF – retired

World Championship Position – Eighth

1985 USA NATIONAL CHAMPIONSHIP

Formula One (Honda RS500)

8/3	Daytona, Florida	DNS
19/5	Sears Point, California	First
9/6	Elkhart Lake, Wisconsin	First
16/6	Loudon, New Hampshire	DNS
23/6	Pocono, Pennsylvania	DNS
14/7	Laguna Seca, California	DNS
4/8	Mid-Ohio	Fourth
9/9	Brainerd, Minnesota	DNF

Championship Position – Eighth

1985 USA NATIONAL CHAMPIONSHIP

Formula Two (Honda RS250)

9/3	Daytona, Florida	DNS
28/4	Willow Springs, California	First
19/5	Sears Point, California	First
9/6	Elkhart Lake, Wisconsin	First
16/6	Loudon, New Hampshire	DNS
23/6	Pocono, Philadelphia	DNS
14/7	Laguna Seca, California	DNS
4/8	Mid-Ohio	First
17/8	Seattle, Washington	First
25/8	Sears Point, California	DNF
1/9	Brainerd, Minnesota	DNF
19/10	Daytona, Florida	DNS

Championship Position – Third

1986 USA NATIONAL CHAMPIONSHIP

Superbike (Honda VFR750)

9/3	Daytona, Florida	Fourth
18/5	Sears Point, California	Third
1/6	Brainerd, Minnesota	First
7/6	Elkhart Lake, Wisconsin	First
15/6	Loudon, New Hampshire	First
21/6	Pocono, Pennsylvania	First
12/7	Laguna Seca, California	First
3/8	Mid-Ohio	DNF – crash
10/8	Atlanta, Georgia	First

Championship Position – Second

1986 USA NATIONAL CHAMPIONSHIP

Formula One (Honda RS500)

18/5	Sears Point, California	Third
1/6	Brainerd, Minnesota	DNF
7/6	Elkhart Lake, Wisconsin	First
15/6	Loudon, New Hampshire	Third
21/6	Pocono, Pennsylvania	Second
13/7	Laguna Seca, California	DNF
3/8	Mid-Ohio	DNS
10/8	Atlanta, Georgia	DNS

Championship Position – Fourth

Combined Superbike/F-One Camel Pro Championship Position – Second

1987 USA NATIONAL CHAMPIONSHIP

Superbike (Honda VFR750)

8/3	Daytona, Florida	First
17/3	Atlanta, Georgia	First
7/6	Brainerd, Minnesota	First
21/6	Loudon, New Hampshire	Second
28/6	Elkhart Lake, Wisconsin	Second
12/7	Laguna Seca, California	Fifth
2/8	Mid-Ohio	Second
9/8	Memphis, Tennessee	Second
30/8	Sears Point	Sixth

Championship Position – First

1988 GRAND PRIX

		Circuit	*Qualifying*	*Race Position*
27/3	Japanese GP	Suzuka	Sixth	Sixth
10/4	United States GP	Laguna Seca	First	Fourth
24/4	Spanish GP	Jarama	Fifth	Sixth
1/5	Portuguese GP	Jerez	Second	Second
22/5	Italian GP	Imola	Fourth	Third
29/5	West German GP	Nurburgring	Second	Second
12/6	Austrian GP	Salzburgring	Eighth	Third
25/6	Dutch TT	Assen	Seventh	Seventh
3/7	Belgian GP	Spa-Francorchamps	Third	Fifth
17/7	Yugoslavian GP	Rijeka	Fourth	Third
24/7	French GP	Paul Ricard	Fifth	Fifth
7/8	British GP	Donington Park	Fifth	First
14/8	Swedish TT	Anderstorp	Third	Fifth
28/8	Czechoslovakian GP	Brno	Second	Third
18/9	Brazilian GP	Goiania	Sixth	DNF – puncture

World Championship Position – Third

1989 GRAND PRIX

		Circuit	Qualifying	Race Position
26/3	Japanese GP	Suzuka	Second	Second
9/4	Australian GP	Phillip Island	Second	Second
16/4	United States GP	Laguna Seca	First	First
30/4	Spanish GP	Jerez	First	Second
14/5	Italian GP	Misano	Fourth	DNF – works rider boycott
28/5	West German GP	Hockenheimring	Second	First
4/6	Austrian GP	Salzburgring	Third	Third
11/6	Yugoslavian GP	Rijeka	Second	Second *
24/6	Dutch TT	Assen	Second	First
2/7	Belgian GP	Spa-Francorchamps	Second	Third
16/7	French GP	Le Mans	Third	Third
6/8	British GP	Donington Park	Third	Third
13/8	Swedish TT	Anderstorp	First	DNF – crash
27/8	Czechoslovakian GP	Brno	Fourth	Third
17/9	Brazilian GP	Goiania	First	Third

World Championship Position – Second

1990 GRAND PRIX

		Circuit	*Qualifying*	*Race Position*
25/3	Japanese GP	Suzuka	First	First *
8/4	United States GP	Laguna Seca	Second	First
6/5	Spanish GP	Jerez	Second	Second
20/5	Italian GP	Misano	First	First *
27/5	West German GP	Nurburgring	Third	Second
10/6	Austrian GP	Salzburgring	Second	Second
17/6	Yugoslavian GP	Rijeka	First	First *
30/6	Dutch TT	Assen	Second	Second
8/7	Belgian GP	Spa-Francorchamps	Second	First *
22/7	French GP	Le Mans	Second	Third
5/8	British GP	Donington Park	Third	Second
12/8	Swedish TT	Anderstorp	Fourth	First *
26/8	Czechoslovakian GP	Brno	Third	First *
2/9	Hungarian GP	Hungaroring	Fourth	DNF – brake failure
16/9	Australian GP	Phillip Island	Fifth	Third

World Championship Position – First

273

1991 GRAND PRIX

		Circuit	Qualifying	Race Position
24/3	Japanese GP	Suzuka	Fifth	Third
7/4	Australian GP	Eastern Creek	First	First *
21/4	United States GP	Laguna Seca	First	First *
12/5	Spanish GP	Jerez	First	Third *
19/5	Italian GP	Misano	First	Ninth *
26/5	German GP	Hockenheimring	Fourth	Second
9/6	Austrian GP	Salzburgring	Third	Second *
16/6	European GP	Jarama	Second	First *
29/6	Dutch TT	Assen	Second	Second
21/7	French GP	Paul Ricard	First	First *
4/8	British GP	Donington Park	Second	Second
18/8	San Marino GP	Mugello	Third	First
25/8	Czechoslovakian GP	Brno	First	First *
8/9	Vitesse du Mans	Le Mans	Third	Third
29/9	Malaysian GP	Shah Alam	DNS	DNS – injured

World Championship Position – First

1992 GRAND PRIX

		Circuit	Qualifying	Race Position
29/3	Japanese GP	Suzuka	Ninth	DNF – crash
12/4	Australian GP	Eastern Creek	Second	Second
19/4	Malaysian GP	Shah Alam	Second	Second *
10/5	Spanish GP	Jerez	Second	Second
24/5	Italian GP	Mugello	Third	DNF – crash
31/5	European GP	Catalunya	Fourth	First
14/6	German GP	Hockenheimring	Second	DNF – retired hurt
27/6	Dutch TT	Assen	DNS	DNS – withdrew
12/7	Hungarian GP	Hungaroring	Second	Fifth
19/7	French GP	Magny Cours	Second	First
2/8	British GP	Donington Park	Third	Second *
23/8	Brazilian GP	Interlagos	Second	First *
25/8	South African GP	Kyalami	Fourth	Third

World Championship Position – First

1993 GRAND PRIX

		Circuit	Qualifying	Race Position
28/3	Australian GP	Eastern Creek	Second	Second *
4/4	Malaysian GP	Shah Alam	Third	First *
18/4	Japanese GP	Suzuka	Third	First
2/5	Spanish GP	Jerez	Third	Second
16/5	Austrian GP	Salzburgring	Seventh	Third
13/6	German GP	Hockenheimring	Sixth	Fifth
26/6	Dutch TT	Assen	Sixth	Fifth
4/7	European GP	Catalunya	Third	First *
18/7	San Marino GP	Mugello	Fifth	Third
1/8	British GP	Donington Park	Eighth	Second
22/8	Czech Republic GP	Brno	First	First *
5/9	Italian GP	Misano	Second	DNF – crash
12/9	United States GP	Laguna Seca	DNS	DNS
26/9	FIM GP	Jarama	DNS	DNS

World Championship Position – Second

WAYNE RAINEY AND KEVIN SCHWANTZ

1988–1993 Comparative 500cc statistics

RAINEY

	1988	1989	1990	1991	1992	1993	Total	1984 (250CC)
GP Calendar	15	15	15	15	13	14	87	(12)
Starts	15	15	15	14	12	12	83	(12)
Did Not Start	0	0	0	1	1	2	4	(0)
Did Not Finish	1	2	1	0	3	1	8	(4)
Race Crash	0	1	0	0	2	1	4	(1)
Pole Position	1	4	3	6	0	1	15	(1)
Front Row Start	8	15	14	13	12	7	69	(4)
Race Win	1	3	7	6	3	4	24	(0)
Race Top Three	7	13	14	13	8	9	64	(1)
Best Race Lap	0	1	6	8	3	4	22	(1)

SCHWANTZ

	1988	1989	1990	1991	1992	1993	Total	
GP Calendar	15	15	15	15	13	14	87	–
Starts	14	15	15	14	12	14	84	–
Did Not Start	1	0	0	1	1	0	3	–
Did Not Finish	3	6	4	2	3	1	19	–
Race Crash	2	2	4	0	3	1	12	–
Pole Positions	0	9	7	5	1	6	28	–
Front Row Starts	6	15	14	12	6	13	66	–
Race Wins	2	6	5	5	1	4	23	–
Race Top Three	4	9	10	8	3	11	45	–
Best Race Lap	2	8	6	4	1	2	23	–

INDEX